THE JEWS OF
LONG ISLAND

THE JEWS OF LONG ISLAND
1705–1918

Brad Kolodny

excelsior editions

AN IMPRINT OF STATE UNIVERSITY OF NEW YORK PRESS

On the cover: Wedding of Dr. Solomon Weingrad and Ruth Esther Siegel in front of the Lindenhurst Hebrew Congregation synagogue, May 19, 1916.

Published by State University of New York Press, Albany

Excelsior Editions is an imprint of State University of New York Press

For information, contact State University of New York Press, Albany, NY
www.sunypress.edu

Library of Congress Cataloging-in-Publication Data

Name: Kolodny, Brad, author.
Title: The Jews of Long Island : 1705–1918 / Brad Kolodny.
Description: Albany : State University of New York Press, [2022] | Series: Excelsior editions | Includes bibliographical references.
Identifiers: LCCN 2021018463 | ISBN 9781438487236 (hardcover : alk. paper) | ISBN 9781438487229 (pbk. : alk. paper) | ISBN 9781438487243 (ebook)
Subjects: LCSH: Jews—New York (State)—Long Island—History—19th century. | Jews—New York (State)—Long Island—History—20th century. | Jews—New York (State)—Nassau County—Registers. | Jews—New York (State)—Suffolk County—Registers.
Classification: LCC F127.L8 K65 2022 | DDC 974.7/21004924—dc23
LC record available at https://lccn.loc.gov/2021018463

10 9 8 7 6 5 4 3 2 1

For Julia and Spencer.
The future is ours to see.

Contents

Part II: Suffolk County

Illustrations

Figures

Tables

Prologue

In June 2019 my first book, *Seeking Sanctuary: 125 Years of Synagogues on Long Island*, was published. In conjunction with its release I embarked on a tour of Long Island, giving presentations at synagogues and local libraries over the next eight months. During the Q&A session at these events I was repeatedly asked what I was working on for my next book, and each time my response was the same: there would not be one. I was pleased by how well the book had been received and felt confident there was no other topic I would be as passionate about or would capture my attention the way *Seeking Sanctuary* did.

Then the coronavirus pandemic hit in the middle of March 2020. With the exception of weekly ventures to the supermarket, I essentially stayed at home over the next three months as most of the country did. I knew I would have a lot of time on my hands moving through 2020 and wanted to do something productive: so I invested several hours each night in online research.

Seeking Sanctuary tells the story of every building on Long Island used as a synagogue and provides a history of how Jewish communities were established and evolved over the decades. There were many individuals who were instrumental in bringing their Jewish neighbors together to form the earliest congregations. Only a handful of these trailblazers are mentioned in *Seeking Sanctuary*, but there are so many more whose contributions were not included because my focus for that book was on the buildings, not the people.

A comprehensive look at the earliest Jews to live on Long Island and identifying as many of them as possible was something that had not been done before on a large scale. Recording the names and piecing together the stories about why Jews settled in Nassau and Suffolk counties became a pursuit I decided to embrace. The only person who did this type of work previously was Helene Gerard, a former librarian at Westhampton Beach Junior High School. Beginning in 1975 she conducted personal interviews with about a hundred Jewish men and women who lived on Long Island around the turn of the century, capturing their experiences both extraordinary and mundane. These oral histories provide essential insight about the early Jewish experience on Long Island with a focus on Suffolk County. Helene's work came together in an exhibit sponsored by the East End Arts and Humanities Council in 1982 called "And We're Still Here: 100 Years of Small Town Jewish Life." In 2018 I acquired the exhibition catalogue from Helene's husband, Lloyd (Helene passed away in 1986), which provided me with the inspiration to continue Helene's work using tools at my disposal that were not available to her forty-plus years ago.

Online resources have made it possible for me to identify over 4,400 Jews who lived in 75 different villages and towns in Nassau and Suffolk counties before the end of World War I, but what has emerged is more than just names. Taken in aggregate there is data that identifies trends and patterns as to when, where, and why Jews settled across the island from Great Neck to Greenport and Cedarhurst to Sag Harbor, but ultimately each story is unique. Helene's firsthand accounts exemplifies that, and I am proud to bring more stories forward by reconstructing people's lives through the historical record they left behind. Census records, naturalization papers, World War I registration cards, old newspapers, certificates of incorporation and other paper trails were utilized to piece together the details, and in some cases I was fortunate to fill in missing information by exchanging emails and speaking with the descendants of these pioneers. Individuals had varying levels of success in earning a living, many found love and had children, some endured tragedies, others had brushes with fame. People whose names were lost to obscurity or are remembered to this day come together here, forming the mosaic of early Long Island Jewish life where the seeds were planted giving rise to Judaism on Long Island that exists today.

Brad Kolodny
Plainview, New York
March 2021

Introduction

Determining Who Is Jewish

Who is a Jew is a question that has been debated for centuries. The answer is not supplied here. But for the purposes of this book the criteria used to determine whether or not someone would qualify as being Jewish and therefore included in this volume are as follows:

1. Buried in a Jewish cemetery.

2. Indicated as Jewish on a census or other records. While the 1910 United States census does not indicate religious affiliation, it does ask the question of language spoken. The 1920 census also asks for the mother tongue of the individual and both of their parents. An answer to this question for some Jews, mostly immigrants, is sometimes noted as Hebrew, Yiddish, or Jewish.

3. Named as a member, officer, or trustee of a synagogue or Jewish organization.

4. A relative of someone identified as Jewish based on one of the prior three requirements.

Use of Records

The sources used most often to find the names of Jewish individuals who lived on Long Island prior to 1919, along with details about their lives, can be found on four websites: familysearch.org, nyshistoricnewspapers.org, fultonhistory.com, and findagrave.com. A typical example of how these sites were utilized to discover and verify information can be illustrated starting with a woman named Sylvia Walsdorf. Findagrave.com lists several but not all interments at the Huntington Jewish Center cemetery. Sylvia is listed as having lived from 1899 to 1966, but did she live in Huntington? And if so, during what years? At the cemetery she is buried next to her husband, Louis Walsdorf. Putting their names in the search field of all newspapers in Suffolk County on NYShistoricnewspapers.org shows the earliest mention in 1925; but a further search for their obituaries was ultimately found in the *Long Islander*. Sylvia's obituary was particularly difficult to find because it lists her name as Mrs. L. J. Walsdorf, but it uncovered a wealth of valuable information. She was born in Glen Cove in 1899, and at the time of her death she had three sisters: Sophie Greenberg, Beatrice Roiser, and Mrs. David Oles. What was not clear for Sylvia or her sisters was their maiden name, which would be critical to finding more about her background in Glen Cove. At familysearch.org the sisters were searched by first name only and as living together, and the 1910 census record showed their family, named Greenberg, living in Glen Cove, including their parents Max and Leah and three other siblings. To find out more about Max Greenberg, his name was searched in NYShistoricnewspapers.org, and the *Nassau Daily Review* newspaper from Freeport reported that he was a trustee at Congregation Tifereth Israel of Glen Cove in 1931. The article lists six other officers that led to a search of those individuals to see if they lived in Glen Cove or elsewhere on Long Island prior to 1919. Max Greenberg, being a somewhat common name, also matched up with an individual living in Hempstead whose name appeared on a list in the *Nassau Post* of 190 men who were slated to be drafted for military service in 1917. This was not the same Max Greenberg from Glen Cove, but I now had to verify that this new Max Greenberg from Hempstead was Jewish. Seems logical that he would be, given his name; but verification was needed. Back at familysearch.org "Max Greenberg" was plugged into the search field, but nothing about him in Hempstead was uncovered. However, yet another Max Greenberg was found living in Great Neck with his brother-in-law Julius Jacoby according to the census of 1920 (a World War I registration card shows Julius lived in Great Neck in 1918). Julius's wife Rose and Max Greenberg are brother and sister, but are they Jewish? Another document on familysearch.org reveals that Rose died in 1937 and is buried in Mt. Carmel Cemetery in Queens, which is a Jewish cemetery. Because it could not be verified that Max Greenberg from Hempstead was Jewish, he does not appear in this book. But a search that began with Sylvia Walsdorf led in several different directions, finding names of Jews in other communities that might not have been uncovered otherwise.

In addition to census records at familysearch.org, there is a significant amount of genealogical information available that proved useful, including birth, marriage, and death certificates; naturalization papers; military registrations; passport applications; and land deeds. Looking through old newspapers at nyshistoricnewspapers.org and fultonhistory.com provided a treasure trove of vital information as well. Back in the nineteenth and early twentieth centuries anything of public record was used to fill the pages of local newspapers, most being published just once a week. This included noteworthy legal proceedings such as jury duty selection, land transactions, assessments, mortgages, taxes, disputes and judgments, legal notices, liens, wills, and licenses issued. Social announcements such as births, engagements, weddings, divorces, and obituaries were common with space also dedicated to letting readers know when local residents left town to visit with relatives or friends and when visitors came to town. New jobs, donations to charitable causes, school records (including grades), and even lists of unclaimed letters left at the post office were part of their editorial content. In the 1910s and 1920s newspapers would publish lists of businesses and homes that acquired a telephone with their phone number, individuals who purchased new cars, men drafted to fight in World War I, and column after column of names of individuals who purchased war bonds. Advertisements in the newspaper, both display ads and classifieds, were also a great source of information and uncovered many details about individuals that help paint the picture of how Jews made a living on Long Island during this period.

Accuracy of Dates, Names, and Spelling

When recording information from different sources it is not uncommon to find variations of important data. Inconsistencies can sometimes be attributed to the original record taker but also to the person whose information is being recorded. There are several examples of immigrants who did not have knowledge of their own birthday or the year they came to the United States. When asked for this information, required for a federal census, it could be remembered differently when the next census was taken ten years later. In other records, including a petition for naturalization or World War I registration, the answer to a question about a specific date can be seen listed as approximate or unknown. Every effort has been made to be as accurate as possible. But when presented with documents that show different years of birth, or the spelling of a first name (such as "Morris" versus "Maurice") or last name ("Brown" versus "Braun") that are not consistent, judgment calls needed to be made.

Lists of Names

At the end of the narrative for each chapter is a list of names of people who lived in that village or nearby town with their year of birth, year of death (if known), maiden name (if known), and small bits of information about the person. They are arranged alphabetically with families separated by surname in bold face type. In many cases a person was born on Long Island, got married, and had children of their own all during the period covered in the book. In this situation certain individuals are listed twice, grouped with their parents as well as with their spouse and children. It should be noted that since this book focuses on the Jews of Long Island from 1705 to 1918, individuals born in 1919 and later are not included. Similarly, for individuals who are listed, details about their lives that occurred after 1918 will generally not be indicated.

A Note about Geography

Any reference made to Long Island here refers to Nassau and Suffolk counties only. While Nassau County was not established until 1899, there were Jews who settled in places like Glen Cove, Hempstead, and Freeport: all of which were part of Queens County when they arrived. The definition of Long Island for this book is the area constituted by the present borders of Nassau and Suffolk.

Chapter 1

In the Beginning . . .

In the 214 years from 1705 to 1918 there were Jewish individuals and families living on Long Island whose experiences intersected with major events in world history. During the Revolutionary War a handful of Jews from Oyster Bay and East Hampton fled British-occupied New York, crossing the Long Island Sound to be among patriots in Connecticut. The son of a merchant from Babylon pitched for the New York Giants baseball team; two individuals with family ties to Long Island were aboard the Titanic; and dozens of men enlisted to fight in the Great War. But the majority of Jews in Nassau and Suffolk counties lived their lives outside of the public eye, many were immigrants who sought a better life for themselves and for their children leaving the hardships they endured in Europe behind. There were observant Jews who worshiped on their own when no community was available, Jews who were instrumental in establishing a synagogue, secular Jews who were affiliated only by birth, and those who left the faith for reasons based on love or convenience.

Records suggest the first Jewish resident of Long Island may have been Nathan Simson. In 1720 he was president of Congregation Shearith Israel in New York City but prior to that may have been a shopkeeper in Brookhaven in 1705. Nathan's nephew Joseph Simson made multiple land purchases with his wife Rebecca Isaacs in Oyster Bay as early as 1726. Others also bought and sold property in the hamlet including Jacob Franks, Abraham Isaacks, Samuel Myers Cohen, and Rachel Levy.

Figure 1. Joseph Simson, 1686–1787. *Source:* American Jewish Historical Society Quarterly, vol. 27, the Lyons Collection, vol. 2, 1920.

The first Jew known to have been born on Long Island was Myer Michaels, the son of Levy Michaels, a resident of South Haven. He utilized the services of the mohel Abraham I. Abrahams from New York City who performed the ritual circumcision for Myer on July 8, 1760.

Solomon Simson, son of Joseph and Rebecca, owned two houses in Oyster Bay in 1775 but left during the Revolutionary War, taking refuge in Connecticut. As a colonist who supported independence, Solomon contributed to the war effort by supplying a cannon to the New York militia and lead for making bullets. Aaron Isaacs was a merchant in East Hampton in the 1770s and owned part of a wharf in Sag Harbor. Like Simson, he decided to cross the sound for Connecticut rather than live under British rule on Long Island.

Joshua Montefiore, uncle of the British philanthropist Sir Moses Montefiore, was a lawyer in Sag Harbor in the 1820s. At the time he was married to Isabella, the second of his three wives, and had three children with her. Isabella was a dressmaker and made trips to New York with her husband, bringing back fashionable items to sell to the women of Sag Harbor.

In the 1850s merchants Jonas Fishel in Riverhead and Bannat Salky in Hempstead opened retail shops in their respective villages. They were

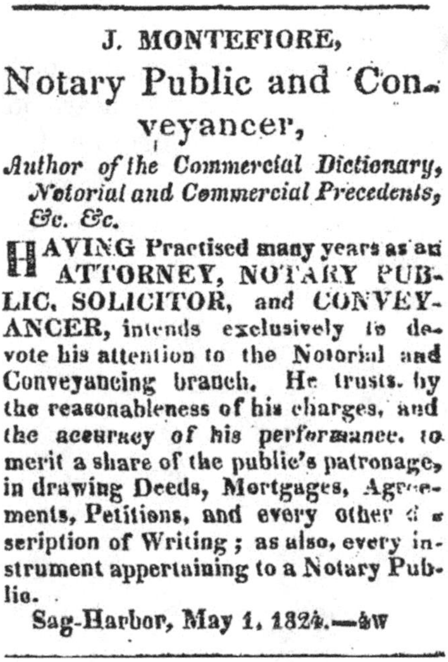

J. MONTEFIORE,

Notary Public and Conveyancer,

Author of the Commercial Dictionary, Notorial and Commercial Precedents, &c. &c.

HAVING Practised many years as an ATTORNEY, NOTARY PUBLIC, SOLICITOR, and CONVEYANCER, intends exclusively to devote his attention to the Notorial and Conveyancing branch. He trusts, by the reasonableness of his charges, and the accuracy of his performance, to merit a share of the public's patronage, in drawing Deeds, Mortgages, Agreements, Petitions, and every other description of Writing ; as also, every instrument appertaining to a Notary Public.

Sag-Harbor, May 1, 1824.—4w

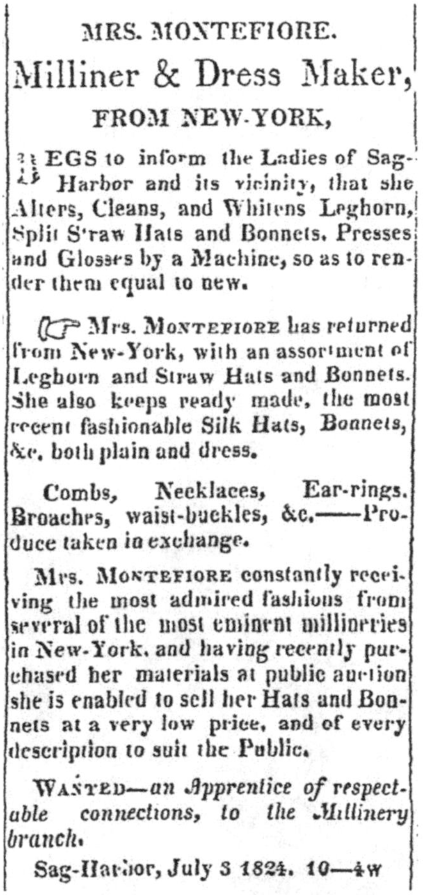

MRS. MONTEFIORE.

Milliner & Dress Maker,

FROM NEW-YORK,

BEGS to inform the Ladies of Sag-Harbor and its vicinity, that she Alters, Cleans, and Whitens Leghorn, Split Straw Hats and Bonnets. Presses and Glosses by a Machine, so as to render them equal to new.

☞ Mrs. MONTEFIORE has returned from New-York, with an assortment of Leghorn and Straw Hats and Bonnets. She also keeps ready made, the most recent fashionable Silk Hats, Bonnets, &c. both plain and dress.

Combs, Necklaces, Ear-rings. Broaches, waist-buckles, &c.——Produce taken in exchange.

Mrs. MONTEFIORE constantly receiving the most admired fashions from several of the most eminent milliorries in New-York, and having recently purchased her materials at public auction she is enabled to sell her Hats and Bonnets at a very low price, and of every description to suit the Public.

WANTED—*an Apprentice of respectable connections, to the Millinery branch.*

Sag-Harbor, July 3 1824. 10—4w

Figures 2 and 3. Advertisements for Joshua Montefiore's legal services and his wife Isabella's women's clothing business. *Source: The Corrector*, May 8, 1824, and July 10, 1824.

followed by Jonas's brother Andrew Fishel in Patchogue, Michael Sandman in Glen Cove, and Bernard Rosenthal in Greenport in the 1860s, Morris Miller in Freeport, Simon Hirschfeld in Huntington, Morris Henschel in Amityville, and Adolph Edelstein in Sag Harbor the 1870s. Up to this point Jewish immigrants were predominantly from Germany, but the 1880s saw the beginning of an influx of over two million Jews from eastern Europe who landed on American shores over the next forty years. Of those who settled in New York City, a very small percentage headed east and established themselves on Long Island. All needed to make a living, and a great many did so as merchants.

Typically, a young man would start out as a peddler selling dry goods or fruits and vegetables, roaming rural towns and venturing out to remote farmhouses across the island. They traversed on foot with packs on their backs while others used a pushcart or made their way by horse and wagon. Max Smith, who arrived in Southampton around 1873, exemplified the life of an itinerant merchant and progression in business. His experience is captured in an article in the *Sea-Side Times* from January 23, 1908,

Figure 4. Simon Hirschfeld in Huntington. *Source:* Courtesy of Susan Hirschfeld Mohr.

where it recalls Smith set out "with a small stock of goods which he sold through the east end villages from a basket carried on his arm. After a few years his stock of goods gradually increased until he was unable to carry it on foot and he bought a horse and wagon which enabled him to carry a much larger stock and do a much larger business." Max's success did not stop there. In 1888 "he established himself in Southampton in the central business section of Main Street and the growth of his business since that has necessitated the enlarging of the plant several times to accommodate his ever increasing stock of goods."

Many hardworking Jewish immigrants who started out small and enjoyed some success would take the next step by opening a merchandise or grocery store. Their presence in a business district contributed to the

Figure 5. Advertisement for Max Smith's Clothing Emporium. *Source: Sea-Side Times*, August 29, 1907.

growth of towns and villages all over the island and endeared them to their non-Jewish neighbors. General stores and larger department stores that sold a variety of items were opened by proprietors such as Harry Freedman in Bay Shore, Louis Cohen in Hempstead, Isaac Jacobson in Lynbrook, Max Saltz and Louis Alter in Northport; grocery stores were run by Benjamin Morris in Hicksville, Abraham Gerstein in Setauket, and Elle Aronson in Huntington. Others focused on a business selling specialty items like Adolph Levy's men's clothing store in Freeport, Maurice Beck's women's clothing store in Patchogue, Samuel Harding's furniture store in Riverhead, and Mark Wolff's rug store in Rockville Centre.

Men who learned a trade opened up shop as a shoemaker like August Sokolowsky in Mineola, a tailor like Louis Cohn in Amityville, a baker like Jacob Feinberg in Glen Cove, a butcher like August Mainzer in East Quogue, or a jeweler like Max Maizels in Sayville. Others ran businesses selling essential and nonessential items. These proprietors included Adolph Dicks in Hempstead who ran a flower shop, Morris Spitzer in Lynbrook

Figure 6. Adolph Levy & Son store on South Main Street in Freeport. *Source:* Freeport Historical Society.

who opened a confectionary store, Benjamin Ballen in Greenport who had a hardware store, Herman Spitz in Sag Harbor who opened a music store, Max Israel in Port Washington who had a liquor store, and Samuel Henschel in Port Jefferson who ran a saloon.

Those who did not exhibit the entrepreneurial spirit to start their own business might have settled in villages on the island where factories

Figure 7. Herman Spitz sold Victrolas in Sag Harbor. *Source: East Hampton Star,* March 23, 1917.

employed a large number of people needed to fill both skilled and manual labor positions. This included J. W. Elberson's rubber factory in Setauket, Jacob Follender's doll factory in East Islip, several companies involved in the embroidery industry in Lindenhurst, Joseph Fahys's watchcase factory in Sag Harbor, and the Patchogue Manufacturing Company that had 650 employees in their lace mill in 1912.

Not everyone went the traditional route earning a living as a merchant, a tradesman, or working for a manufacturer. Living on an island meant there was money to be made from the sea by fishing and oystering. In Huntington, Joseph Schramm was a bayman, in West Sayville Cornelius De Ruiter was an oysterman, and in Sag Harbor Joseph Schapiro worked for the Gardiners Bay Oyster Company. Samuel and Julius Levine lived in Greenport as observant Jews who kept kosher but were encouraged by their mother to sell scallops in their small store. The brothers would gather and open the bivalves but never ate them.

Other less common job choices during this early period included professionals working in an office like insurance salesman Sigmund Reiss in Freeport, stockbroker Victor Barton in Cedarhurst, and advertising executive Harry Rascovar from Lawrence. Two involved in the newspaper business included Morris Friedman, editor and publisher of the *Hicksville Courier*, and Isaac Gobetz, who worked for the *Freeport Review*, *Brooklyn Daily Eagle*, and *New York Herald*. And some like Harry Davidow and Leopold Michnoff held jobs that required an education beyond high school: Davidow started a law firm in Patchogue, and Michnoff had a dental office in Rockville Centre. Dorothy Ollswang from Amagansett was a pioneer as one of thirty graduates from Women's Medical College in Philadelphia in 1915. She became a doctor with a practice in Albion, New York.

Women at this time were predominantly homemakers, but some were involved in work outside the home. As their peddler husbands made the transition to opening a store, in many cases the men continued to maintain and deliver to customers who did not have easy access to the new establishment. These stores often were on the ground level of a two-story building with a residence above. While the merchant was away, his wife would take care of the family and conduct business with incoming customers. Sole proprietors in their own businesses included Rose Steinberg, who owned a variety store in Roslyn; Johanna Friedman, who had a liquor store in Huntington; Rebecca Eisenberg, who managed a grocery store in Sag Har-

Figure 8. Abraham Ingerman's dry goods store in Northport was in a typical building of the period, with the store on the street level and apartments for the family above. *Source:* Courtesy of Marcia Clark.

bor; and Rachael Leder, who operated Leder's Bazaar in Rockville Centre.

Perhaps the most plentiful resource available on Long Island, particularly in Suffolk County, was land. Some families made their living as farmers. Harris Karlin and his son Jacob grew crops on their farm in Calverton, Israel Katz and his son Abraham had a wholesale milk and cattle business in Holtsville appropriately known as I. Katz and Son; and Harry Bernstein started a duck farm in Center Moriches. Aaron Stern took advantage of the plentiful local cucumber bounty to start his Farmingdale wholesale and retail pickle business in 1899. Land was also an investment, with property being bought and sold for income. Nathan Kaplan in Greenport registered hundreds of land transactions from 1873 to 1911 at locations all over the east end. Hugo Stearns purchased eight connecting farms in 1905 and established a high-end real estate development in Freeport known as Stearns Park. These ventures saw varying levels of success but without a doubt the most profitable land speculator was Samuel Cohn. He owned a men's clothing store in Patchogue and purchased seventy acres in Montauk including ocean frontage for $15 per acre. This investment of $1,050 made in 1879 was still in Cohn's possession in 1926 when the value had increased two hundred times to $210,000.

Titans of industry whose businesses were based in New York City also lived on Long Island in large estates used as summer residences. Investment banker Otto Kahn purchased 443 acres in West Hills and built Oheka Castle, the second-largest private home in the country. Daniel, Isaac, and William Guggenheim each had their own estate in Sands Point during the 1910s. Their brother Benjamin, who died aboard the Titanic in 1912, may have crossed paths with another first-class passenger on the fateful voyage named Edith Russell, who survived the tragedy. Born Edith Rosenbaum, she was a fashion buyer and a Paris correspondent for *Women's Wear Daily* whose parents, Harry and Sophia Rosenbaum, lived in Rockville Centre.

Once established in a career many Jewish Long Islanders became involved in supporting various causes, some even entered the political arena. Adolph Rosenthal was president of the Hempstead Democratic Club and was elected as one of five trustees for the Village of Hempstead in 1893. Isidore Mayer ran for police justice of Freeport in 1915 but lost. Andrew Fishel was elected inspector of the Patchogue Fire District in 1885. With an eye on the needs of local citizens the Daughters of Israel was formed in Patchogue with Caroline Manus as president in 1905. They were a philanthropic organization that gave to those in need regardless of their religion. Lillian Schloss from Freeport was president of the Ladies Aid Society in Hempstead for twenty-five years. Causes on a national and international level received support as well. Andrew Fishel's niece Lillian Fishel was a founder of the Babylon Library and active in the suffrage movement as the chair of the committee of arrangements for the Babylon Equal Franchise society. She attended a meeting for suffragists from the Second Assembly District of Suffolk County on May 22, 1913, and was elected vice president. Another Jewish woman Maude Henschel from Kings Park was elected secretary of the organization. Max Ollswang supported the Women's Political Union in Amagansett by posting information about the suffrage movement in his store window in 1915. Benjamin Rosen was chairman of the Southampton chapter of the American Jewish Relief Committee for Sufferers from the War in 1917. That same year Benjamin Schindler and over a dozen Jewish Freeport residents contributed to the Jewish Consumptive Relief Society, as did Samuel Jaffe from Roosevelt.

By 1918 there were seven synagogue buildings in Suffolk County and two in Nassau that provided an opportunity for communal gathering, primarily for religious purposes. But becoming engrained in the social fabric of a town or village meant being involved in groups and organizations that were instrumental in seeing a community grow and prosper. Several Jews took an active role by becoming volunteers at the local fire department, or even organizing one if it did not exist. Max Schramm was an elected trustee of the Islip Fire Department in 1890. Charter members of the Freeport Fire Department in 1893 included Henry Ackerman, Henry Gobetz, Abraham Goldsmith, Hyman Schloss, Israel Schloss, and Morris Miller (who was also the treasurer). Harry Goldstein was a founder of the Eastport Fire Department in 1913 and was treasurer for thirty-nine years. Community banks were an important part of the financial well-being of a village, so it is not surprising that Jewish merchants with expertise in this area took on leadership positions. Isaac Levenbron was a founder and longtime director of the Huntington Station Bank. Leopold Fishel was a director of the Babylon National Bank, and his brother Jonas Fishel was a charter member and trustee of the Riverhead Savings Bank. In social circles Bernard and Milton Hirschfeld were members of Old Town Lodge in Southampton, Louis Friedman of Freeport was part of the Odd Fellows, and Harry Weiss was a member of both the Odd Fellows and Royal Arcanum in Hicksville.

Life on Long Island was not only about earning a living, as sports and leisure activities played an important role in everyday life. Isaac Miller was a centerfielder and pitched for the Freeport club in the Long Island South Shore Base Ball League in 1899, Max Lipetz from Riverhead played basketball in 1911 for a team called the Good Ground Crescents, and George Morton Levy suited up for the Freeport High School football team in 1904. Later in life Levy founded Roosevelt Raceway and was inducted into the Harness Racing Hall of Fame in 1967. One Jewish athlete from Long Island even made it to the major leagues when Babylon's Leo Fishel appeared in a game for the New York Giants on May 3, 1899. At the time Leo was a college man matriculated at Columbia University, located just forty blocks south of the Polo Grounds where the Giants played their home games. Fishel pitched a complete game in a 7–3 loss to the Philadelphia Phillies but made history that day becoming the first Jewish pitcher in the history of Major League Baseball. In their account of the game the *New York Times* said Fishel "has a variety of curves, both slow and speedy, and at times he mixes these up in such clever style that the hard-hitting Philadelphias were made to look foolish." The *Morning Telegraph* newspaper reported that Giants Manager John Day would sign the twenty-one-year-old to a contract by the end of the month once Leo graduated from Columbia. But it was not meant to be. It was the only game Fishel ever appeared in at the big-league level. He chose instead to become a lawyer, perhaps at the urging of his parents.

As part of his residential development in Freeport Hugo Stearns had a nine-hole golf course constructed on his property that was expanded to eighteen holes and became Manhattan Country Club (later known as Milburn Country Club). Jacob Jaffe from Roosevelt played a match on this course in 1917 but was not able to take home the gold cup awarded to the winner. Moses Feltenstein had a tennis court adjacent to his home in

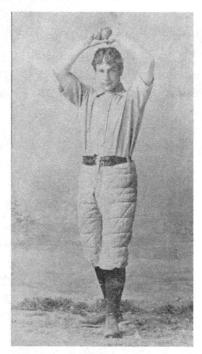

Figure 9. Leo Fishel from Babylon, the first Jewish pitcher in Major League Baseball history. *Source:* Courtesy of Fred Fishel.

Freeport that he would flood in the winter to become an ice-skating rink. Also in Freeport Isaac DaSilva entered a Ping-Pong tournament in 1902 losing in the quarterfinals, Isidore Mayer opened a roller rink in 1909, and Jacob Kegel managed the Woodcleft Channel Bathing Pavilion during the summer months. Benjamin Rosen was a member of the Southampton string quartet in 1908, Regina Sturmdorf was a concert pianist in Southold, and Hannah Weiss from Hicksville earned some notoriety playing cards as "the champion woman euchre player of the Island" in 1912.

When it was necessary to support their country in military service, Long Island's Jewish men proved up to the task. From just a handful of Jewish families living on the island in the early 1860s two men were involved with the armed forces during the Civil War years, both via the draft. Andrew Fishel from Patchogue registered in June of 1863, and Jacob Sidenberg from Hempstead was drafted into the New York State militia in 1864.

Once the United States entered the Great War in 1917 there was no shortage of young men willing to sign up and serve. Some of those who enlisted were Isaac Jaspin from Rockville Centre; Bernard Gobetz, Harry Puck, Lawrence Puck, and Jacob Shapero from Freeport; Jesse Schramm from Babylon; Harry Leavitt from Riverhead; Milton Hirschfeld and William Tisnower from Southampton; and Herbert Wimpfheimer from Westhampton Beach. At least ten men from Patchogue served including three of Daniel and Ethel Davidow's five sons and brothers Dewitt and Leonard Cohn. Dewitt was on board the SS *Tuscania* when the luxury cruise liner turned military transport was torpedoed by a German submarine in the Irish Sea. He survived the ship's sinking, but 210 of his comrades did not. Sergeant Harry Golden from Setauket, part of the 307th Infantry 77th Division was killed in France on May 29, 1918. Isaac Tisnower from Southampton suffered the same fate when he was killed in action on September 14 as was Isaac Solomonoff from Halesite on September 27, just six weeks before Germany surrendered and ended the war.

These are just some of the individuals who left a mark through public records that is discoverable more than a hundred years after the fact. The presence of early Jewish residents on Long Island can also be remembered today by seeing their names listed on plaques in synagogues, their gravestones, and streets that bear their names including Kaplan Avenue in Greenport, Bernstein Boulevard in Center Moriches, Karlin Drive in Calverton, and

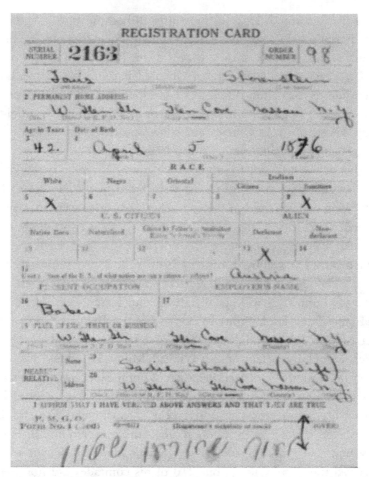

Figure 10. Presumably Louis Shorenstein from Glen Cove did not know how to write in English, so he signed his name in Hebrew at the bottom of his WWI registration card. *Source:* National Archives and Records Administration accessed from familysearch.org.

Sterns Court in Farmingdale. There are thousands more identified in the pages that follow who had an impact in their own way, within their families and communities, that paved the way for the generations of Jewish Long Islanders to come.

The Jewish population of Long Island that followed had its first spike in growth following World War I and was the beginning of what American

Figure 11. Leonard Cohn from Patchogue. *Source:* Celia M. Hastings Local History Room, Patchogue-Medford Library.

Jewish historian Jacob Rader Marcus referred to as the "voluntary suburban ghetto." Reliable figures by ethnicity are hard to come by, but it is believed there were six thousand Jews living in Nassau County in 1930 who made up just 1.9 percent of the population. Following World War II there was an unprecedented explosion of Jews who moved out to Long Island, creating one of the largest Jewish communities in the diaspora. By 1960 there were 345,000 Jews living in Nassau accounting for 26.5 percent of the population of the county. Trends in recent years have led to a decrease in synagogue affiliation causing the merger of multiple congregations among Conservative and Reform Jews. At the same time growth in the Orthodox community has emerged in certain areas, and the popularity of Chabad has given many an appreciation for thousands of years of Jewish tradition.

Figure 12. Memorial in Setauket for Harry Golden who was killed in the line of duty during WWI. *Source:* Photo by Brad Kolodny.

As Judaism on Long Island continues to evolve the constant that will not change is the history of how these Jewish communities began, why Jews decided to settle in Nassau and Suffolk counties, and their early prosperity that planted the seed for the growth that followed.

Part I
Nassau County

Chapter 2

Cedarhurst

Including Lawrence and Woodmere

In the late nineteenth and early twentieth century every sizable town on Long Island had a main street or central area where stores and shops engaged in commerce of goods and services. In some larger villages there were factories that employed individuals to manufacture goods, and in more rural areas farmers produced crops to bring to market. In most cases an individual would earn a living within the confines of the town they lived in or in a neighboring town; however, this was not necessarily true in Cedarhurst. Because of its location on the western edge of Nassau County and ease of getting to New York City there were several men who became among the first commuters to find employment in Manhattan, taking the train on a daily basis from home to work. This was particularly true after 1910 when the East River tunnels opened, allowing riders of the Long Island Rail Road (LIRR) to go directly into Penn Station, making the time to and from work considerably shorter. Prior to that, Long Islanders wishing to access Manhattan by mass transit rode the LIRR to Long Island City in Queens and transferred to a ferry to cross the river docking at the East Thirty-Fourth Street terminal.

Working in Manhattan opened a world of opportunity to earn a living in a variety of different industries. Some Cedarhurst residents were employed as traders of stocks and bonds, while others worked in the garment district or in the jewelry business. Henry Rosenfelt, an attorney from Philadelphia, took a different path as a fundraiser and philanthropist working for the American Jewish War Relief Committee on East Fortieth Street. As the assistant executive director Henry coordinated the appeal to raise funds across the United States for Jews in Europe who were displaced or affected during World War I. In January 1915, $275,000 had been raised: but less than three years later, in December 1917 after the United States had entered the conflict, Rosenfelt had the distinction of making a major announcement. Through the generosity of donors around the country the organization's fundraising tally had reached $10 million.

Figure 13. Grave of Henry Rosenfelt in West Palm Beach, Florida. *Source:* Photo by Julia Kolodny.

Residential dwellings in the heart of any village on Long Island could be found in small apartments above stores in the central business district. In Cedarhurst this was the case along Central Avenue, but many Jews lived in single-family homes on tree-lined streets. It was not uncommon to find Jewish households that included one or more individuals who lived in the home as a servant, maid, or other domestic helper. Wealthy families were settling in Cedarhurst, including Rudolf and Miriam Kohn and their children Edward and Janet who lived at 49 Columbia Avenue. Rudolf, born in Vienna in 1883, came to the United States in 1905 and was general manager of the De Luxe Clock & Manufacturing Company on East Seventeenth Street in Manhattan. Business interests led to trips overseas that included stops in England, France, Germany, Switzerland, Austria, Czechoslovakia, and Holland. On at least one occasion Miriam joined Rudolf on his European excursions.

Abraham Adelberg was from a different generation than the newer Jewish residents who were moving into the area in the later 1910s. Adelberg, a Russian immigrant, was established in business as the head of a

Figure 14. Rudolf Kohn. *Source:* National Archives and Records Administration accessed from familysearch.org.

prominent clothing firm in Manhattan around the turn of the century before moving to Cedarhurst in 1907. Having achieved success in the garment industry, Adelberg turned his focus toward civic involvement, becoming a trustee of the Nassau County Police Relief Fund and chairman of the Sanitary Commission of District 1. When the Village of Cedarhurst was incorporated in 1910, Adelberg was one of the three trustees and soon after became a real estate developer, purchasing one hundred acres of farmland north of the LIRR train tracks. Roads were built and gas, electric, water, and telephone systems were installed to service more than thirty homes to be built in the community known at the time as Cedarhurst Park North. As part of this high-end residential development Adelberg established Cedarhurst Country Club in 1914 with his son Max and a third partner Max Greenwald. The trio, along with club officers and committee chairmen, unveiled the $50,000 clubhouse with much fanfare at a gala reception on June 6 for five hundred people, which included a hundred club members and their guests.

Over the next several years the country club would host dances, concerts, motion picture entertainment and other social gatherings for its members. On occasion the clubhouse would be used by nonmembers for weddings, meetings, and in 1917 as a staging area for local men from southwestern Nassau County who were drafted to serve in the armed forces. As a veteran of the Spanish-American War, Adelberg was happy to do his duty for the war effort and volunteered the Cedarhurst Country Club to be used as barracks. Seventy-five men were housed there, meals were prepared for as many as three hundred, and a memorable sendoff banquet was held on September 5 for the first round of recruits who were to become soldiers. Adelberg felt it was his obligation to ensure that each drafted man was well fed, entertained, and had a good night's sleep before transitioning from civilian to military life. At the banquet Adelberg addressed the men and was given a long, thunderous ovation as a token of their appreciation.

Without a synagogue nearby, Adelberg and others joined Temple Israel in Far Rockaway, founded in 1908 and located across the county line in Queens. In later years Rudolf Kohn and his family became members of Temple Israel once that congregation relocated to Lawrence and built a new synagogue in 1930. Prior to that the first congregation organized in Cedarhurst was Temple Beth El founded in 1922. They built a synagogue shortly after on Locust Avenue that was dedicated on September 14, 1924, and is still in use today.

CEDARHURST COUNTRY CLUB, CEDARHURST, L. I.

Figures 15 and 16. Memorial plaque for Abraham Adelberg located in Cedarhurst Park. *Source:* Photo by Brad Kolodny; and the Cedarhurst Country Club he founded in 1914. *Source:* From the collection of the author.

Abraham Adelberg continued to be a force for good in the community. He raised his profile among residents of the village and ascended the political ranks becoming village president in 1926. Due to a law change in 1927 the new head official of Cedarhurst would become mayor. Adelberg was elected mayor of Cedarhurst in 1928 and served the public in that capacity until 1932.

Table 2.1. Residents of Cedarhurst

Abraham	**Adelberg**		1874	1936	First wife Sarah Braun died 1905
Max	Adelberg	son	1892		
Sadie	Adelberg	daughter	1894		m. Joseph Steinberg
Rose	Adelberg	daughter	1898		
Ida	Adelberg	daughter	1900		
Nora	(Braun) Adelberg	second wife	1886		Sister of Abraham's first wife Sarah
Donald	Adelberg	son	1906		
Irene	Adelberg	daughter	1910	1948	
Victor	**Barton**		1894	1966	Son of Anna Frank
Clifford	**Barton**		1896	1958	Son of Anna Frank
Max	**Berg**		1882		Dry goods merchant
Minnie	Berg	wife	1886		
Emmanuel	Berg	son	1908		
Morris	**Berman**		1860		
Anna	(Scholn) Berman	wife	1864		
Israel	**Bernfeld**		1858	1921	
Rose	(Fein) Bernfeld	wife	1870		
Mollie	Bernfeld	daughter	1887		
William	Bernfeld	son	1888		
Dora	Bernfeld	daughter	1896		
Sophia	Bernfeld	daughter	1899		
Bertha	**Dreyfus**		1844	1928	
Frederick	Dreyfus	son	1876	1950	
Rubin	**Endler**		1874		Coat manufacturer in NYC
Anna	Endler	wife	1884		
Herbert	Endler	son	1904		
David	Endler	son	1906		
Alice	Endler	daughter	1910		
Nathan	**Frank**		1874		
Anna	(Rosenbaum) Frank		1874		Second marriage, first husband was Frank Barton
Leo	**Goldberger**		1881		Cleaner and dyer
Louise	Goldberger	wife	1884		
Frank	Goldberger	son	1912		
Hilda	Goldberger	daughter	1914		
Michael	**Goldstein**		1872		Merchant
Hattie	(Wiener) Goldstein	wife	1886		
Travis	Goldstein	son	1912		

Table 2.1. Continued.

Myrna	Goldstein	daughter	1915		
Leonard	Goldstein	son	1918		
Charles	**Hepner**		1873		Brother of Samuel
Rae	(Samuels) Hepner	wife	1877		
Elizabeth	Hepner	daughter	1906		
Florence	Hepner	daughter	1909		
Samuel	**Hepner**		1864		Brother of Charles
Joanna	**Hirsch**		1870		Sister of Bertha Dreyfus
George	**Hirschhorn**		1879	1962	Middle name Washington
Blanche	Hirschhorn	wife	1882		
Rosamond	Hirschhorn	daughter	1907		
Carol	Hirschhorn	daughter	1910		
Morris	**Jacobs**		1854		Insurance salesman
Annie	(Schick) Jacobs	wife	1861		
Morris	**Kirsner**		1863		Tailor
Minnie	Kirsner	wife	1875		
Harry	Kirsner	son	1898		
Rebecca	Kirsner	daughter	1902		
Charles	Kirsner	son	1911		
Rudolf	**Kohn**		1883		Clock manufacturer in NYC
Miriam	(Burgheim) Kohn	wife	1886		
Edward	Kohn	son	1915		
Janet	Kohn	daughter	1917	2005	
Benjamin	**Lesser**		1881		Salesman in NYC
Sally	Lesser	wife	1883		
Isabel	Lesser	daughter	1912		
Annette	Lesser	daughter	1915		
Henry	**Levine**		1875		Grocer
Eva	Levine	wife	1877		
Sadie	Levine	daughter	1898		
Esther	Levine	daughter	1902		
Joseph	Levine	son	1903		
Jacob	**Mayblum**		1878		Grocer
Olga	Mayblum	wife	1878		
Lillian	Mayblum	daughter	1905		
Benjamin	**Meyer**		1879		Jewelry merchant
Sylvia	(Sobel) Meyer	wife	1896		
Elsie	Meyer	daughter	1916		
Shirley	Meyer	daughter	1918		

continued on next page

Table 2.1. Continued.

Louis	**Moss**		1877		Cloth business in NYC
Miriam	(Wolf) Moss	wife	1882	1952	
Sidney	Moss	son	1902		
Mildred	Moss	daughter	1904		
Frank	Moss	son	1913		
Samuel	**Perper**		1880	1943	Importer in NYC
Lillian	(Sturman) Perper	wife	1890		
Sylvia	Perper	daughter	1914		
Dorothy	Perper	daughter	1914		
Howard	Perper	son	1916		
Charles	**Press**		1881		Tailor
Sarah	Press	wife	1882		
Rosa	Press	daughter	1908		
Isador	Press	son	1909		
Edith	Press	daughter	1912		
Abraham	Press	son	1914		
Yetta	Press	daughter	1916		
Arthur	Press	son	1918		
Henry	**Rosenfelt**		1877	1959	Worked for American Jewish War Relief Committee
Celia	(Cohn) Rosenfelt	wife	1884		
Marc	Rosenfelt	son	1910		
Samuel	**Rosenthal**		1877		Tailor
Tessie	Rosenthal	wife	1888		
Sylvia	Rosenthal	daughter	1909		
Lillian	Rosenthal	daughter	1911		
Herbert	Rosenthal	son	1915		
Sidney	Rosenthal	son	1915		
Israel	**Saul**		1886		Clothing merchant
Charlotte	(Berman) Saul	wife	1892		
Lucille	Saul	daughter	1915		
Juliet	Saul	daughter	1917		
Isidore	**Schweitzer**		1885		Ladies wear manufacturer in NYC
Sadie	Schweitzer	wife	1889		
Helen	Schweitzer	daughter	1913		
Florence	Schweitzer	daughter	1915		
Austin	Schweitzer	son	1918		
George	**Shaskan**		1883	1950	Dealer in stocks and bonds

Table 2.1. Continued.

Fannie	(Luber) Shaskan	wife	1880	1969	
Gertrude	Shaskan	daughter	1902		
Sidney	Shaskan	son	1903	1985	
Donald	Shaskan	son	1910	1995	
Gladys	Shaskan	daughter	1913	2003	
George	Shaskan	son	1917	2007	
Samuel	**Siegel**		1891		Owned a furniture store
Ethel	Siegel	wife	1891		
Pearl	Siegel	daughter	1916		
Joseph	**Steinberg**		1888		
Sadie	(Adelberg) Steinberg	wife	1894		Daughter of Abraham and Sarah
Sophie	Steinberg	daughter	1917		
Max	**Weisenberg**		1855		
Yetta	Weisenberg	wife	1868		
Sadie	Weisenberg	daughter	1887		m. Henry Wohl
Rose	Weisenberg	daughter	1896		
Honora	Weisenberg	daughter	1900		
Regina	Weisenberg	daughter	1903		
Henry	**Wohl**		1880		Manufacturer in NYC
Sadie	(Weissberg) Wohl	wife	1887		Daughter of Max and Yetta
Alfred	Wohl	son	1915		
Eleanor	Wohl	daughter	1918		

Table 2.2. Residents of Lawrence

Samuel	**Bernstein**		1878		Shirtwaist manufacturer in NYC
Yetta	Bernstein	wife	1889		
Martin	Bernstein	son	1907		
Edith	Bernstein	daughter	1909		
Joseph	**Cohen**		1881		Glazier
Annie	Cohen	wife	1884		
Henry	Cohen	son	1906		
Dorothy	Cohen	daughter	1914		
Anna	Cohen	daughter	1918		
Abraham	**Dobkin**		1890	1938	Worked in a grocery store
Edward	**Fleming**		1876		Chauffer
Gussie	Fleming	wife	1890		

continued on next page

Table 2.2. Continued.

Charles	Fleming	son	1907		
James	Fleming	son	1909		
Rosie	Fleming	daughter	1912		
Joseph	**Fried**		1862		Lawyer
Flora	(Shamberg) Fried	wife	1879		
Muriel	Fried	daughter	1904		
Walter	Fried	son	1905		
Caroline	Fried	daughter	1907		
Anita	Fried	daughter	1909		
Lorna	Fried	daughter	1912		
John	**Logunow**		1883	1942	Mechanic
Fannie	(Shapiro) Logunow	wife	1886		
Ray	Logunow	daughter	1904	1948	
Dorie	Logunow	daughter	1906		
Abraham	Logunow	son	1907		
Eva	Logunow	daughter	1910		
Goldie	Logunow	daughter	1912		
Samuel	Logunow	son	1918		
James	**Loucheim**		1845	1938	Liquor merchant
Bessie	(Wachenheimer) Loucheim	wife	1851	1931	
Myra	Loucheim		1876		m. Harry Rascovar
Jerome	**Loucheim**		1878		Son of James and Bessie
Elsa	Loucheim	wife	1880		
Jerome	Loucheim	son	1906		
Elsa	Loucheim	daughter	1910		
Harry	**Rascovar**		1872		Advertising
Myra	(Loucheim) Rascovar	wife	1876		Daughter of James and Bessie
Stanley	Rascovar	son	1905		
Bessie	Rascovar	daughter	1908		
Louis	**Simon**		1861		Dry goods merchant
Fannie	Simon	wife	1867		
Ida	Simon	daughter	1890		
Joseph	Simon	son	1891		
Louis	Simon	son	1893		
Rosie	Simon	daughter	1894		
Jacob	Simon	son	1895		
Mary	Simon	daughter	1897		

Table 2.2. Continued.

Matilda	Simon	daughter	1899		
Barney	**Spitzer**		1885	1970	
Sarah	Spitzer	wife	1888		
Arthur	Spitzer	son	1910		
Alfred	Spitzer	son	1911		
Jesse	Spitzer	son	1913		

Table 2.3. Residents of Woodmere

Morris	**Milk**		1860	1947	Dry goods merchant
Hilda	(Miller) Milk	wife	1868	1913	
Edith	Milk	daughter	1890	1951	
Gertie	Milk	daughter	1893	1947	
Alexander	Milk	son	1894	1987	
Harry	Milk	son	1896	1946	
William	Milk	son	1897	1976	
Albert	Milk	son	1904	1981	
Meyer	**Mosko**		1883		Tailor
Sarah	(Silverman) Mosko	wife	1891		
Robert	Mosko	son	1913		
Samuel	**Pearlman**		1878		Tailor
Esther	Pearlman	wife	1892		
Catherine	Pearlman	daughter	1918		
Sigfried	**Rosenthal**		1875		Shirtwaist manufacturer in NYC
Alpha	(Korn) Rosenthal	wife	1890		
Lawrence	Rosenthal	son	1912		
Edwin	Rosenthal	son	1915		
Robert	Rosenthal	son	1917		
Jacob	**Sachs**		1883	1943	
Carrie	(Miller) Sachs	wife	1882	1951	
Hattie	Sachs	daughter	1913		
Moritz	**Wormser**		1878		Banker
Adele	(Zellner) Wormser	wife	1880	1920	
Samuel	Wormser	son	1907		
Charles	Wormser	son	1912		
Carolyn	Wormser	daughter	1916		

Chapter 3

Freeport

Including Roosevelt and Wantagh

Originally known as Raynortown, the name Freeport was adopted in 1853 because ships during the colonial period were not charged a fee for docking and unloading cargo. It was predominantly a fishing village where oystering was a popular occupation due to its location on the Great South Bay. This began to change in the years following the Civil War thanks in part to the Southside Railroad that brought people out from New York City, including merchants who set up shop on Main Street and established the village as an area for commerce.

The first Jew to arrive was Morris Miller. He lived in Baldwin briefly but came to Freeport in 1871, establishing his store on the north side of Pine Street between South Grove (today Guy Lombardo Avenue) and Church Streets. Ten years later Miller moved his growing establishment to the ground level at 90 South Main Street and took up residence with his wife and three children above the store. Hyman Schloss had a department store in the heart of the village at the corner of Fulton Avenue (today Merrick Road) and South Main Street. He was an innovator, being the first in Freeport to install hanging gas lamps to illuminate his store in the evening and was also the first to have electric lighting inside his store.

Schloss and Miller, along with Henry Gobetz, were three prominent Freeport businessmen who were influential in establishing early Jewish gatherings in Nassau County. Residents from Freeport, Hempstead, and Rockville Centre were involved in the Hebrew Union of the Town of

Figure 17. Fiftieth wedding anniversary invitation for Hyman and Lillian Schloss. Hyman was active in organizing Jewish associations in the Town of Hempstead beginning in 1897 and was a vice president at Temple B'nai Israel in Freeport for twenty years. Lillian was president of the Ladies Aid Society in Hempstead for twenty-five years and treasurer of the sisterhood at B'nai Israel for twenty-two years. *Source:* Freeport Historical Society.

Hempstead that was formed in October 1897. Morris Miller hosted a meeting at his home on November 21 where by-laws were adopted and officers elected, including Miller as vice president and Gobetz as messenger. The organization was short lived, disbanding after just six months, but before too long the Nassau County Hebrew Association was established. Henry Gobetz hosted the first meeting held on November 30, 1902, with Hyman Schloss as a trustee. The long-term stability of this group was not meant to be, as their operation ceased in 1904. Schloss decided to align with a group of men from Rockville Centre and Lynbrook who started a new iteration of the Nassau County Hebrew Association in 1906. This led to the formation of a congregation in 1907 called B'nai Sholom located in Rockville Centre. Schloss was one of the original ten members, but no other Freeporters joined him at its inception.

The majority of Jewish immigrants in the United States who settled on Long Island came from either Germany or eastern Europe. Henry Gobetz was one of a small group who were exceptions. He hailed from London and came to America in the 1860s as did the Nykerk and DaSilva families. It seems likely that members of these three families who ended up in Freeport knew each other back in England.

Moses DaSilva, a cigar maker from Amsterdam, married Rachel Baruch in 1855 and shortly after moved to London. The young couple had three children, Isaac, Rachel, and Sophia, all of whom were born in London and would make the voyage to America with their mother in 1860. On the same ship were Ezekiel and Elizabeth Nykerk, also natives of Amsterdam, and their children Esther and Louis who were born in London. Upon arrival in the United States they all settled in New York City with the DaSilvas living at 170 Christopher Street in 1868. A year later Henry Gobetz left London and in 1870 was living with Moses and Rachel DaSilva. Henry must have spent a considerable amount of time with their daughter Rachel as they formed a relationship and decided to get married in 1874. By 1878 Henry and Rachel Gobetz were living in Freeport with Henry running a cigar and stationery store.

Cigars sold in Gobetz's store were presumably supplied by Henry's father-in-law Moses and brother-in-law Isaac who were in the cigar manufacturing business. In the 1870s the father and son duo had cigar factories in Sayville and Rockaway and also had a retail establishment M. DaSilva & Son in Westville (today Inwood) in 1880. By 1887 the DaSilva family had moved to Freeport with an eye on more than just cigars. Isaac at this point was married with children of his own and firmly at the helm of the family business. After running two stores in Freeport, one on Fulton Street (today Merrick Road) and the other on the southeast corner of Main Street and Olive Boulevard (today Sunrise Highway), Isaac decided to open additional locations in other villages that would become the first chain of five- and ten-cent stores on Long Island. Isaac's son Jacob opened a DaSilva's store in Huntington followed by five more in Rockville Centre, Oyster Bay, Babylon, Bay Shore, and Glen Cove.

At the dawn of the twentieth century the village continued to grow with the arrival of the Long Island Traction Company in 1902 that ran a trolley from Brooklyn to Freeport. Part of the route included South Main Street, where anyone riding between Olive Boulevard and Merrick Road would have encountered a plethora of Jewish-owned businesses. Shoppers along this central part of the village could have stopped in at Harry Barasch's department store, Simon Baumann's furniture store, Louis Bender's butcher shop, Harry Glaser's delicatessen, Jacobson's shoe store, Adolph Levy & Son men's clothing store, the Victor Stationery and Cigar store owned by Louis Michnoff, Abraham Miller's jewelry store, Ralph Samet's women's clothing store, Mervin Schloss's dental practice, Abraham Siegel's paint store, and the American Theater owned by Mark Levy and Michael Hirschthal.

After Glen Cove, Freeport had the second-largest Jewish population in Nassau County prior to World War I, yet there was no organization that

Figure 18. Two of the eight DaSilva chain stores were located in Freeport, this one on Fulton Street (today Merrick Road) in 1905. Adolph Levy's original store can be seen across the street. *Source:* Freeport Historical Society.

Figure 19. Harry Barasch in front of his store on Main Street. *Source:* Courtesy of Betsy Plevan.

brought them together as a Jewish community. While there were attempts to form a congregation with residents from Hempstead and Rockville Centre those efforts did not pan out due to irreconcilable differences among the membership. The issues that led to the demise of these groups included whether to put financial resources toward establishing a cemetery or building a synagogue. When a synagogue became the priority, a debate raged about where to build it, causing a territorial squabble with no solution resulting in the geographic factions going their separate ways. Max Stockman, a tailor living in Freeport by 1910, was not involved in these early iterations of Jewish communal gathering but must have felt a need to fill the void when he formed the Freeport Hebrew Association in 1913.

In addition to the merchants who lined South Main Street in the 1910s there were individuals from another industry who found Freeport to be a popular destination. Entertainers of the stage and screen made their way to what had become a resort community during the summertime when Broadway theaters were closed. These actors banded together to form the

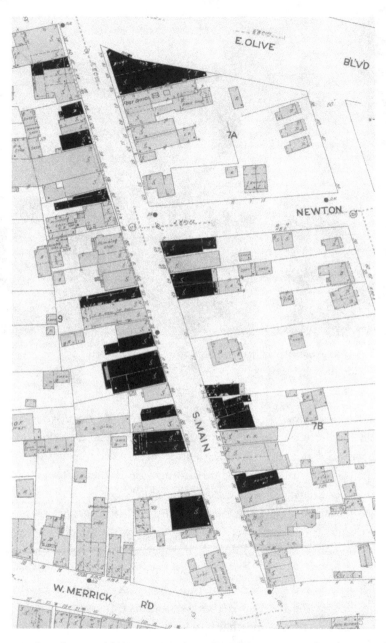

Figure 20. Jewish-owned businesses and residences by 1920 on South Main Street between Olive Boulevard (today Sunrise Highway) and Merrick Road are shaded in black. *Source:* Sanborn Fire Insurance Map from Freeport, Nassau County, New York. Sanborn Map Company, March 1917.

Long Island Good Hearted Thespian Society (LIGHTS) and held performances to the delight of the locals. Among the Jewish entertainers who came to Freeport were singer Sophie Tucker, comedienne Fanny Brice, and composer/pianist Harry Ruby. Others stayed beyond the summer, as was the case for Adolph "Harpo" Marx who came out to Freeport for a few months in 1907. He worked as a piano player earning $8 per month plus room and board at Schang's Hotel, a brothel on Fulton Street east of Liberty Avenue. Abraham and Lena Puck had two children, Harry and Eva, who performed in a song-and-dance act known as Two Little Pucks. They were a hit in New York and other cities but also performed locally at annual fundraising events in 1916, 1917, and 1918 to benefit the building fund for a synagogue in Freeport.

Initially the Freeport Hebrew Association was social and educational in nature, holding discussions about topics including politics, government, and civic responsibilities. A banquet and dance were held on February 11,

Figure 21. Eva and Harry Puck, 1916. *Source:* From the collection of the author.

1914, giving chairman Max Stockman the opportunity to address the 150 attendees. Over a dinner of salmon with hollandaise sauce and fricassé roast duck he laid out the goals of the organization: "To promote brotherly love and to assist one another in the hour of need, and to uplift the moral and intellectual standard of its fellows." Other than Stockman's leadership as chairman, Harry Barasch served as vice chairman, Henry Strauss from nearby Roosevelt was secretary, and Philip Jacobson treasurer. The following year plans were put in place to hold worship services for the High Holidays at Brooklyn Hall led by Rabbi Isaac Epstein and Samuel Jaffe as the cantor. The first gathering of Jews for religious purposes in Freeport was a success, with over a hundred attending. On September 12, 1915, the Sunday evening between Rosh Hashanah and Yom Kippur, a meeting was held at the home of Louis Friedman, and Congregation B'nai Israel was formally established. Momentum continued into October when the congregation began holding Hebrew school on Sunday mornings, also at Brooklyn Hall.

The next step for the fledgling congregation was to seek out a suitable piece of property where a synagogue could be built. A 200' × 200' lot at Broadway and Mount Avenue was purchased in 1916 and architect Christian E. Kern, a Freeport resident, was selected to design the building. By October that year over $1,000 had been pledged by members of B'nai Israel, but because of the war construction was delayed. At a ceremony on August 22, 1920, Morris Miller, the oldest member of the congregation and a merchant who had arrived in Freeport some fifty years prior, was given the honor of laying the cornerstone.

As was the case in many communities across the island following World War II, a surge in the Jewish population of Freeport led to the congregation building a new synagogue. Groundbreaking for the current synagogue located on North Bayview Avenue took place in 1956 with a formal dedication ceremony held on October 24, 1965.

Table 3.1. Residents of Freeport

Henry	**Ackerman**		1853		Paint and wallpaper store owner
Mary Elizabeth	(Nykerk) Ackerman	wife	1858		Daughter of Ezekiel and
Hannah	Ackerman	daughter	1877	1946	m. James Gobetz
Elizabeth	Ackerman	daughter	1881		
Morris	Ackerman	son	1883	1968	m. Catharine Meehan
Aaron	Ackerman	son	1885	1931	
Abraham	Ackerman	son	1891	1892	
Birdie	Ackerman	daughter	1894	1961	m. Jacob DaSilva
Morris	**Ackerman**		1883	1968	Son of Henry and Mary
Catharine	(Meehan) Ackerman	wife	1884		
Beatrice	Ackerman	daughter	1913		
Henry	Ackerman	son	1915		
Louis	**Appleton**		1890	1985	Hardware store owner
Ruth	(Sonenblick) Appleton	wife	1892		
Norman	Appleton	son	1915		
Arnold	Appleton	son	1918		
Harry	**Barasch**		1877	1937	Son of George and Hilda from Lindenhurst
Regina	(Rattner) Barasch	wife	1881	1956	
Herman	Barasch	son	1906	1961	
Beatrice	Barasch	daughter	1910		
William	Barasch	son	1918	1959	
Seymour	**Baumann**		1884	1947	Ran furniture store owned by his father-in-law Simon
Florence	(Baumann) Baumann	wife	1888		Daughter of Simon and Carrie
Lester	Baumann	son	1915		
Janette	Baumann	daughter	1917		
Simon	**Baumann**		1862	1944	Owned five furniture stores
Carrie	(Schlenker) Baumann	wife	1862	1928	
William	Baumann	son	1887		
Florence	Baumann	daughter	1888		m. Seymour Baumann
Jerome	Baumann	son	1890		
Eugene	**Bender**		1881	1946	Brother of Louis
Marie	Bender	wife	1892		
Louis	**Bender**		1874	1932	Butcher
Minnie	(Nachman) Bender	wife	1874	1923	

continued on next page

Table 3.1. Continued.

Sylvia	Bender	daughter	1898	1995	
Arthur	Bender	son	1898	1968	
Jefferson	Bender	son	1900	1963	
Frank	**Brown**		1900		Brother-in-law of Louis Posner
Harry	**Cohen**		1869	1941	
Mary	(Duffy) Cohen	wife	1870		
Harry Jr	Cohen	son	1906		
Felix	Cohen	son	1909		
Louis	**Cohen**		1886		Furniture salesman
Annie	(Viertel) Cohen	wife	1887		Daughter of Nathan and Fanny
Jules	Cohen	son	1908		
Serviar	Cohen	son	1910		
George	**Comer**		1863	1934	Singer and entertainer
Daniel	**DaSilva**		1885	1965	Son of Isaac and Annie
Carrie	(Kramer) DaSilva	wife	1893	1918	
Isaac	**DaSilva**		1855	1919	Son of Moses and Rachel
Annie	(Horowitz) DaSilva	wife	1863	1919	Sister of Benjamin Horowitz
Moses	DaSilva	son	1881	1954	m. Ella Cammaun lived in Valley Stream
Daniel	DaSilva	son	1885		m. Carrie Kramer
Louise	DaSilva	daughter			
Louis	DaSilva	son	1887	1958	
Jacob	**DaSilva**		1888		Son of Isaac and Annie
Birdie	(Ackerman) DaSilva	wife	1894	1961	Daughter of Henry and Mary
Edwin	DaSilva	son	1915	1919	
Moses	**DaSilva**		1835	1894	Cigar manufacturer
Rachel	(Baruch) DaSilva	wife	1834	1917	
Thomas	**Davison**		1841		Father of Rose Henschel
Philip	**Dobkin**				Owned Nu Mode Millinery
Isaac	**Epstein**				Rabbi
Moses	**Feltenstein**		1873		Lawyer
Sidonia	(Holland) Feltenstein	wife	1882		
Sidney	Feltenstein	son	1903		
Roslyn	Feltenstein	daughter	1906		
Bernice	Feltenstein	daughter	1917		
Leo	**Fishel**		1877	1960	Son of Leopold and Theresa from Babylon

Table 3.1. Continued.

Laura	(Duerstein) Fishel	wife	1895	1971	
Leo Jr.	Fishel	son	1917	2003	
Louis	**Friedman**		1886		
Belle	Friedman	wife	1888		
Julius	Friedman	son			
Joseph	Friedman	son			
Pearl	Friedman	daughter	1912		
Edwin	Friedman	son	1915		
Bernard	Friedman	son	1915		
Harry	**Glaser**		1881		In the liquor business
Lena	(Mayer) Glaser	wife	1883		Daughter of Judith
Henry	**Gobetz**		1852	1925	Owned a cigar and stationery store
Rachel	(DaSilva) Gobetz	first wife	1857	1898	Daughter of Moses and Rachel
James	Gobetz	son	1875		
Rosie	(Greebel) Gobetz	second wife	1873	1921	Daughter of Sophie
Bernard	Gobetz	son	1901		
Jessie	Gobetz	daughter	1902		
James	**Gobetz**		1875		Son of Henry and Rachel
Hannah	(Ackerman) Gobetz	wife	1877	1946	Daughter of Henry and Mary
Henry	Gobetz	son	1894		
Estelle	Gobetz	daughter	1895		
Leroy	Gobetz	son	1898		
Lafayette	Gobetz	son	1900	1965	
Arthur	Gobetz	son	1903	1962	
Harold	Gobetz	son	1907	1990	
Robert	Gobetz	son	1909		
Wallace	Gobetz	son	1916	1973	
Joseph	**Goldberg**		1878		Children's garment manufacturer
Katie	(Kress) Goldberg	wife	1882		
Lily	Goldberg	daughter	1903		
Arthur	Goldberg	son	1905		
N.	**Goldberg**				Attended first meeting B'nai Israel 1915
Herman	**Goldfarb**		1873		Tailor
Rose	Goldfarb	wife	1872		
Joseph	Goldfarb	son	1895		
Cecilia	Goldfarb	daughter	1897		

continued on next page

Table 3.1. Continued.

Annie	Goldfarb	daughter	1901		
Tillie	Goldfarb	daughter	1903		
Sadie	Goldfarb	daughter	1906		
Emanuel	Goldfarb	son	1910		
Abraham	**Goldsmith**		1863	1928	
Sarah	(DaSilva) Goldsmith	wife			Daughter of Moses and Rachel
Max	**Goldsmith**		1879		
Jennie	(Markowitz) Goldsmith	wife	1881		Daughter of Jacob and Regina
Irving	Goldsmith	son	1904		
Philip	Goldsmith	son	1905		
Charles	Goldsmith	son	1907		
Henry	Goldsmith	son	1909		
Sophie	**(Heiman) Greebel**		1832	1920	
Rosie	Greebel	daughter	1871	1921	m. Henry Gobetz
Edith	Greebel	daughter	1873	1941	m. Henry Hirschfeld lived in Southampton
William	**Greenblatt**		1867	1921	Owned a stationery store
Helen	Greenblatt	wife	1872		
Sylvester	Greenblatt	son	1896	1956	
Aaron	**Henschel**		1872		Son of Morris and Rachel from Amityville
Rose	(Davison) Henschel	wife	1872		Daughter of Thomas Davison
Samuel	**Herzfield**		1876	1947	Shoe store owner
Ida	(Bloom) Herzfield	wife	1878		
Mervin	Herzfield	son	1903		
Ruth	Herzfield	daughter	1905		
Max	Herzfield	son	1907		
Leonard	Herzfield	son	1909		
Sara	Herzfield	daughter	1911		
Lillian	Herzfield	daughter	1913		
Michael	**Hirschthal**		1884	1948	Brother of Mary Levy
Ann	Hirschthal	wife	1896	1968	
Benjamin	**Horowitz**				Brother of Annie DaSilva
Louis	**Israel**				
Morris	**Jacobs**		1883		Metallurgist
Anna	(Deutch) Jacobs	wife	1887		
Lydia	Jacobs	daughter	1915		
Morris	**Jacobson**		1875	1938	Brother of Isaac from Lynbrook and Philip

Table 3.1. Continued.

Rosie	Jacobson	wife	1880		
David	Jacobson	son	1903		
Harry	Jacobson	son	1905		
Beatrice	Jacobson	daughter	1912		
Sylvia	Jacobson	daughter	1912		
Philip	**Jacobson**				Brother of Isaac from Lynbrook and Morris
Alfred	**Jonas**		1876		Son of Bernard and Regina from Wantagh
Lillie	(Klein) Jonas	wife			
Sigmund	**Kalban**		1889		
Sarah	(Knapp) Kalban	wife	1884		Daughter of Abraham and Fannie
Bernard	Kalban	son	1917		
Edward	**Kegel**		1889		Son of Jacob and Minnie
Bertha	Kegel	wife	1893		
Jacob	**Kegel**		1862	1917	Manager Woodcleft Channel Bathing Pavilion
Minnie	Kegel	wife			
Edward	Kegel	son	1889		m. Bertha
Abraham	**Knapp**		1857	1934	
Fannie	(Dobus) Knapp	wife			
Sarah	Knapp	daughter	1884		m. Sigmund Kalban
David	Knapp	son	1896		
Lillian	Knapp	daughter	1899		
Joseph	Knapp	son	1901		
William	**Kowitz**		1887		Artist
Miriam	(Rosenberg) Kowitz	wife	1887		
Nathaniel	Kowitz	son	1915		
Bertha	Kowitz	daughter	1917		
Joseph	**Kramer**		1879		Window washer
Gussie	Kramer	wife	1888		
Fanny	Kramer	daughter	1908		
Isadore	Kramer	son	1909		
Edith	Kramer	daughter	1912		
Bertie	Kramer	daughter	1914		
Rose	Kramer	daughter	1916		
Soll	**Lenden**		1884		Nephew of Hyman Schloss
Henri	**Leschziner**				Worked for Bedell & Co.
Harris	**Levine**		1867		Jeweler

continued on next page

Table 3.1. Continued.

Rosa	Levine	wife	1869	1920	
Jack	Levine	son	1901		
Sadie	Levine	daughter	1903		
Louise	Levine	daughter	1904		
Adolph	**Levy**		1854	1918	Men's clothing store owner
Anna	(Katz) Levy	wife	1864		
David	Levy	son	1887		m. Florence Friedman
George M.	Levy	son	1888	1977	Attorney
Jeanette	Levy	daughter	1894		m. Henry Miller
David	**Levy**		1887		Son of Adolph and Anna
Florence	(Friedman) Levy	wife	1894		
Mark	**Levy**		1869		Owned American Theatre with his brother-in-law Michael Hirschthal
Mary	(Hirschthal) Levy	wife	1878		Sister of Michael
Abraham	Levy	son	1910	1985	
Fanny	**Lieberman**		1875		
Herman	Lieberman	son	1896	1955	
Mabel	Lieberman	daughter	1905		
Jacob	**Loberfald**				
Lottie	(Behr) Loberfald	wife			
Rose	Loberfald	daughter	1888		
Louis	**Markheim**		1882		Wholesale silk salesman
Charlotte	(Cestonicker) Markheim	wife	1887		
Annette	Markheim	daughter	1909		
Dorothy	Markheim	daughter	1912		
Jacob	**Markowitz**		1847	1920	
Regina	(Marks) Markowitz	wife	1851		
David	Markowitz	son	1874		
Jennie	Markowitz	daughter	1881		m. Max Goldsmith
Adolph	**Marx**		1888	1964	"Harpo" lived in Freeport 1907
Isidore	**Mayer**		1871		First president B'nai Israel 1915
Etta	(Jonas) Mayer	wife	1877		Daughter of Bernard and Regina from Wantagh
Hortense	Mayer	daughter	1902		
Judith	**Mayer**		1842		
Isidore	Mayer	son	1871		m. Etta Jonas
Lena	Mayer	daughter	1877		m. Harry Glaser

Table 3.1. Continued.

Leopold	Mayer	son	1880		
Simon	Mayer	son	1882		
Louis	**Michnoff**		1876		Son of Benjamin and Minnie from Bay Shore
Ray	(Kahn) Michnoff	wife	1884		
Meyer	**Michnoff**		1884		Son of Benjamin and Minnie from Bay Shore
Edith	Michnoff	wife	1893		
Henriette	Michnoff	daughter	1913		
Abraham	**Miller**		1888		Jeweler
Ethel	Miller	wife	1896		
Mildred	Miller	daughter	1917		
Henry	**Miller**		1890		
Jeanette	(Levy) Miller		1894		Daughter of Adolph and Anna
Isaac	**Miller**		1878	1948	Son of Morris and Fannie
Florence	(Klepperman) Miller	wife	1884		First husband Max Stockman
Morris	**Miller**		1845	1922	Merchant
Fannie	Miller	wife	1850	1922	
Carrie	Miller	daughter	1877		
Isaac	Miller	son	1878	1948	m. Florence Klepperman
Hattie	Miller	daughter	1883	1914	
William	**Millheiser**				
?	Millheiser	wife			
Bernard	Millheiser	son			
Harold	Millheiser	son	1898	1917	
Philip	**Nickelsburg**		1887	1963	Attended first meeting B'nai Israel 1915
Dina	Nickelsburg	wife	1888		
Elizabeth	**(Gobetz) Nykerk**		1834	1910	Mother of Mary Ackerman
Louis	**Posner**		1889	1961	Owned a cigar store
Francis	Posner	wife	1893		
Bertram	Posner	son	1918		
Abraham	**Puck**		1866		
Lena	(Salmon) Puck	wife	1874		
Harry	Puck	son	1891	1964	Song writer and actor
Eva	Puck	daughter	1892	1979	Actress
Lawrence	Puck	son	1896		
Lauretta	Puck	granddaughter	1912	1972	Daughter of Eva and Aaron Kessler

continued on next page

Table 3.1. Continued.

Sigmund	**Reiss**		1877		Insurance salesman
Bertha	(Sachter) Reiss	wife	1878	1948	
Estelle	Reiss	daughter	1902		
Mortimer	Reiss	son	1905		
Gertrude	Reiss	daughter	1909		
Abraham	**Rosenstein**		1873		Lawyer
Lena	Rosenstein	wife	1883		
Grace	Rosenstein	daughter	1907		
Ralph	**Samet**		1885		Owned a women's apparel shop
Lottie	Samet	wife	1894		
Tina	Samet	daughter	1914		
Warren	Samet	son	1917		
Max	**Samuels**				
Herman	**Schieber**		1871		
Yetta	Schieber	wife	1872		
Samuel	Schieber	son	1896		
Irving	Schieber	son	1899		
Francia	Schieber	daughter	1904		
Lillian	Schieber	daughter	1907		
Benjamin	**Schindler**		1890		
Rose	Schindler	wife	1890		
Edna	Schindler	daughter	1911		
Sylvia	Schindler	daughter	1917		
Nathan	**Schless**		1881		Wholesale silk merchant
Martha	(Fox) Schless	wife	1888		
Hortense	Schless	daughter	1911		
Janice	Schless	daughter	1914		
Hyman	**Schloss**		1870	1947	Department store owner
Lillian	(Livingstone) Schloss	wife	1875	1962	
Mervin	Schloss	son	1895	1985	
Lawrence	Schloss	son	1901	1999	
Isador	**Schloss**		1861		Butcher
Bertha	(Baer) Schloss	wife	1868		
Tessie	Schloss	daughter	1889		
Sidney	Schloss	son	1891	1919	
Alfred	Schloss	son	1892	1962	
Leo	Schloss	son	1896	1980	
Israel	**Schloss**		1871		Brother of Hyman
Joseph	Shapero		1888		Dentist

Table 3.1. Continued.

Julius	**Shapiro**		1879	1932	Upholsterer
Stella	(Cohen) Shapiro	wife	1885		
Irene	Shapiro	daughter	1906		
Harold	Shapiro	son	1909		
Abraham	**Shebar**		1882	1977	
Sadie	(Klein) Shebar	wife	1888		
Gustave	Shebar	son	1904		
Paul	Shebar	son	1906		
Sidney	Shebar	son	1908		
Joseph	Shebar	son	1910		
Bernard	Shebar	son	1912		
Martin	Shebar	son	1914		
Mildred	Shebar	daughter	1918		
Abraham	**Siegel**		1895		Paint store owner
Martha	Siegel	wife	1898		
A.	**Spierengen**				Attended first meeting B'nai Israel 1915
Hugo	**Stearns**		1866		Real estate developer
Erna	(Althof) Stearns	wife	1885		
Bessie	**Stockman**		1847		Mother of Max Stockman
Max	**Stockman**		1878		Chairman Freeport Hebrew Assn. 1914
Florence	(Klepperman) Stockman	wife	1884		Divorced 1913, second husband Isaac Miller
Ruth	Stockman	daughter	1907		
Abe	Stockman	son	1911		
Nathan	**Viertel**		1858	1930	
Fanny	Viertel	wife	1859	1936	
Annie	Viertel	daughter	1887		m. Louis Cohen
Jacob	Viertel	son	1895	1981	
Harry	**Wolfson**		1883		
Rose	Wolfson	wife	1884		
Esther	Wolfson	daughter	1906		
Celia	Wolfson	daughter	1910		

Table 3.2. Residents of Roosevelt

B.	**Jaffe**				
David	**Jaffe**		1892		Son of Samuel and Lena
Beatrice	(Blumberg) Jaffe	wife	1899	1976	

continued on next page

Table 3.2. Continued.

Ira	Jaffe	son	1917		
Samuel	**Jaffe**		1873	1945	Treasurer Freeport Hebrew Assn. 1915
Lena	Jaffe	wife	1867	1929	
David	Jaffe	son	1892		m. Beatrice Blumberg
Solomon	Jaffe	son	1893	1962	m. Minnie
Harry	Jaffe	son	1894		
Jacob	Jaffe	son	1898		
Rose	Jaffe	daughter	1900		
Herbert	Jaffe	son	1902	1980	
Solomon	**Jaffe**		1893	1962	Son of Samuel and Lena
Minnie	Jaffe	wife	1900		
Harry	**Katz**		1885		Son of Benjamin and Annie from Deer Park
Cecilia	(Kranzler) Katz	wife	1893		Daughter of Jacob and Dora from Farmingdale
Sadie	Katz	daughter	1912		
Mildred	Katz	daughter	1916		
Henry	**Strauss**		1882	1925	Secretary Freeport Hebrew Assn. 1914
Ray	(Friedman) Strauss	wife	1888	1934	
Maurice	Strauss	son	1908		
Elias	Strauss	son	1914		

Table 3.3. Residents of Wantagh

Ernestina	**Gruled**		1864		Niece of Bernard Jonas
Bernard	**Jonas**		1837	1928	Owned a hotel
Regina	(Heyman) Jonas	wife	1838	1917	
Moses	Jonas	son	1872		
Alfred	Jonas	son	1876		m. Lillie Klein, lived in Freeport
Etta	Jonas	daughter	1877		m. Isidore Mayer, lived in Freeport
Hortense	Jonas	daughter			

Chapter 4

Glen Cove

*Including Brookville, Locust Valley,
Oyster Bay, and Sea Cliff*

As early as 1829 steamboats carried leisure travelers from New York City via Long Island Sound out to Glen Cove on the north shore of the island. Additional visitors would come by train once the LIRR reached the village in 1867. This is around the time Michael Sandman and his family arrived as the first Jews to live in Glen Cove.

Michael Sandman was the proprietor of a clothing store in the village of Glen Cove by 1870. While a successful merchant, his life was also marked by criminal activity and civic squabbles. In 1875 Sandman was fined $75 and sentenced to fifteen days in jail for selling liquor without a license, which was not an uncommon offense in the day. But it was an incident three years later that caused the *Glen Cove Gazette* to refer to Michael as "the crazed Israelite," a derogatory description that may not have been entirely unwarranted. Sandman initiated controversy with his neighbor claiming a fence dividing their property was positioned incorrectly and unjustly encroached on his land. The difference was negligible. Even if Sandman was

Figure 22. The grave of Michael Sandman and his second wife Caroline. *Source:* Photo by Brad Kolodny.

proven correct in his assertion the resolution would not bring any significant additional value to his property. Land surveys were conducted on multiple occasions, and legal proceedings ensued. Shortly after the case was closed, Sandman was committed to an asylum in Poughkeepsie, New York, for a period of several weeks with a diagnosis of temporary aberration of mind. In the fall of 1890 he was taken to another asylum in Middletown, New York, where he died on October 27.

It is not known if Sandman was an observant Jew, but what we do know is that he never had the opportunity to gather in a formal synagogue setting with his fellow Jews in Glen Cove. The Jewish community did gather for services in the home of Isaac and Esther Bessel for the simple reason that they owned a Torah. Isaac, a horse dealer who also had a feed and grain business, was instrumental in organizing Congregation Tifereth Israel in 1897 along with Benjamin Cohen who was their first president. Cohen ran a hotel at the northeast corner of North Hempstead Turnpike (today route 25A) and Cedar Swamp Road. This area for many years was referred to as "Cohen's Corner" and could be found as such on maps. Bessel

Figure 23. Isaac and Esther Bessel. *Source:* Congregation Tifereth Israel, Glen Cove.

became president of Tifereth Israel in 1899, and Cohen was vice president guiding the congregation to become officially incorporated on November 6. Services for Yom Kippur were held that year in the Vincent Opera House on Continental Avenue.

The other officers of Tifereth Israel at the time of incorporation included Theodore Jospe as secretary, Barney Freedman as treasurer, Nathan Simon

Figure 24. Advertisement for Theodore Jospe's store. *Source: Sea Cliff News,* April 21, 1900.

as collector, and trustees Philip Goodman, Michael Kobachnik, and Wolf Kotler. Jospe started out in the jewelry business operating a store in Hicksville and lived there when he married his wife Dora in 1894. The couple moved to Glen Cove the following year; however, Theodore maintained a business presence going back to Hicksville once a week to take orders from customers. The store in Glen Cove went beyond his jewelry expertise to offer the sale of pianos, organs, and other musical instruments, as well as sewing machines. The expansion of his product line was successful enough for Jospe to begin construction on a new building on School Street that was completed in 1904. It was a three-story structure with the store occupying the ground level and apartments on the second and third floors.

But Jospe was not just a businessman. He became embedded in the community by serving on committees within the village including membership chairman of the Glen Cove Neighborhood Association in 1915. That same year he was president of Tifereth Israel when they purchased land at Montefiore Cemetery in Queens and dedicated their sacred ground on September 5. In 1916 Jospe was second vice president of the Boy Scout Council and in 1917 served on a subcommittee charged with formulating plans for Glen Cove to incorporate as an independent city. In November, Jospe was on the ballot as the Republican candidate for commissioner of accounts in the newly established City of Glen Cove. He lost the election by forty-eight votes.

A new mass transportation option came to Glen Cove in 1905 with the arrival of the Glen Cove Railroad, a trolley line that ran from the Sea Cliff station of the LIRR all the way to the steamboat landing on the shore of Hempstead Bay. This benefited the many proprietors whose stores lined the business district along Glen Street including Joseph and Philip Bernstein. The brothers from Russia opened their department store in 1897 and continued for nearly twenty years until the partnership was dissolved in 1915. As part of the agreement Philip would own the building, and Joseph would continue to run the store under a ten-year lease from his brother.

While Tifereth Israel rented space in the Vincent Opera House for services beginning in 1899 the leaders of the congregation envisioned having a building they could call their own. On October 23, 1906, Tifereth Israel purchased the First Presbyterian Church building and all its contents for $1,000 that was to be moved to another location due to the fact that the church did not own the land the building was situated on. Trouble arose

Figure 25. Bernstein Brothers Department Store, located on the southwest corner of Glen Street and Mill Street (now Pulaski Street), in an unusually tall four-story building. *Source:* From the collection of the author.

when it became necessary to remove some trees from the property, owned by Charles Danis, in order to move the building. When Danis refused a lawsuit was brought by the congregation seeking $7,000, the case went to trial, and the jury awarded Tifereth Israel $3,500 in damages. It is not known exactly what that money was used for, but within a few years the congregation would purchase the Vincent Opera House and convert it for use as their synagogue.

In 1920 a $50,000 fundraising drive was initiated to tear down the opera house and build a new synagogue in its place that opened in 1928. The post–World War II generation brought an entirely new influx of Jews to Glen Cove that necessitated an expansion to another new building. Land was purchased on Landing Road in 1955 and the current synagogue opened in 1961. The Bessel Torah is still in use today at Congregation Tifereth Israel, the oldest congregation in Nassau County.

Singer's Department Store,
a Ninety-Year Fixture in Glen Cove

As an immigrant from Lithuania in his early thirties, Bernard Singer was working as a night watchman when he first arrived in New York City but decided to become a peddler at the urging of a relative who started him out with $5. Bernard sold his goods on Long Island mostly in Hicksville, but once he could afford a horse and wagon, he also called on some wealthy families in Oyster Bay. Four years after his arrival in America, Bernard was able to bring his family over to live with him in Hicksville. Wife Pearl, son Benjamin, and daughter Rebecca were reunited with Bernard in 1901.

Life in Hicksville for the family lasted just a few months as anti-Semitic sentiments caused an uneasiness leading the Singers to seek a residence elsewhere. A larger Jewish community with an existing congregation in Glen Cove was attractive to Bernard and Pearl as was the bustling village where Bernard was able to open a small dry goods store on School Street in the fall of 1901. The family lived behind the store in meager quarters consisting of just two rooms. And while Bernard was out on the road selling to some of his regular customers Benjamin and Rebecca ran the store. In 1913 Benjamin assumed ownership over the family business when Bernard passed away.

After about a decade as sole proprietor Benjamin moved to a new location on Glen Street with an eye on further expansion. In 1928 Benjamin had his store razed and had a much larger three-story building constructed in its place. Singer's Department Store was one of five retail establishments located on the ground floor, with eighteen offices on the second and third floors.

Singer's was truly a family-run business. Shortly after Benjamin married Lena Bermstein in 1931 he brought on Rebecca and her husband William Zatlin as partners focused on supplying goods for women. William was a corsetiere and Rebecca a millinery specialist going into New York City to buy the latest styles of hats to be sold at the store. The next generation took an interest in the store starting with Benjamin and Lena's son Burt who, at the age of seven or eight, helped out during the busy Christmas holiday season. Burt remembers selling embroidered handkerchief sets to mothers in need of a gift for their children's teachers in school. By the time he was twenty-five Burt had taken over his father's responsibilities at the store as a partner alongside his uncle William.

Figures 26 and 27. Bernard Singer (upper), and his children Benjamin and Rebecca in front of the store on School Street (lower). *Source:* Courtesy of Burt Singer.

Eventually William and Rebecca's son, also named Burt, assumed control of the Zatlin half of Singer's. Cousins Burt Singer and Burt Zatlin upheld the family legacy for over thirty years together selling popular items including women's clothing, undergarments, handbags, and items for babies and young children. Burt Zatlin's son Dave became the fourth-generation owner of Singer's Department Store for just a couple of years before closing the store in the 1990s.

Figure 28. Burt Singer, third-generation merchant in Glen Cove, sharing his family history. *Source:* Photo by Brad Kolodny.

Table 4.1. Residents of Glen Cove

Ernest	**Ables**		1869		
Emma	Ables	wife	1879		
Elsie	Ables	daughter	1897		
Rosia	Ables	daughter	1898		
Ida	Ables	daughter	1900		
Laura	Ables	daughter	1902		
Morris	Ables	son	1903		
Julius	**Ain**		1891	1968	
Clara	Ain	wife	1892	1960	
Jacob	Ain	son	1915	2009	
Sarah	Ain	daughter	1918		
Joseph	**Averick**		1873	1932	Dry goods store owner
Sophie	Averick	wife	1874	1936	
Leona	Averick	daughter	1902		
Martha	Averick	daughter	1905		
Bessie	**Bernstein**				
Samuel A.	Bernstein	son	1876		
Isaac	**Bernstein**				Member of Cong. Tifereth Israel 1915
Joseph	**Bernstein**		1890	1922	Nephew of Nathan
Anna	Bernstein	wife	1890		
Julia	Bernstein	daughter	1912		
Seymour	Bernstein	son	1914		
Esther	Bernstein	daughter	1918		
Joseph A.	**Bernstein**		1874	1931	Brother of Philip and Walter
Henriette	(Goldstein) Bernstein	first wife	1875	1906	Daughter of Harris and Anne from Huntington
Pearl	Bernstein	daughter	1900		
Maurice	Bernstein	son	1902		
Ethel	Bernstein	second wife	1878	1956	
Sumner	Bernstein	son	1908	1969	
Julius	**Bernstein**		1872	1921	Dry goods peddler
Bessie	Bernstein	wife	1876		
Esther	Bernstein	daughter	1903		
Edith	Bernstein	daughter	1908		
Mildred	Bernstein	daughter	1910		
Morris	**Bernstein**		1887		Nephew of Nathan
Nathan	**Bernstein**		1862	1926	Second Trustee Cong. Tifereth Israel 1915
Sarah	Bernstein	wife	1876		

Table 4.1. Continued.

Jacob	Bernstein	son	1904		
Abraham	Bernstein	son	1905		
Maurice	Bernstein	son	1907		
Pearl	Bernstein	daughter	1913		
Samuel	Bernstein	son	1915		
Norman	Bernstein	son	1917		
Philip	**Bernstein**		1870	1949	Brother of Joseph A. and Walter
Bessie	Bernstein	wife	1871	1956	
Herbert	Bernstein	son	1897		
Marion	Bernstein	daughter	1901		
Mildred	Bernstein	daughter	1904		
Sylvia	Bernstein	daughter	1911		
Sidney	Bernstein	son	1914		
Samuel	**Bernstein**		1877		Member of Cong. Tifereth Israel 1899
?	Bernstein	brother	1883		
Sidney	**Bernstein**		1883		Dry goods merchant
Jennie	(Bernstein) Bernstein	wife	1886		
Bernard	Bernstein	son	1909		
Zelda	Bernstein	daughter	1914		
Herman	Bernstein	son	1917		
Walter	**Bernstein**				Brother of Joseph A. and Philip
Bella	Bernstein	wife			
Leonard	Bernstein	son			
David	**Bessel**		1872	1919	
Rose	(Siegel) Bessel	wife	1875	1953	
Florence	Bessel	daughter	1904		
Samuel	Bessel	son	1906		
Abraham	Bessel	son	1908		
George	Bessel	son	1908		
Theodore	Bessel	son	1913		
Isaac	**Bessel**		1844	1924	President of Cong. Tifereth Israel 1899
Esther	(Sussman) Bessel	wife	1848	1930	
Samuel	Bessel	son	1870	1941	m. Yetta Schuman
Louis	Bessel	son	1874		
James	Bessel	son	1878	1918	m. Fannie Miller

continued on next page

Table 4.1. Continued.

Simon	Bessel	son	1882		
Sarah	Bessel	daughter	1884		
Ida	Bessel	daughter	1887	1947	
James	**Bessel**		1878	1918	Son of Isaac and Esther
Fannie	(Miller) Bessel	wife	1885	1935	
Israel	Bessel	son	1912	1968	
Gertrude	Bessel	daughter	1913	1954	
Abraham	Bessel	son	1917	1976	
Morris	Bessel	son	1918	1974	
Samuel	**Bessel**		1870	1941	Treasurer of Cong. Tifereth Israel 1915
Yetta	(Schuman) Bessel	wife	1874	1958	
Max	Bessel	son	1897	1974	
Bessie	Bessel	daughter	1897		
Florence	Bessel	daughter	1898		
Abraham	Bessel	son	1900		
Catherine	Bessel	daughter	1902		
Anna	Bessel	daughter	1907		
Max	**Bloom**		1884	1938	Fourth Trustee Cong. Tifereth Israel 1915
Anna	(Berkowitz) Bloom	wife	1889		
Silvia	Bloom	daughter	1913		
Daniel	Bloom	son	1917		
Adolph	**Brause**		1872	1923	Brother of Louis and Harry
Marcella	Brause	wife	1877	1950	
Esther	Brause	daughter	1902		
Della	Brause	daughter	1904		
Archibald	Brause	son	1906		
Edward	Brause	son	1909		
Harry	**Brause**		1879	1948	Brother of Adolph and Louis
Rose	Brause	wife	1882	1942	
Louis	**Brause**		1870	1945	Brother of Adolph and Harry
Rebecca	Brause	wife	1878	1945	
Miriam	Brause	daughter	1902		
Ethel	Brause	daughter	1905		
Rose	Brause	daughter	1907		
Florence	Brause	daughter	1910		
Alexander	**Buxenbaum**		1879	1951	House decorator
Rose	(Berkowitz) Buxenbaum	wife	1881	1952	

Table 4.1. Continued.

Arthur	Buxenbaum	son	1901	1997	
Herman	Buxenbaum	son	1905	1971	
Abraham	Buxenbaum	son	1909		
Milton	Buxenbaum	son	1911	1985	
Mervin	Buxenbaum	son	1913	1972	
Morris	**Canarick**		1888	1970	Merchant
Ray	(Hornstein) Canarick	wife	1893	1976	
Ruth	Canarick	daughter	1911		
Sarah	Canarick	daughter	1915		
Sidney	Canarick	son	1918	2007	
Morris	**Cantor**		1865	1932	Cigar merchant
Hannah	Cantor	wife	1869	1931	
Abraham	Cantor	son	1898	1935	
Miriam	Cantor	daughter	1902	1977	
Meyer	Cantor	son	1903		
Leskar	Cantor	son	1905		
Wolf	Cantor	son	1907		
Abraham	**Cohen**		1890		Son of Benjamin and Leah
Molly	Cohen	wife	1893		
Aaron	Cohen	son	1917		
Benjamin	**Cohen**		1861	1924	President of Cong. Tifereth Israel 1897
Leah	(Kaplan) Cohen	wife	1862	1916	
Maurice	Cohen	son	1882		m. Hattie Sandman
Sadie	Cohen	daughter	1883		
Jacob	Cohen	son	1887	1949	
Samuel	Cohen	son	1889		
Abraham	Cohen	son	1890		
Isaac	Cohen	son	1893		
Maurice	**Cohen**		1882		Son of Benjamin and Leah
Hattie	(Sandman) Cohen	wife	1883		Daughter of Samuel
Bertha	Cohen	daughter	1906		
Muriel	Cohen	daughter	1908		
Morris	**Cohen**		1871		Member of Cong. Tifereth Israel 1899
Pinchus	**Cohen**		1848		Farmer
Sarah	Cohen	wife	1875		
Fanny	Cohen	daughter	1901		
Archie	Cohen	son	1902		

continued on next page

Table 4.1. Continued.

David	Cohen	son	1905		
Jacob	**Feinberg**		1876		Member of Cong. Tifereth Israel 1915
Pauline	Feinberg	wife	1880		
Joseph	Feinberg	son	1898		
Louis	Feinberg	son	1901		
Ruben	Feinberg	son	1908		
Esther	Feinberg	daughter	1910		
Charlie	Feinberg	son	1912		
Charles	**Fractenberg**				Member of Cong. Tifereth Israel 1899
Barney	**Freedman**		1855		Member of Cong. Tifereth Israel 1899
Bessie	(Marks) Freedman	wife	1866		
Annie	Freedman	daughter	1891		
Bertha	Freedman	daughter	1892		
Meyer	Freedman	son	1895		
Louis	Freedman	son	1897		
Fannie	Freedman	daughter	1901		
David	Freedman	son	1906		
William	Freedman	son	1910		
Joseph	**Freedman**		1881	1967	Member of Cong. Tifereth Israel 1899
Sadie	Freedman	wife	1884	1938	
Florence	Freedman	daughter	1903		
Merwin	Freedman	son	1906		
Herald	Freedman	son	1908		
Joshua	**Freedman**		1900		Nephew of Joseph A. Bernstein
Robert	**Freedman**		1871		Grocery store owner
Dora	(Henschel) Freedman	wife	1874	1963	Daughter of Morris and Rachel from Amityville
Ethel	Freedman	daughter	1898		
Robert	Freedman	son	1901		
Raymond	Freedman	son	1907		
Nathan	**Friedman**				Member of Cong. Tifereth Israel 1899
Abraham	**Gell**		1890		Jeweler
Samuel	**Gershowitz**		1884	1962	
Ida	(Levitz) Gershowitz	wife	1884	1945	

Table 4.1. Continued.

Max	Gershowitz	son	1908		
Samuel	Gershowitz	son	1910		
Archie	Gershowitz	son	1911		
Philip	Gershowitz	son	1913		
Dora	Gershowitz	daughter	1914		
Julius	Gershowitz	son	1916		
Abraham	**Glickfield**		1880		Merchant
Annie	(Horowitz) Glickfield	wife	1882		
Peter	Glickfield	son	1908		
Vivien	Glickfield	daughter	1912		
Samuel	**Goldberg**		1866	1924	Brother of Silas
Carrie	(Strauss) Goldberg	wife	1884	1978	
Rosella	Goldberg	daughter	1904	2002	
Alexander	Goldberg	son	1905	2004	
Louis	Goldberg	son	1908		
Evelyn	Goldberg	daughter	1914		
Silas	**Goldberg**		1870	1947	Brother of Samuel
Amelia	(Stone) Goldberg	wife	1888	1952	
Lionel	Goldberg	son	1916	1997	
Lillian	Goldberg	daughter	1918	1967	
Max	**Goldstein**		1885		Oil man
Lena	Goldstein	wife	1888		
Julius	Goldstein	son	1907		
Philip	Goldstein	son	1909		
Dorothy	Goldstein	daughter	1912		
Isadore	Goldstein	son	1914		
Meyer	Goldstein	son	1916		
Philip	**Goodman**		1861	1938	Trustee of Cong. Tifereth Israel 1899
Bessie	(Newman) Goodman	wife	1865		
Emil	Goodman	son	1883	1946	
Lena	Goodman	daughter	1886		
Anna	Goodman	daughter	1889		
Bernard	Goodman	son	1905		
Max	**Greenberg**		1868	1940	Member of Cong. Tifereth Israel 1899
Leah	(Tash) Greenberg	wife	1876	1953	
Sidney	Greenberg	son	1898	1958	

continued on next page

Table 4.1. Continued.

Sylvia	Greenberg	daughter	1900		
Sophia	Greenberg	daughter	1904		
Adelaide	Greenberg	daughter	1908		
Philip	Greenberg	son	1909		
Beatrice	Greenberg	daughter	1910		
Anita	Greenberg	daughter	1915		
Harry	**Hirschfeld**		1876		Insurance salesman
Bertha	Hirschfeld	wife	1887		
Hilda	Hirschfeld	daughter	1916		
Julius	Hirschfeld	son	1918		
Morris	**Ideleivitz**		1889		Dairy man
Annie	Ideleivitz	wife	1896		
Joshua	Ideleivitz	son	1915		
Benjamin	**Jacobs**				Member of Cong. Tifereth Israel 1899
Henry	**Jacobs**				Member of Cong. Tifereth Israel 1899
Bessie	**Jospe**		1884	1927	Sister-in-law of Theodore Jospe
Essie Jospe	**Jospe**		1876	1949	Sister-in-law of Theodore
Lena	**Jospe**		1875	1952	Sister of Theodore
Theodore	**Jospe**		1869	1934	Secretary Cong. Tifereth Israel 1899
Dora	Jospe	wife	1869	1932	
Leah	Jospe	daughter	1896	1947	
Jacob	Jospe	son	1899	1923	
Leon	Jospe	son	1905	1954	
William	**Kahn**		1882	1951	Grocer
Teresa	(Sandman) Kahn	wife	1883	1949	Daughter of Morris and Hannah
David	**Kaufman**		1885		Junk dealer
Ida	Kaufman	wife	1887		
Annie	Kaufman	daughter	1907		
Cecelia	Kaufman	daughter	1912		
Harvey	Kaufman	son	1914		
Jennie	Kaufman	daughter	1915		
Solomon	Kaufman	son	1918		
Morris	**Kaufman**		1881		Junk man
Rebecca	Kaufman	wife	1882		

Table 4.1. Continued.

Tessie	Kaufman	daughter	1905		
Max	Kaufman	son	1908		
Lena	Kaufman	daughter	1910		
David	Kaufman	son	1914		
Isadore	Kaufman	son	1916		
Dorothy	Kaufman	daughter	1918		
Michael	**Kobachnik**		1863		Trustee of Cong. Tifereth Israel 1899
Elizabeth	Kobachnik	wife	1870		
Libbie	Kobachnik	daughter	1892		
Benjamin	Kobachnik	son	1895		
Abraham	Kobachnik	son	1897		
Herbert	Kobachnik	son	1902		
David	Kobachnik	son	1905		
Arthur	Kobachnik	son	1907		
Wolf	**Kotler**				Trustee of Cong. Tifereth Israel 1899
David	**Lavine**		1865		Merchant
Sarah	Lavine	wife	1869		
Philip	Lavine	son	1890		
Harry	Lavine	son	1891		
Mervin	Lavine	son	1896		
Ruth	Lavine	daughter	1901		
Israel	**Lebendiger**		1886	1964	Rabbi at Cong. Tifereth Israel 1915
Abe	**Levin**		1870	1940	Fin. Secy. Cong. Tifereth Israel 1915
Fannie	Levin	wife	1868	1964	
Nathan	Levin	son	1899	1985	
Sigmond	Levin	son	1901		
Theresa	Levin	daughter	1903		
Ruth	Levin	daughter	1905		
Isidor	**Levin**		1879	1959	Son of Louis and Dora from Rockville Centre
Fannie	(Jacobson) Levin	wife	1880	1967	
Anita	Levin	daughter	1908		
Norman	Levin	son	1910		
Gabriel	Levin	son	1912		
Ruth	Levin	daughter	1914		
Sylvia	Levin	daughter	1916		

continued on next page

Table 4.1. Continued.

Harris	**Lipschitz**		1873	1962	Butcher, was also a mohel
Gladys	Lipschitz	wife	1883	1977	
Benjamin	Lipschitz	son	1909		
Morris	Lipschitz	son	1911		
Harry	Lipschitz	son	1915		
Belle	Lipschitz	daughter	1917		
Jacob	**Margolis**		1878		Member of Cong. Tifereth Israel 1915
Perl	Margolis	wife	1882		
Tillie	Margolis	daughter	1908		
Bessie	Margolis	daughter	1911		
Dora	Margolis	daughter	1915		
Beckie	Margolis	daughter	1917		
Charles	**Miller**		1888		
Mary	(Raff) Miller	wife	1892		Daughter of Barnett and Rebecca from Sea Cliff
Mildred	Miller	daughter	1918		
Bella	**Mintz**		1893		Niece of Abe Levin
Bess	**Mintz**				
David	**Nosovitz**		1864		Record. Sec. Cong Tifereth Israel 1915
Pearl	(Spector) Nosovitz	wife	1870		
George	Nosovitz	son	1892	1918	
Herman	Nosovitz	son	1896		
Harry	Nosovitz	son	1898		
Etta	Nosovitz	daughter	1900		
Israel	Nosovitz	son	1902		
Maxwell	Nosovitz	son	1903		
Moses	Nosovitz	son	1905		
Mollie	Nosovitz	daughter	1907	1908	
Joshua	Nosovitz	son	1909		
Nathan	**Rabinosky**				Member of Cong. Tifereth Israel 1899
Joseph	**Rodoshefsky**		1880	1963	
Lillie	(Belle) Rodoshefsky	wife	1884	1959	
Joseph, Jr.	Rodoshefsky	son	1915		
Benjamin	Rodoshefsky	son	1917		
Abraham	**Rofheart**				Trustee of Cong. Tifereth Israel 1899

Table 4.1. Continued.

Frank	**Rose**		1881		
Dora	Rose	wife	1889		
Sylvia	Rose	daughter	1911		
Seymour	Rose	son	1912		
Clarence	Rose	son	1915		
Evelyn	Rose	daughter	1918		
Michael	**Sandman**		1816	1890	Clothing store owner
Henry	Sandman	son	1855		
Nancy	Sandman	daughter	1858		
Caroline	(Rosenfeld) Sandman	second wife	1828	1914	
Henrietta	Sandman	daughter	1862		
Gussie	Sandman	daughter	1863	1945	
Lena	Sandman	daughter	1865	1950	
Emanuel	Sandman	son	1868		
David	Sandman	son	1872	1957	m. Cecelia Thorman lived in Babylon
Samuel	Sandman	son	1874	1966	m. ?
Morris	**Sandman**		1844	1941	Grocer
Hannah	(Lefkowitz) Sandman	wife	1846	1911	
Henry	Sandman	son	1879		
Hattie	Sandman	daughter	1882		
Teresa	Sandman	daughter	1883	1949	m. William Kahn
Samuel	**Sandman**		1874	1966	Son of Michael and Caroline
?	Sandman	wife			
Hattie	Sandman	daughter	1883		m. Maurice Cohen
Morris	**Sharp**		1881		Furniture store owner w/Max Bloom
Louis	**Shorenstein**		1876	1940	Baker
Sadie	(Schwartz) Shorenstein	wife	1881	1958	
Joseph	Shorenstein	son	1898	1931	
Eva	Shorenstein	daughter	1902		
William	Shorenstein	son	1903	1991	
Samuel	Shorenstein	son			
Benjamin	Shorenstein	son	1906		
Maurice	Shorenstein	son	1911		
Lillian	Shorenstein	daughter	1911		

continued on next page

Table 4.1. Continued.

Rosa	Shorenstein	daughter	1912		
Edward	**Siegel**		1896	1973	Son of Louis and Yetta from Sea Cliff
Sallie	(Miller) Siegel	wife	1895	1985	
Mildred	Siegel	daughter	1918		
Benjamin	**Simon**				Member of Cong. Tifereth Israel 1899
Jacob	**Simon**				Member of Cong. Tifereth Israel 1899
Nathan	**Simon**		1876	1940	Collector of Cong. Tifereth Israel 1899
Yetta	Simon	wife	1877	1949	
Bernard	**Singer**		1865	1913	Dry goods merchant
Pearl	Singer	wife	1858	1935	
Benjamin	Singer	son	1890	1957	
Rebecca	Singer	daughter	1893		
Abraham	**Solomon**		1860		Leather worker
Rebecca	Solomon	wife	1870		
Atel	Solomon	daughter	1899		
Sarah	Solomon	daughter	1904		
Annie	Solomon	daughter	1906		
Louis	Solomon	son	1909		
Louis	**Solomon**		1866		Shoemaker
Teckler	Solomon	wife	1876		
Max	Solomon	son	1896		
Morris	Solomon	son	1899		
Edward	Solomon	son	1903		
Fannie	**Spector**		1840		Mother of Pearl Nosovitz
Israel	**Spencer**		1882		
Fannie	Spencer	wife	1891		
Maurice	**Steisel**		1887	1963	Hardware store owner
Laura	Steisel	wife	1888	1974	
Sylvia	Steisel	daughter	1914		
Pearl	Steisel	daughter	1916		
Abraham	**Tobias**		1894		Tailor
Celia	Tobias	wife	1895		
Sarah	Tobias	daughter	1916		
Harry	**Weinstein**				Member of Cong. Tifereth Israel 1899
Louis	**Wolpert**		1868		Cigar maker

Table 4.1. Continued.

Ida	Wolpert	wife	1875	
Samuel	Wolpert	son	1896	
Nathan	Wolpert	son	1899	
Esther	Wolpert	daughter	1901	
Helen	Wolpert	daughter	1905	
Julia	Wolpert	daughter	1909	
Philip	**Zendle**		1890	In the milk business
Bessie	(Idelwitz) Zendle	wife	1888	
Henry	Zendle	son	1914	
Ettie	Zendle	daughter	1916	
Edward	Zendle	son	1918	
Leopold	**Zimmerman**			Member of Cong. Tifereth Israel 1915

Table 4.2. Residents of Brookville

Joseph	**Sugarman**		1848	Real estate agent
Annie	(Schonlank) Sugarman	wife	1858	
Martin	Sugarman	son	1880	
Harry	Sugarman	son	1882	
Samuel	Sugarman	son	1884	
Morris	Sugarman	son	1887	
Nathan	Sugarman	son	1889	
William	Sugarman	son	1893	
Mortimer	Sugarman	son	1898	

Table 4.3. Residents of Locust Valley

Samuel	**Greenberg**		1875	Tailor
Rebecca	Greenberg	wife	1880	
Rose	Greenberg	daughter	1904	
Maurice	Greenberg	son	1909	
Victor	Greenberg	son	1911	
Max	**Levi**		1864	Hotel keeper
Fannie	Levi	wife	1868	
Bessie	Levi	daughter	1890	
B. Samuel	Levi	son	1892	
Joseph	Levi	son	1906	

continued on next page

Table 4.3. Continued.

| Sarah | Levi | daughter | 1907 | | |
| Morris | **Levi** | | 1889 | | Nephew of Max |

Table 4.4. Residents of Oyster Bay

Sidney	**Bernstein**		1883		Dry goods store owner
Jennie	Bernstein	wife	1886		
Bernard	Bernstein	son	1909		
Zelda	Bernstein	daughter	1914		
Herman	Bernstein	son	1917		
Philip	**Kahn**		1869	1947	Shoe store owner
Katie	Kahn	wife	1877	1958	
Julius	Kahn	son	1900		
Celia	Kahn	daughter	1902		
Mamie	Kahn	daughter	1906		
Solomon	**Simson**				Owned two houses in 1775

Table 4.5. Residents of Sea Cliff

Benjamin	**Feingold**		1883		Jewelry dealer
Elizabeth	Feingold	wife	1885		
Alfred	Feingold	son	1905		
Beatrice	Feingold	daughter	1908		
Janis	Feingold	daughter	1916		
Harry	**Meritzer**		1884		Traveling salesman
Tillie	(Silver) Meritzer	wife	1891		
Roberta	Meritzer	daughter	1910		
Barnett	**Raff**		1863		Tailor
Rebecca	(Brause) Raff	wife	1871		
Mary	Raff	daughter	1892		m. Charles Miller, lived in Glen Cove
Elias	Raff	son	1893		
Yetta	Raff	daughter	1896		
Isaac	Raff	son	1899		
Samuel	Raff	son	1903		
Isaac	**Ritzeir**		1880		Tailor
Louis	**Siegel**		1872		Fruit merchant
Yetta	(Marcus) Siegel	wife	1873		
Samuel	Siegel	son	1891		

Table 4.5. Continued.

Sadie	Siegel	daughter	1896		
Edward	Siegel	son	1896	1973	m. Sallie Miller, lived in Glen Cove
Harry	Siegel	son	1898		
Morris	Siegel	son	1900		
Emil	Siegel	son	1904		
David	Siegel	son	1908		
Beatrice	Siegel	daughter	1912		

Chapter 5

Hempstead

Including Franklin Square and Malverne

The Village of Hempstead has been known for its ethnic and religious diversity that has existed for over 350 years. Dutch and English settlers lived among Native Americans with an African presence by 1651, and in the nineteenth century Irish, Polish, and German immigrants began arriving. The earliest Jewish residents were merchants from Germany who helped establish Hempstead as a center for commerce by building retail businesses selling clothing and dry goods.

The first to arrive was Bannat Salky, who came to Hempstead in 1858. He owned a clothing store in the heart of the village at 27 Main Street and ran the business for more than three decades. His success was evident with an estate worth $75,000 at the time of his death in 1892 left for his wife Mary and daughter Eliza, a value that equates to over $2 million today.

Another early Jewish merchant located on Main Street beginning in 1883 was Louis Cohen. Other than running a large department store, Cohen also bought and sold land and owned properties including the Utowana Hotel and the post office building. In 1894 he expanded his retail operation by opening a second store location in Rockville Centre on Village Avenue. Cohen purchased a car in 1909, had a maid, a cook, and a waitress living with his family in 1910 and was the largest single taxpayer in the Village of Hempstead. At the same time, he was also committed to organizing Jewish communal gatherings and played a role in the formation of both the Hebrew Union of the Town of Hempstead and the Nassau County Hebrew Association. Cohen invested his time as well as his financial resources in getting these groups off the ground but

CLOTHING

AND

GENTLEMEN'S FURNISHING GOODS.

BANNAT SALKY,

MERCHANT TAILOR,

MAIN STREET, HEMPSTEAD, L. I.

The subscriber invites attention to his superior stock of

Cloths, Cassimeres, Vestings, &c., &c.

Of every variety and style, and of very superior quality.

Also a superior stock of READY-MADE CLOTHING, of all styles for men's or boys' wear, such as Coats, Vests, Pants. &c., &c., which are equal, if not superior, to that of any establishment on Long Island. Also, FURNISHING GOODS, Hats, Caps, &c.

All Cloths and Cassimeres bought at this establishment will be cut free of charge.

BANNAT SALKY.

Hempstead, February 1, 1866.

Figure 29. Advertisement for Bannat Salky's store. *Source: Queens County Sentinel,* December 5, 1867.

was not wholly successful. Because the Jewish population on the south shore of Nassau County at the time was still small, these organizations were made up of individuals from a number of different villages including Hempstead, Freeport, Rockville Centre, Baldwin, and Wantagh. They all wanted to create a successful synagogue, but their geographic disparity was too much to overcome. By 1912 enough Jews were living in the Village of Hempstead to form their own congregation. Two years later Louis Cohen became president of Congregation Beth Israel, while his wife Isabella became the first president of the sisterhood the same year.

Figure 30. Louis Cohen's new department store building, 1892. *Source:* Hempstead Public Library.

Jacob Sidenberg immigrated to the United States from Germany in 1856 and moved to Hempstead in 1861, going into business with Lewis Clark. Sidenberg was one of just two Jewish men from Long Island drafted into the armed forces for service in the Civil War in 1864. He was part of the New York State militia but did not see any active combat duty. The partnership with Clark dissolved in April 1865, leading Jacob to go out on his own as a peddler selling his wares along the north shore of Long Island. In 1874 when Main Street in Hempstead was still largely residential Sidenberg opened a clothing store on the ground level of a three-story building with a residence above the store for his family. He grew his business by opening a second location in Roslyn in 1883, but the Hempstead store at 16 Main Street remained in the same location with Sidenberg in charge for forty-four years. "Uncle Jake," as he became affectionately known within the village, passed away in 1918, leaving his niece Betty Morrison, who had worked for her uncle beginning in 1880, to take over the business.

Perhaps the most civic-minded Jew in town was not a retail merchant like his contemporaries. Adolph D. Rosenthal was born in Philadelphia, the son of a diplomat from Germany who served as American consul there. Adolph graduated from Jefferson Medical College in Philadelphia and later attended Philadelphia Dental College. He moved to New York City in 1883 and to Hempstead by 1885, opening his dental practice at 50 Main Street. It didn't take long for Dr. Rosenthal to become connected with other residents of Hempstead and the neighboring areas through his involvement in various community groups. He was elected warden of the Royal Arcanum in 1886, and five years later became vice regent of the fraternal organization. In 1887 Adolph was the senior master of the Shield of Honor lodge and became the treasurer of the Hempstead Fire Department, a position he held for several years. Rosenthal also thrust himself into the political arena, becoming president of the Hempstead Democratic Club and in 1893 was elected one of five trustees of the Village of Hempstead.

Before the end of the century Rosenthal would find himself at the center of an effort to organize Jewish residents of Hempstead and the neighboring villages of Rockville Centre and Freeport with the intention of forming a congregation. The first meeting of this small group took place on October 24, 1897, and two weeks later they became known as the Hebrew Union of the Town of Hempstead. Morris Miller of Freeport hosted the next meeting at his home on November 21 where bylaws were adopted

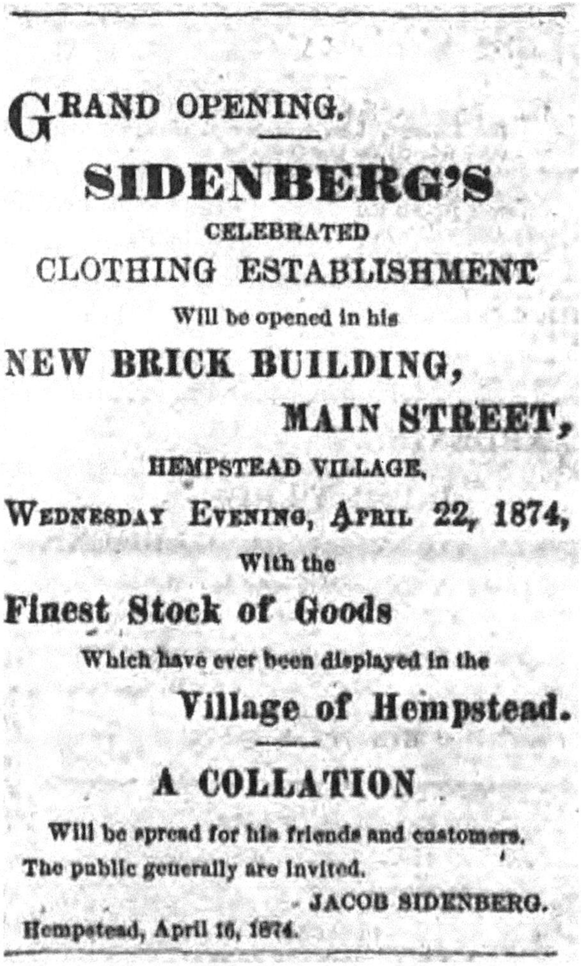

Figure 31. Advertisement for the grand opening of Jacob Sidenberg's store. *Source: Queens County Sentinel*, April 23, 1874.

and officers elected. Dr. Rosenthal was voted in as president, Miller as vice president, Michael Morrison of Hempstead as secretary, Louis Aronson of Rockville Centre as treasurer, and Henry Gobetz of Freeport as messenger. Funds were raised, with the largest donations of $150 each coming from Rosenthal, Louis Cohen, and Jacob Sidenberg all from Hempstead. On November 28 the first service of worship was held in Rosenthal's office. Over the next several months dissension among the group surfaced with disagreement about the importance of building a synagogue versus establishing a cemetery and which should come first. On May 1, 1898, the membership voted unanimously to disband.

A meeting of the group to be known as the Nassau County Hebrew Association was held November 30, 1902, at Gobetz's Hall in Freeport with many of the same individuals who were part of the defunct Hebrew Union of the Town of Hempstead. Once again Rosenthal was elected to lead the fledgling group as president, while Morris Gutowitz of Rockville Centre was elected vice president, Isidor Schloss of Freeport was secretary, and Louis Aronson of Rockville Centre became treasurer. Trustees included Louis Cohen of Hempstead, Hyman Schloss of Freeport, and Joseph Scheffer of Baldwin.

Membership had grown to nearly 50 members in February and a women's auxiliary group was established. Plans for a synagogue and cemetery were underway with a committee of six appointed to lead the task. A

Figure 32. Dr. Adolph Rosenthal's dental office at 50 Main Street, location of the first religious service held for the Hebrew Union of the Town of Hempstead. *Source:* Freeport Historical Society.

twenty-acre property in Roosevelt owned by Louis Cohen, located along the trolley line that ran from Mineola to Freeport, was considered as a possible site but ultimately not selected. As regular meetings continued in the following months the association also began organizing social and religious gatherings. A Purim Ball was held March 16 at Atheneum Hall in Rockville Centre and the first services held under the auspices of the Nassau County Hebrew Association took place on April 19, hosted by Louis Cohen in Hempstead. In September 1903 Rosh Hashanah and Yom Kippur services were conducted at the Masonic Temple in Hempstead.

In the year that followed significant disagreement emerged among members who became divided about the location to build a synagogue and religious observance. Members of the association from Hempstead wanted the synagogue built in their village and favored adoption of Reform movement beliefs. It would appear they had the financial clout to rule the day, but Rockville Centre had a larger contingency who preferred Orthodox traditions, so a synagogue in Hempstead would be too far for them to travel on shabbat. A third group from Freeport seemed indifferent to both location and ritual. Consternation led to an impasse with no resolution on the issues at hand. By December 1904 a split ensued, and all factions went their separate ways.

It wasn't until 1912 that the Hempstead Hebrew Congregation was formed with services held at Liberty Hall on Front Street. The congregation was officially incorporated in 1915, and in the summer of that year they purchased land on the south side of Centre Street east of Franklin Avenue to build a synagogue. Plans had to be put on hold because of World War I, so construction did not begin until September 1919 with the synagogue in use by January 1921.

Growth over the next thirty years led to building a larger second synagogue, this one on Fulton Avenue, which was dedicated in 1950. In the 1960s and 1970s a demographic shift occurred with fewer Jewish families moving to Hempstead. Beth Israel made the decision to sell their building and downsized to a smaller facility, moving to their current location on Hilton Avenue in 1981.

Table 5.1. Residents of Hempstead

Abraham	**Abel**		1881		Trustee Hempstead Hebrew Con. 1915
Anne	(Herzfeld) Abel	wife	1883	1940	
John	Abel	son	1907		
Birdie	Abel	daughter	1909		
Dorothy	Abel	daughter	1915		
Leo	**Baumann**		1884		Son of Simon and Carrie from Freeport
Esther	(Schachewitz) Baumann	wife	1898		Daughter of Joseph and Sarah
Justin	Baumann	son	1917		
Louis	**Cohen**		1857	1921	Pres. Hempstead Hebrew Cong. 1914
Isabella	Cohen	wife	1864	1924	
Nettie	Cohen	daughter	1885		m. Samuel Stein
Clarence	Cohen	son	1889		
Miriam	Cohen	daughter	1891		
Samuel	**Cohen**		1890		Trustee Hempstead Hebrew Con. 1915
Mimie	Cohen	wife	1886		
Lily	Cohen	daughter	1914		
Ruth	Cohen	daughter	1916		
Adolph	**Dicks**		1864		Florist
Sophia	(Finck) Dicks	wife	1862		Daughter of Julenne
Emma	Dicks	daughter	1898		
Hugh	Dicks	son	1901		
George	Dicks	son	1902		
Julenne	**Finck**		1836		Mother of Sophia Dicks and William Finck from Malverne
Abraham	**Frank**		1882		Trustee Hempstead Hebrew Con. 1915
Theresa	Frank	wife	1889		
Hyman	**Franklyn**		1883	1927	Furniture store owner
Leona	Franklyn	wife	1885		
Jerome	Franklyn	son	1908		
Evelyn	Franklyn	daughter	1910		
Irving	Franklyn	son	1913		
Seymour	Franklyn	son	1918		
Samuel	**Geller**		1883	1960	Tailor
Fannie	Geller	wife	1890	1945	

Table 5.1. Continued.

Herman	Geller	son	1909		
Charlie	Geller	son	1911		
David	Geller	son	1913		
Minnie	Geller	daughter	1917		
Zacharias	**Goldberg**		1885		Upholstery worker
Florence	(Steinberg) Goldberg	wife	1894		
Irving	Goldberg	son	1915		
Annette	Goldberg	daughter	1917		
David	**Goldstein**		1880		Dry goods store owner
Esther	Goldstein	first wife	1881		
Leo	Goldstein	son	1903		
Joseph	Goldstein	son	1905		
Annie	Goldstein	second wife	1878		
Arthur	Goldstein	son	1916		
Benjamin	**Greenberg**		1890		Salesman in department store
Israel	**Greenberg**		1875		Trustee Hempstead Hebrew Con. 1915
Celia	(Hurwitz) Greenberg	wife	1876		
Herman	Greenberg	son	1901		
Rosaline	Greenberg	daughter	1906		
Harold	Greenberg	son	1908		
David	Greenberg	son	1910		
Harry	**Greenstein**		1886		Chauffer
Fanny	Greenstein	wife	1886		
George	Greenstein	son	1911		
Blanche	Greenstein	daughter	1916		
Irving	**Jaffe**		1892	1949	Driver
Beatrice	Jaffe	wife	1899		
Ira	Jaffe	son	1917		
William	**Krebs**		1883		Nephew of Louis Cohen
Betty	**Morrison**		1860		Worked for her uncle Jacob Sidenberg
Esther	**Morrison**		1874	1894	Sister of Michael, Betty, Minnie, and Nanse
Michael	**Morrison**		1865	1917	Secretary of Hebrew Union of the Town of Hempstead 1897
Minnie	**Morrison**		1870		Started a Hebrew Sunday school 1910

continued on next page

Table 5.1. Continued.

Nanse	**Morrison**		1872		m. William Finck lived in Malverne
Elias	**Rogow**		1871	1920	Trustee Hempstead Hebrew Con. 1915
Jennie	(Goodman) Rogow	wife	1879		
Archibald	Rogow	son	1900		
Morton	Rogow	son	1902		
Solomon	**Rosenberg**		1871		Brother of Pauline Rosenthal
Rose	(Springer) Rosenberg	wife	1875		
Julis	Rosenberg	son	1908		
Adolph	**Rosenthal**		1856	1933	President of Hebrew Union of the Town of Hempstead 1897
Pauline	(Rosenberg) Rosenthal	wife	1863	1928	
William	**Rosenthal**		1867		Brother of Adolph
W. S. V.	**Roth**				Member Hebrew Union of the Town of Hempstead 1897
Bannat	**Salky**		1825	1892	Clothing store owner
Mary	Salky	wife	1827	1897	
Eliza	Salky	daughter			
Tillie	Salky	daughter	1868	1891	
Joseph	**Schacewitz**		1857		
Sarah	(Shapiro) Schacewitz	wife	1864		
Esther	Schacewitz	daughter	1898		m. Leo Baumann
Abraham	Schacewitz	son	1905		Middle name Lincoln
Benjamin	**Shapiro**		1874		Brother of Isaac from Huntington
Lillian	(Cooper) Shapiro	wife	1880		
Ezra	Shapiro	son	1905		
Josephine	Shapiro	daughter	1909		
Adolph	Shapiro	son	1915		
Leonard	Shapiro	son	1917		
Leon	**Shore**		1895		Son of Morris and Lena from Rockville Centre
Lillian	(Hirschfield) Shore	wife	1899		

Table 5.1. Continued.

Jacob	**Sidenberg**			1841	1918	Member Hebrew Union of the Town of Hempstead 1897
Ernestine	Sidenberg	wife		1831	1901	
Morris	**Smith**			1874		Tailor
Hilda	Smith	wife		1880		
Louis	Smith	son		1901		
Samuel	**Stein**			1876		Trustee Hempstead Hebrew Con. 1915
Nettie	(Cohen) Stein	wife		1885		Daughter of Louis and Isabella
Thiresa	Stein	daughter		1908		
Max	**Weisberg**			1872	1947	Member Hempstead Hebrew Con 1915
Mollie	(Weiss) Weisberg	wife		1872	1954	Sister of Harry Weiss from Hicksville

Table 5.2. Residents of Franklin Square

Charles	**Frank**					
Anna	Frank	wife				
Rose	Frank	daughter		1896	1958	m. Jacob Karlin, lived in Calverton

Table 5.3. Residents of Malverne

Walter	**Bange**			1893		Nephew of William Finck
William	**Finck**			1871		Florist
Nanse	(Morrison) Finck	wife		1872		Sister of Michael, Betty, Minnie, and Esther from Hempstead
Carl	Finck	son		1911		
Elsa	Finck	daughter		1914		

Chapter 6

Rockville Centre

Including Baldwin, Lynbrook, and Valley Stream

Following the unsuccessful attempts at forming a Jewish congregation in 1897 and 1902 with residents from Rockville Centre, Freeport, and Hempstead, Hyman Schloss from Freeport approached Abraham Mintz from Rockville Centre about organizing a new congregation. The religious affiliation would be strictly Orthodox, and the group would be centered in Rockville Centre, two major points that were vehemently opposed by the faction from Hempstead. Mintz, a liquor store owner, offered his home as a location to host High Holiday services in 1906, and on September 30, the day after Yom Kippur, the new Nassau County Hebrew Association was formed. Other than Schloss and Mintz, the founders included Max Levy,

A. Levin, Edward Stavenhagen, George Joseph, Louis Aronson, Lazarus Leder, and Nathan Cohen from Rockville Centre, and Isaac Jacobson from Lynbrook. By 1907 the congregation had adopted the name B'nai Sholom.

Louis Aronson, the owner of a dry goods and clothing store, was one of the original ten members of B'nai Sholom but was active in Jewish affairs of the community from the outset. He lived in Rockville Centre by 1891, and his business there was growing to the point where he was able to open a larger department store in 1898. His success could be attributed in part to his knowledge of haberdashery, having worked in similar stores selling men's clothing in Berlin and Paris before coming to America in 1890. Louis's wife Augusta also had experience working at Hearn's department store in New York and was a significant contributor in selling women's goods. Their success allowed Louis to make a $50 pledge toward building a synagogue for the Hebrew Union of the Town of Hempstead in 1897, but his support was not just financial, as he also volunteered to be the treasurer of the Nassau County Hebrew Association in 1902. Aronson wanted to see a synagogue built and dedicated his efforts toward that goal.

Without a public location for gatherings in the early years of B'nai Sholom services and meetings were held in private homes. Abraham and Sophie Mintz continued to offer their home for services at 83 Lincoln Avenue while Philip and Julia Goldberg hosted Hebrew school classes in their home at 116 Morris Avenue in 1908. Educating the Jewish children of the community about their history, religious observance, learning to read and write in Hebrew, and honoring holiday traditions were all of paramount importance and became a driving force behind wanting to construct a synagogue building of their own.

Tragedy struck B'nai Sholom in October 1911 when President Edward Stavenhagen passed away. A meeting was held two months prior, but a period of inactivity followed that lasted nearly two years. The congregation reconvened on April 6, 1913, with new officers elected and revived enthusiasm for the future. Documentation from the meeting states, "Among the things the organization recognized was that the soul of the Jewish community is religious education." Fundraising began for the purchase of land where a synagogue could be built, and before too long a plot was chosen on Windsor Avenue, south of Merrick Road, adjacent to the trolley tracks of the New York and Long Island Traction Company.

Figure 33. The synagogue for B'nai Sholom was located on Windsor Avenue alongside the tracks of the trolley line that ran from Brooklyn to Freeport. *Source:* B'nai Sholom Beth David, Rockville Centre.

The congregation was gaining in popularity with a need for larger space before the new synagogue could be built. Private homes were no longer viable to accommodate the growing number of worshipers, so Atheneum Hall was secured for use during the High Holidays. Mr. O. Reissman from New York City was hired to be the architect, and a cornerstone-laying ceremony was held on September 6, 1914. President Philip Goldberg made opening remarks and called upon his son Clarence along with other teenage boys Harold Cohen, Myron Elias, and Daniel Goldberg to present a ceremonial trowel. Myron's father Joseph Elias, vice president of the congregation and chairman of the building committee, was given the honor of laying the cornerstone in place.

By February 1915 the synagogue was in use; however, the formality of an official opening was put off until the spring and held on Sunday, May 2. The eternal lamp was ignited, the Torahs were placed into the ark, and Philip Goldberg's seven-year-old daughter Gladys delivered the

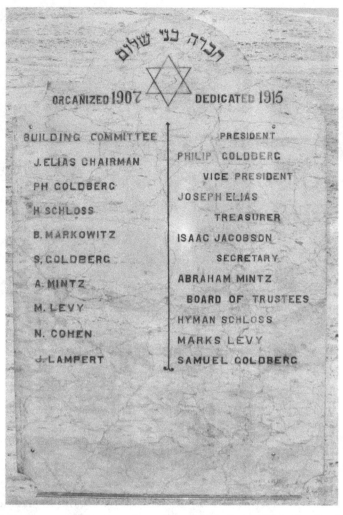

Figure 34. Synagogue dedication plaque from 1915. *Source:* Photo by Brad Kolodny.

golden key to the building on a white satin pillow. In his remarks to the assembly Goldberg thanked Mary Stavenhagen, wife of Edward who had passed away four years prior, for her work and dedication as head of the Ladies Auxiliary that was instrumental in raising funds for the project. He praised her by saying, "As Rebecca was dear to her people in her days, so are you Mrs. Stavenhagen, considered by our people now."

Figure 35. Ceremonial golden key to the synagogue inscribed with the date of dedication. *Source:* Photo by Brad Kolodny.

The sanctuary encompassed the entire upper level of the building, and space for classrooms and social gatherings was located on the lower level. The cost of the building was $10,000, and at the time there were fewer than fifty members. This was the first building constructed in Nassau County for use as a synagogue. Growth in the post–World War II era led B'nai Sholom to build a larger synagogue on Hempstead Avenue that opened in 1949 and is still in use today.

Leder's in Business in Rockville Centre since 1903

Lazarus Leder, a founder of B'nai Sholom, married Rachael Friede in 1892 and was living in Rockville Centre by 1898. Lazarus was a tailor with a shop on Village Avenue while Rachael, commonly known as Ray, was also a merchant in town. A renaissance woman in her day, Ray took over Van Fleat's Bazaar in 1903, selling a variety of household items, toys, and gifts. The store was appropriately renamed Leder's Bazaar and was located south of the railroad tracks on the east side of Village Avenue, the opposite side of the street from where Lazarus did his tailoring.

Lazarus and Ray's son Hamilton assumed ownership of Leder's Bazaar in 1920. Hamilton's son Allen had aspirations to enter the jewelry trade, perhaps inspired by his wife Thelma's father, Benjamin Hoffman, who was

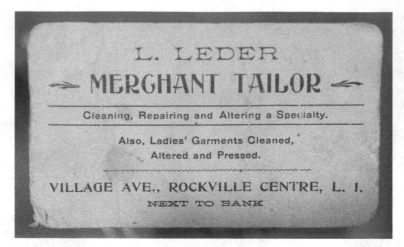

Figure 36. Lazarus Leder's business card. *Source:* Courtesy of Lloyd Leder.

Figure 37. Father and son, Lloyd and Benjamin Leder. *Source:* Photo by Brad Kolodny.

a jeweler in Freeport. Allen honed his craft at the Taus School of Watchmaking in New York City and opened Leder's Jewelers at 15 North Village Avenue in 1948. The store was located next door to Leder's Bazaar at 17 North Village Avenue.

The two family-owned businesses continued to operate adjacent to each other into the 1950s until the stores began moving away from selling general merchandise to focusing solely on jewelry. In 1973 Allen brought his son Lloyd into the fold, and today Lloyd works side by side with his son Benjamin. The store has remained at the same location for 118 years with Benjamin as the fifth-generation Leder in the family business.

Table 6.1. Residents of Rockville Centre

Louis	**Aronson**		1859		Founding member B'nai Sholom 1906
Augusta	(Tuch) Aronson	wife	1863		
Hortense	Aronson	daughter	1892	1916	
Lillian	Aronson	daughter	1894		
Herbert	Aronson	son	1906	1891	
Helen	**Aronson**		1880		Niece of Louis Aronson
Michael	**Barasch**		1884	1944	Son of George and Hilda from Lindenhurst
Eva	(Bogasky) Barasch	wife	1888		
Samuel	Barasch	son	1911		
Lewis	Barasch	son	1915	2006	
Lena	**Bloom**		1855		Mother of Mamie Goldberg
Samuel	**Blumenthal**		1872		Butcher
Rose	(Meyer) Blumenthal	wife	1875		
Harry	Blumenthal	son	1899	1980	
Harold	**Blumenthal**		1905		Nephew of Samuel Cohen
Nathan	**Cohen**		1869	1937	Founding member B'nai Sholom 1906
Rebecca	(Berger) Cohen	wife	1872	1935	B'nai Sholom Ladies Auxiliary 1915
Harold	Cohen	son	1898		
Samuel	**Cohen**		1885		
Sadie	Cohen	wife	1884		
Isaac	**Davis**		1877		
Emma	(Rasener) Davis	wife	1881	1947	Daughter of Jacob and Myriam
Levi	**Davis**		1862	1944	
Joseph	**Elias**		1874		VP B'nai Sholom 1913
Gussie	(Goldberg) Elias	wife	1873		
Caroline	Elias	daughter	1899		
Myron	Elias	son	1900		
Herbert	Elias	son	1902		
Irving	Elias	son	1906		
Robert	Elias	son	1912		
Benjamin	**Fishkind**		1892	1989	Dentist
Clara	Fishkind	wife	1896	1953	
Philip	**Goldberg**		1874		President B'nai Sholom 1913
Julia	(Weisenberg) Goldberg	wife	1877		B'nai Sholom Ladies Auxiliary 1915

Table 6.1. Continued.

Clarence	Goldberg	son	1899		
Harold	Goldberg	son	1902		
Gladys	Goldberg	daughter	1908		
Samuel	**Goldberg**		1880	1915	Trustee B'nai Sholom 1913
Mamie	(Bloom) Goldberg	wife	1876		
Daniel	Goldberg	son	1900		
Harold	Goldberg	son	1906		
Clarence	Goldberg	son	1909		
Raymond	Goldberg	son	1911		
Bertram	Goldberg	son	1914		
William	**Goldberg**		1885		
Francis	(Scheer) Goldberg	wife	1898		
Louis	**Greenwald**		1883		
Hedwig	Greenwald	wife	1893		
Sophie	**Hepner**		1861	1937	
Charles	Hepner	son	1885	1979	
Cecilia	Hepner	daughter	1895	1949	m. Max Barasch 1916 first wedding at B'nai Sholom, lived in Lindenhurst
Martin	Hepner	son	1898		
Isaac	**Jaspin**		1878	1946	Ice cream store owner
Lena	(Abramowitz) Jaspin	wife	1884	1972	
Leon	Jaspin	son	1907		
Harry	Jaspin	son	1908	1991	
George	Jaspin	son	1910		
George	**Joseph**		1867		Founding member B'nai Sholom 1906
Henrietta	(Hellman) Joseph	wife	1871		
Alice	Joseph	daughter	1895		
Benjamin	Joseph	son	1898		
Louis	**Kirschbaum**		1862		Farmer
Julia	(Goodman) Kirschbaum	wife	1862	1928	
Bertram	Kirschbaum	son	1890		
Florence	Kirschbaum	daughter	1893		
Charles	Kirschbaum	son	1895	1961	
Otto	**Klein**		1877		Cousin of Samuel Blumenthal
Samuel	**Kolbou**		1887		Cousin of Abraham Mintz
Henry	**Kramer**		1867		

continued on next page

Table 6.1. Continued.

Mamie	(Kahn) Kramer	wife	1877		
Janet	Kramer	daughter	1899		
Paula	Kramer	daughter	1902		
Miriam	Kramer	daughter	1906		
Jacob	**Lampert**		1880		Jewelry merchant
Frances	(Gray) Lampert	wife	1885		B'nai Sholom Ladies Auxiliary 1914
Gladys	Lampert	daughter	1908		
Naomi	Lampert	daughter	1914		
Lazarus	**Leder**		1868	1926	Founding member B'nai Sholom 1906
Rachael	(Friede) Leder	wife	1870	1939	Variety store owner
Marian	Leder	daughter	1892		m. Gustave Weiner from Hicksville
Hamilton	Leder	son	1896	1971	
Simon	Leder	son	1902		
Louis	**Leder**		1864		Brother of Lazarus
A.	**Levin**				Founding member B'nai Sholom 1906
Louis	**Levin**				
Dora	Levin	wife	1845	1925	
Sophie	Levin	daughter	1878		m. Abraham Mintz
Max	**Levy**				Founding member B'nai Sholom 1906
Benjamin	**Markowitz**		1879	1937	
Sophia	(Newmark) Markowitz	wife	1883	1936	B'nai Sholom Ladies Auxiliary 1914
Sanford	Markowitz	son	1904		
Mordecai	Markowitz	son	1909		
Bernice	Markowitz	daughter	1913		
Jerome	Markowitz	son	1918		
Edward	**Michnoff**		1885		Son of Benjamin and Minnie from Bay Shore
Sadie	(Willensky) Michnoff	wife	1891		
Grace	Michnoff	daughter	1908		
Robert	Michnoff	son	1913		
Muriel	Michnoff	daughter	1917		
Leopold	**Michnoff**		1874		Son of Benjamin and Minnie from Bay Shore

Table 6.1. Continued.

Bessie	(Wallach) Michnoff	wife	1887		
Romola	Michnoff	daughter	1911		
David	Michnoff	son	1913		
Roslyn	Michnoff	daughter	1916		
Robert	**Michnoff**		1887		Son of Benjamin and Minnie from Bay Shore
Beatrice	(Gallin) Michnoff	wife	1892		
Leo	Michnoff	son	1915		
Ethel	Michnoff	daughter	1915		
Abraham	**Mintz**		1873	1929	Founding member B'nai Sholom 1906
Sophie	(Levin) Mintz	wife	1878		Daughter of Louis and Dora
Bella	Mintz	daughter	1904		
Irving	Mintz	son	1908		
Seymour	Mintz	son	1912		
Bella	**Mintz**		1894		Niece of Abraham Mintz
Ralph	**Moolten**		1874	1930	Dentist
Minnie	(Tigner) Moolten	wife	1883		B'nai Sholom Ladies Auxiliary 1914
Sylvan	Moolten	son	1905		
Lenore	Moolten	daughter	1908		
Elsa	Moolten	daughter	1915		
Hugh	**Newman**		1897	1979	Secretary B'nai Sholom 1914
Marion	Newman	wife	1898		
Jeanne	Newman	daughter	1916		
Jacob	**Rasener**		1859	1925	Shoe merchant
Myriam	(Hoffman) Rasener	wife	1859	1926	
Emma	Rasener	daughter	1881	1947	m. Isaac Davis
Hilda	Rasener	daughter	1886		
Herman	Rasener	son	1889	1926	
Marcus	**Ratheim**		1856	1946	Merchant
Emily	(Sichel) Ratheim	wife	1867		
Julius	Ratheim	son	1889		
Rudolph	Ratheim	son	1891		
Alfred	Ratheim	son	1896		
Harry	**Rosenbaum**		1851	1927	
Sophia	(Hollstein) Rosenbaum	wife	1865		
Morris	**Shore**		1870		Grocery store owner

continued on next page

Table 6.1. Continued.

Lena	(Stoller) Shore	wife	1876		
Leon	Shore	son	1895		m. Lillian Hirshfield lived in Hempstead
Marie	Shore	daughter	1897		
David	Shore	son	1898		
Arthur	Shore	son	1907		
Edward	**Stavenhagen**		1836	1911	Founding member B'nai Sholom 1906
Mary	Stavenhagen	wife	1844	1927	B'nai Sholom Ladies Auxiliary 1914
Amelia	**Tuch**		1815		Mother of Augusta Aronson
Gustav	**Zadeck**		1875	1957	
Anna	(Sichel) Zadeck	wife	1872	1953	

Table 6.2. Residents of Baldwin

Abraham	**Allen**		1868		
Anna	Allen	wife	1869		
Ida	Allen	daughter	1893		
Phillip	Allen	son	1896		
Mary	Allen	daughter	1900		
David	**Goldstein**		1875		Dry goods merchant
Esther	Goldstein	wife	1881		
Leo	Goldstein	son	1903		
Joseph	Goldstein	son	1904		
Arthur	Goldstein	son	1916		
Joseph	**Sheffer**		1876	1947	Trustee Nassau County Hebrew Assoc. 1902
Annie	(Reich) Sheffer	wife	1878	1937	
Bella	Sheffer	daughter	1899		
Harry	Sheffer	son	1901		
Simpson	Sheffer	son	1902		
Eugene	Sheffer	son	1905		
Samuel	Sheffer	son	1914		

Table 6.3. Residents of Lynbrook

Morris	**Ackerman**		1883	1968	Son of Henry and Esther from Freeport
Catharine	(Meehan) Ackerman	wife	1885		

Table 6.3. Continued.

Beatrice	Ackerman	daughter	1913		
Henry	Ackerman	son	1915	1955	
Jonas	**Adelson**		1877		
Lulu	(Cohen) Adelson	wife	1878		
Samuel	Adelson	son	1906		
Hazel	Adelson	daughter	1914		
Morris	**Brown**		1881		Tailor
Fannie	(Barnett) Brown	wife	1881		
Isadore	Brown	son	1901		
Herman	Brown	son	1904		
Samuel	Brown	son	1911		
Milton	Brown	son	1913		
Daniel	Brown	son	1918		
Abraham	**Chisel**		1881		Worked in a knitting mill
Ida	Chisel	wife	1883		
Mollie	Chisel	daughter	1914		
Abraham	**Goldberg**		1877		Shoemaker
Annie	Goldberg	wife	1885		
Jacob	Goldberg	son	1905		
Martha	Goldberg	daughter	1911		
John	**Goldstein**		1884	1954	
Elsa	(Zilges) Goldstein	wife	1884		
Marjorie	Goldstein	daughter	1911		
Edith	Goldstein	daughter	1914		
Moses	**Goldstein**		1876	1933	
Martha	(Spitzer) Goldstein	wife	1886		
Henrietta	Goldstein	daughter	1905		
Lawrence	Goldstein	son	1908		
Morton	Goldstein	son	1918		
Rosa	**Gorlen**		1862		
Maer	Gorlen	son	1890		Milk dealer
Morris	**Hirsch**		1874		Tailor
Minnie	Hirsch	wife	1874		
Jacob	Hirsch	son	1901		
Abraham	Hirsch	son	1903		
Tobah	Hirsch	daughter	1904		
Chepak	Hirsch	daughter	1908		
Isaac	**Jacobson**		1869	1952	Founding member B'nai Sholom 1906

continued on next page

Table 6.3. Continued.

Rebecca	(Brenner) Jacobson	wife	1870	1945	
Rose	Jacobson	daughter	1894		
Sarah	Jacobson	daughter	1897		
Solomon	Jacobson	son	1898	1968	
Dora	Jacobson	daughter	1902		
Samuel	**Jacobson**		1880		Brother of Isaac as well as Philip and Morris from Freeport
Mildred	(Simon) Jacobson	wife	1890		
David	Jacobson	son	1909		
Dorothy	Jacobson	daughter	1912		
Harold	Jacobson	son	1917		
Harry	**Katz**		1903		Brother-in-law of Lawrence Schwartz
Jacob	**Leff**		1897		
Yetta	Leff				Either wife or mother of Jacob
Joseph	**Levy**				Store owner
Marks	**Levy**		1863		Trustee B'nai Sholom 1915
Sarah	Levy	wife	1863		
David	Levy	son	1889		
Alice	Levy	daughter	1891		
Joseph	Levy	son	1892		
Rebecca	Levy	daughter	1895		
Isabel	Levy	daughter	1898		
Lawrence	**Schwartz**		1886	1967	Shoemaker
Sadie	Schwartz	wife	1888		
Jeannette	Schwartz	daughter	1912		
Ruby	Schwartz	son	1914		
Leo	**Spitzer**		1886		Salesman
Clara	(Wolf) Spitzer	wife	1890		
Margery	Spitzer	daughter	1914		
Adel	Spitzer	daughter	1917		
Morris	**Spitzer**		1874		Confectionery merchant
Julia	Spitzer	wife	1885		
Samuel	Spitzer	son	1907		
Ruth	Spitzer	daughter	1909		
Jesse	Spitzer	son	1910		
Mark	**Wolf**		1877		Rug store owner
Bessie	(Woldowsky) Wolf	wife	1888	1950	

Table 6.3. Continued.

Albert	Wolf	son	1912		
Lenore	Wolf	daughter	1915		

Table 6.4. Residents of Valley Stream

Moses	**DaSilva**	1882	1954	Son of Isaac and Annie from Freeport
Ella	(Cammaun) DaSilva	wife	1884	
Jacob	**Eisenberg**		1892	Nephew of Louis and Edith
Annie	(Eisenberg) Eisenberg	wife	1895	Daughter of Louis and Edith
Louis	**Eisenberg**		1867	Barrel maker
Edith	Eisenberg	wife	1869	
Samuel	Eisenberg	son	1892	m. Lena
Annie	Eisenberg	daughter	1895	m. Jacob Eisenberg
Morris	Eisenberg	son	1897	
Fannie	Eisenberg	daughter	1901	
William	Eisenberg	son	1903	
Yetta	Eisenberg	daughter	1907	
Hyman	Eisenberg	son	1911	
Samuel	**Eisenberg**		1892	Son of Louis and Edith
Lena	Eisenberg	wife	1895	

Chapter 7

Central Nassau

Including Central Park (Now Bethpage),
Farmingdale, Floral Park, Hicksville, Mineola,
New Hyde Park, and Westbury

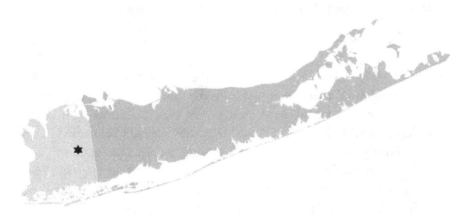

The earliest villages established on Long Island in the eighteenth and nineteenth centuries all have something in common. While agriculture was the dominant contributor to the local economies, they were also dependent on fishing, whaling, and oystering. Being able to move goods for trade occurred by boat, and therefore the most populated towns were situated near the water. These coastal communities were connected by a main road that ran along the north (today known as route 25A) and south (Montauk Highway) shores of the island. Merchants made their way east and west along these routes. And when factories were first built, they were situated in these villages where labor could be supplied, leading to additional growth of the waterfront towns.

Figure 38. Sam Schwartz business advertisement. *Source: The Long-Islander*, May 8, 1908.

Real estate values were at their highest in the central business district with land becoming more affordable away from the coast. With the exception of Hempstead, communities in the central part of Nassau County were slower to develop even with the arrival of the LIRR that was built primarily to ship goods to Boston via Greenport, not for moving people. Like the north and south shores, the middle of the island had a central thoroughfare, and Jews settled in the towns situated along Jericho Turnpike including Floral Park, New Hyde Park, Mineola, and Westbury as well as the villages of Hicksville and Farmingdale located south of the turnpike.

Samuel Schwartz immigrated to the United States as a ten-year-old boy in 1894 and moved to Hicksville with his wife Bessie in 1907. Sam operated a secondhand furniture business run out of a storage warehouse he built on Duffy Avenue near his home in 1909. The couple had three children before 1912 when their fourth was born, a son named Julius. Friends and family from around Long Island and New York City made their way to Hicksville, eight days after the birth, for Julius's bris. Other than the mohel Harris Lipschitz from Glen Cove, who performed the ritual circumcision, attendees included August Sokolowsky and Joseph Katz from Mineola, and Hicksville residents Abe Schwartz (Sam's brother), Isaac Spiro, J. Wolf, I. Ginsberg, Frank Marrs, A. G. Heitz, Karl Hoffman, and Harry Weiss.

New York Clothing Co.

Kallert Building
Broadway and Mary St., Hicksville, L. I.

—

Men's and Young Men's Fall
Suits at **$10** and **$12**, made of Pure
Worsted materials in all the latest
shades and cuts.

A large assortment to select
from.

Also a full line of

Gent's Furnishings
Hats
Caps
Shoes

NEW YORK CLOTHING COMPANY
Broadway and Mary St., Hicksville, L. I.

Figure 39. Advertisement for Harry Weiss's store. *Source: The Long-Islander,* November 19, 1909.

Harry Weiss was a proprietor of clothing stores with his brothers. By 1901 the Weiss family business had six locations in New York and New Jersey. Harry and his wife Hannah were married in 1899 and lived in Rockville Centre where Harry ran the New York Clothing Company branch on Village Avenue. Hannah's parents Meyer and Elizabeth Goodman also lived in Rockville Centre with Meyer earning a living as a merchant selling liquor. Harry moved his store to Hicksville in 1904, located in the business hub on Broadway, and soon after the Goodmans also moved east, finding a new home in nearby Farmingdale where Meyer had a shoe store in 1906. A year later Meyer expanded his business by teaming up with his son-in-law and opened a shoe department in the New York Clothing Company store that was run by Meyer's son Lester.

Another proprietor located on Broadway in Hicksville was Abraham Katz, younger brother of Joseph Katz from Mineola. Joe was an active member of the Jewish community serving as president of the Nassau Hebrew

Figure 40. Joe and Anna Katz started out living in Glen Cove by 1898, then Westbury in 1899, Roslyn in 1900, and finally settled in Mineola in 1912. L to R, back row: Esther, Anna, Maurice, Joe, and Jacob; front row: Ethel and Harry, c. 1907. *Source*: Courtesy of Gary Katz.

Association in 1913, 1924, and 1938. He married Anna Rosenthal in 1896 and had seven children who were all born on Long Island. In his professional life Joe was in the furniture business opening North Shore Furniture Company in 1916 but started out as a peddler selling his wares in various towns and villages in Nassau County. When traveling through Mineola on his regular route Joe would often stop and visit with Joseph and Minnie Saul whose home was known as a good resting place for Jewish itinerant merchants. It is not known exactly how or when, but Joe introduced his brother Abe to Joseph and Minnie's daughter Emma. Abe Katz and Emma Saul were married in 1909 and made their home in New Hyde Park until 1915 when Abe opened his clothing store in Hicksville.

Abe Katz, the son of a stone cutter from Russia, earned a good living selling men's and women's clothing from his store located at the northeast corner of Broadway and Marie Street. He had the reputation around Hicksville as something of a pugnacious character. In his sixties Abe initiated a physical confrontation with a man half his age over a business dispute, and he also severed ties with his brother-in-law due to a financial matter that was not repaired until some ten years later. At the same time Abe was known for his empathy and generosity displayed through dealings with his loan officer at the bank. Abe and the banker carried on a cantankerous relationship for years. But when the banker was down on his luck and without a job during the Depression, Abe supported him financially.

As more young Jewish families moved to Hicksville an education in Hebrew studies became increasingly important. Religious observance and Jewish tradition were important to Sam Schwartz, who was vice president of the Nassau Hebrew Association and had organized services in his home on Duffy Avenue for Rosh Hashanah in 1912. He stepped up again, offering his new building, at the corner of Broadway and Cherry Street, as the location for a Hebrew school in 1917. It was around this time the Jewish men of Hicksville were organizing and planning to establish a congregation. Their efforts came to fruition when Congregation Shaarei Zedek Anshei Hicksville was incorporated on February 25, 1919.

A synagogue was built for the congregation in Hicksville on East Barclay Street that opened in 1926 and a second on Old Country Road in 1965. The Nassau Hebrew Association, with the majority of its members centered in Mineola, became an incorporated entity in 1925 and built a synagogue on Willis Avenue that opened in 1932. At the dedication on February 28, President Mack Markowitz accepted the ceremonial golden key to the synagogue from the chairman of the building committee Joe Katz.

Covering Floors in Nassau County for Ninety Years

Joe Katz started in business as a peddler just as many other young Jewish men did around the turn of the century on Long Island. By 1910 he was an employee in a furniture store, and six years later he opened North Shore Furniture Company in Mineola. Success enabled Joe to expand, moving to a 10,500-square-foot showroom on Main Street that he boasted was the largest furniture store on Long Island when it opened in October 1924. Joe's sons joined him in the business through the 1920s but fell on hard times during the Depression and had to close down the store in 1932.

Joe's son Harry took the remaining rugs, rolls of linoleum, and some ice boxes from North Shore Furniture to start his own business he named

Figures 41 and 42. Employees at Harry Katz Floor Coverings, c. 1950. *Source*: Courtesy of Gary Katz; and two of Harry's grandchildren Gary and Cyndy. *Source:* Photo by Brad Kolodny.

Harry Katz Floor Coverings and Appliances. The store was located on Main Street in 1932, moved to 204 Jericho Turnpike, then was located at 167 Mineola Boulevard until 1955 when they opened a new showroom at 450 Jericho Turnpike, where the store is still located today. Having Harry's name front and center was appropriate for this gregarious businessman who knew how to schmooze and make connections. Being active in civic associations was beneficial for his public persona, leading Harry to become a star in local politics as a trustee for the village of Mineola for twelve years and eventually becoming deputy mayor. But the fact is that Harry's wife, Yetta, was the real brains behind the success of the store. She was a valedictorian at Mineola High School who had her eye on Harry at an even younger age. People recognized Yetta's brilliance and referred to her as being the world's first computer because she carried everything around in her brain with a capacity for storing endless amounts of information.

Upon his return to Mineola from service during the Korean War, Harry and Yetta's son Kenneth began working at the store and took over in 1970 when his parents decided to retire. The baton was passed to the next generation with Ken's four children Ron, Cyndy, Doug, and Gary all taking an active role in various aspects of the retail and wholesale divisions of the family business. In 1987 the company strengthened their purchasing power and exposure through advertising by joining a flooring cooperative and changed the store's name to Harry Katz Carpet One. As they approach ninety years of selling carpeting, linoleum, and other floor coverings, the current owners take pride in being the fourth generation of the Katz family to conduct business in Mineola, beginning with their great-grandfather Joe.

Table 7.1. Residents of Central Park (Now Bethpage)

Morris	**Friedman**		1881		Publisher Hicksville Courier
Grace	(Ross) Friedman	wife	1882		
Evelyn	Friedman	daughter	1902		
Mildred	Friedman	daughter	1909	1938	
Robert	Friedman	son	1913		
Sarah	**Ross**		1860		Mother of Grace Friedman

Table 7.2. Residents of Farmingdale

Benjamin	**Blumberg**		1846	1906	Worked at Queens Brick Co.
Harris	**Brower**		1854	1936	Trustee Lindenhurst Hebrew Con. 1913
Sarah	Brower	wife	1857	1942	
Isaac	Brower	son	1875	1957	m. Rose
Louis	Brower	son	1889		
Annie	Brower	daughter	1892		m. Samuel Cohen lived in Lindenhurst
Isaac	**Brower**		1875	1957	Son of Harris and Sarah
Rose	Brower	wife	1879	1952	
Bertha	Brower	daughter	1902		
Joseph	Brower	son	1904		
Aaron	Brower	son	1906		
Dorothy	Brower	daughter	1908		
Irwin	Brower	son	1913		
Edith	Brower	daughter	1915		
Milton	Brower	son	1918		
Meyer	**Goodman**		1855	1925	Shoe store owner
Elizabeth	(Levi) Goodman	wife	1857		
Hannah	Goodman	daughter	1876		m. Harry Weiss, lived in Hicksville
Florence	Goodman	daughter	1880		
Morris	Goodman	son	1882		
Lester	Goodman	son	1886		
Jacob	**Kranzler**		1869		Dry goods merchant
Dora	(Gettinger) Kranzler	wife	1869		
Cecilia	Kranzler	daughter	1892		m. Harry Katz, lived in Roosevelt
Anna	Kranzler	daughter	1894		m. Benjamin Waldner
Charles	Kranzler	son	1897		

Table 7.2. Continued.

Bessie	Kranzler	daughter	1899		
Edward	Kranzler	son	1901		
Morris	**Slotnick**		1882		Dry goods merchant
Rose	Slotnick	wife	1883		
Anna	Slotnick	daughter	1904		
Samuel	Slotnick	son	1908		
Benjamin	**Waldner**		1889	1966	Dry goods merchant
Anna	(Kranzler) Waldner	wife	1894		Daughter of Jacob and Dora
Daniel	Waldner	son	1914		
Perry	Waldner	son	1918		

Table 7.3. Residents of Floral Park

Max	**Kaslow**		1876		Hardware merchant
Etta	Kaslow	wife	1886		
Ruvin	Kaslow	son	1905		
May	Kaslow	daughter	1910		
Harry	Kaslow	son	1913		
Bertram	Kaslow	son	1914		
Jacob	**Oshansky**		1878	1936	Merchant
Sophia	Oshansky	wife	1882		
Louis	Oshansky	son	1902		
Harry	Oshansky	son	1904		
Esther	Oshansky	daughter	1909		
Molly	Oshansky	daughter	1910		
Samuel	**Sokolowsky**		1862	1941	Shoemaker
Rachel	Sokolowsky	wife	1859	1940	
Max	Sokolowsky	son	1896		
Rose	Sokolowsky	daughter	1901		

Table 7.4. Residents of Hicksville

Samuel	**Albert**		1875		
Jennie	Albert	wife	1882		
Morris	Albert	son	1907		
Sarah	Albert	daughter	1910		
Nathan	Albert	son	1912		
Sophia	Albert	daughter	1915		
Ethel	Albert	daughter	1917		

continued on next page

Table 7.4. Continued.

Jacob	**Cristel**		1860		Junkman
Rosie	Cristel	wife	1865		
Morris	Cristel	son	1895		
Isadore	**Ginsberg**		1880		Trustee Nassau Hebrew Assoc. 1913
Fanny	Ginsberg	wife	1883		
Tilly	Ginsberg	daughter	1908		
Julius	Ginsberg	son	1913		
Karl	**Hoffman**		1870		Junkman
Yetta	Hoffman	wife	1872		
David	Hoffman	son	1896		
Rose	Hoffman	daughter	1900		
May	Hoffman	daughter	1901		
Anna	Hoffman	daughter	1904		
Mary	Hoffman	daughter	1906		
Sidney	Hoffman	son	1908		
Jacob	Hoffman	son	1912		
Philip	**Jacobson**		1883		Shoe store owner
Esther	Jacobson	wife	1885		
Rose	Jacobson	daughter	1908		
Sadie	Jacobson	daughter	1910		
David	Jacobson	son	1917		
Irving	Jacobson	son	1918		
Samuel	**Kantor**		1888		
Gertrude	Kantor	wife	1888		
Morris	Kantor	son	1911		
David	Kantor	son	1912		
Nathan	Kantor	son	1916		
Abraham	**Katz**		1882	1951	Brother of Joseph from Mineola and David from Roslyn
Emma	(Saul) Katz	wife	1886	1967	Daughter of Joseph and Minnie from Mineola
Celia	Katz	daughter	1910		
Lawrence	Katz	son	1912	1999	
Joseph	Katz	son	1912	1988	
Harry	Katz	son	1914	1997	
Lillian	Katz	daughter	1918	1995	
Benjamin	**Morris**		1859		Member Nassau Hebrew Assoc. 1913

Table 7.4. Continued.

Anna	Morris	wife	1865		
Lena	Morris	daughter	1893		
Sarah	Morris	daughter	1894		
Harry	Morris	son	1899		
May	Morris	daughter	1901		
Samuel	**Ruhig**		1842	1932	
Mary	Ruhig	wife	1850	1921	
Alex	Ruhig	son	1883		
Bertha	Ruhig	daughter	1887		m. David Weiner
Jacob	**Scheiner**		1868	1955	Merchant
Rose	Scheiner	wife	1875	1946	
Nathan	Scheiner	son	1898		
Jennie	Scheiner	daughter	1903		
Abraham	**Schwartz**		1885		Brother of Samuel
Rosie	Schwartz	wife	1893		
Sam	Schwartz	son	1917		
Morris	Schwartz	son	1918		
Samuel	**Schwartz**		1884		VP Nassau Hebrew Association 1913
Bessie	Schwartz	wife	1884		
Harry	Schwartz	son	1906		
Annie	Schwartz	daughter		1907	Five months old at time of death
Isidore	Schwartz	son	1909		
Julius	Schwartz	son	1912		
Isaac	**Spiro**		1873	1919	Member Nassau Hebrew Assoc. 1913
Sarah	(Saiger) Spiro	wife	1873		
Hiram	Spiro	son	1897	1936	
Morris	Spiro	son	1901		
Clarence	Spiro	son	1906	1937	
Solomon	**Swba**		1871		Dry goods merchant
?	Swba	first wife			
Louise	Swba	daughter	1899		
Annie	Swba	second wife	1887		
Rosie	Swba	daughter	1908		
Sarah	Swba	daughter	1910		
David	**Weiner**		1882		Printer
Bertha	(Ruhig) Weiner	wife	1887		Daughter of Samuel and Mary

continued on next page

Table 7.4. Continued.

Herman	Weiner	son	1906		
Julia	Weiner	daughter	1909		
Gustave	**Weiner**		1887		Printer
Marian	(Leder) Weiner	wife	1892		Daughter of Lazarus and Rachael from Rockville Centre
Harry	**Weiss**		1876	1928	Brother of Louis from Huntington
Hannah	(Goodman) Weiss	wife	1876		Daughter of Meyer and Elizabeth from Farmingdale
Isabelle	Weiss	daughter	1900		
Gertrude	Weiss	daughter	1902		
Sadie	Weiss	daughter	1904		
Arthur	Weiss	son	1905		
Sanford	Weiss	son	1907		
William	Weiss	son	1908		
Helen	Weiss	daughter	1911		
Lillian	Weiss	daughter	1915		
Samuel	**Yondelman**		1883		Member Nassau Hebrew Assoc. 1913
Bertha	Yondelman	wife	1887		
Tessie	Yondelman	daughter	1908		
Jacob	Yondelman	son	1910		
David	Yondelman	son	1910		

Table 7.5. Residents of Mineola

Julius	**Braunstein**		1880		Store owner
Fanny	Braunstein	wife	1888		
Percy	Braunstein	son	1911		
Anna	Braunstein	daughter	1916		
Frieda	Braunstein	daughter	1918		
Menie	**Dollinger**		1882		Tailor
Ethel	Dollinger	wife	1888		
William	**Dubowsky**		1891		Baker
?	Dubowksy	wife			
?	Dubowsky	child			Born before 1918
Adolph	**Flesch**		1877	1935	Member Nassau Hebrew Assoc. 1913
Gussie	(Markowitz) Flesch	wife	1879	1959	
Charles	Flesch	son	1903		

Table 7.5. Continued.

Emanuel	Flesch	son	1905	1960	
Sadie	Flesch	daughter	1907		
Joseph	Flesch	son	1909		
Pearl	Flesch	daughter	1913		
Ignatz	**Flesch**		1855		Father of Adolph
Joseph	**Flesch**		1880	1953	
Samuel	**Flesch**		1882	1952	Auto supply business
Fanny	Flesch	wife	1883		
Helen	Flesch	daughter	1903		
Martin	Flesch	son	1908		
Harold	Flesch	son	1912		
Ira	Flesch	son	1918		
Samuel	**Golden**		1879	1944	Member Nassau Hebrew Assoc. 1913
Tillie	(Farman) Golden	wife	1886		
Michael	Golden	son	1904		
Annie	Golden	daughter	1906		
Joseph	**Katz**		1871	1957	President Nassau Hebrew Assoc. 1913
Anna	(Strauss) Katz	wife	1877	1967	
Maurice	Katz	son	1898		
Esther	Katz	daughter	1899		
Jacob	Katz	son	1902		
Harry	Katz	son	1904	1985	
Ethel	Katz	daughter	1906		
Lillian	Katz	daughter	1908		
Louis	Katz	son	1910		
Hilda	Katz	daughter	1914		
Morris	**Poross**		1884	1952	Painter
Anna	(Golden) Poross	wife	1890		
Joseph	**Saul**		1856	1912	Dry goods merchant
Minnie	Saul	wife	1865	1923	Maiden name Cohen or Teyson
Emma	Saul	daughter	1882		m. Abraham Katz lived in Hicksville
Fannie	Saul	daughter	1886		
Delia	Saul	daughter	1888		
Leon	Saul	son	1898	1948	
Harry	**Siegel**		1887		Tailor

continued on next page

Table 7.5. Continued.

Tina	(Rachman) Siegel	wife	1886		
Lillie	Siegel	daughter	1907		
Yetta	Siegel	daughter	1908	1999	
Morris	Siegel	son	1912		
Louis	Siegel	son	1914		
Aaron	**Sokolinsky**		1886		Member Nassau Hebrew Assoc. 1913
Rose	(Fahrman) Sokolinsky	wife	1890		
Dorothy	Sokolinsky	daughter	1916		
Gus	**Sokolinsky**		1885	1969	Member Nassau Hebrew Assoc. 1913
Tillie	Sokolinsky	wife	1892	1961	
Dorothy	Sokolinsky	daughter	1914		
Philip	Sokolinsky	son	1916		
Bernie	**Sokolinsky**		1891		Brother of Gus
Adolph	**Smith**		1878		Tailor
Miriam	Smith	wife	1886		
Roslyn	Smith	wife	1913		
Carl	Smith	son	1918		
Martin	Smith	son	1918		

Table 7.6. Residents of New Hyde Park

Annie	**Frank**		1860		
Samuel	Frank	son	1888		
Rosie	Frank	daughter	1892		
Nathan	**Friedman**		1870		Vegetable peddler
Anna	Friedman	wife	1870		
Julius	Friedman	son	1895		
Jacob	Friedman	son	1896		
Ida	Friedman	daughter	1897		
Samuel	Friedman	son	1899		
Tilly	Friedman	daughter	1903		
Harry	Friedman	son	1909		
Aaron	**Holman**		1873		Merchant
Lena	(Farman) Holman	wife	1885		
David	Holman	son	1904		
Eveline	Holman	daughter	1912		

Table 7.6. Continued.

Harry	**Rosenberg**		1858	1942	Member Nassau Hebrew Assoc. 1913
Annie	(Kroresk) Rosenberg	wife	1863	1929	
Lena	Rosenberg	daughter	1888		
Morris	Rosenberg	son	1889		
Rosy	Rosenberg	daughter	1893		
Frank	Rosenberg	son	1895		
Minnie	Rosenberg	daughter	1900		
Benjamin	Rosenberg	son	1903		
Aaron	**Shapiro**		1882		Grocery store owner
Esther	(Frank) Shapiro	wife	1886		Daughter of Annie
Charles	Shapiro	son	1911		
Herman	Shapiro	son	1912		
Jacob	Shapiro	son	1917		

Table 7.7. Residents of Westbury

Harry	**Baer**		1883	Member Nassau Hebrew Assoc. 1913
Bessie	(Simon) Baer	wife	1884	Daughter of Benjamin and Minnie
Joseph	**Dollinger**		1876	Tailor
Hannah	Dollinger	wife	1882	
Aaron	Dollinger	son	1908	
Sadie	Dollinger	daughter	1912	
Benjamin	Dollinger	son	1916	
Zacharias	**Goldenberg**		1886	Upholsterer
Florence	Goldenberg	wife	1894	
Irving	Goldenberg	son	1915	
Annette	Goldenberg	daughter	1918	
Arthur	**Harris**		1885	Motorcycle dealer
Jeannette	Harris	wife	1892	
John	Harris	son	1913	
Hilda	Harris	daughter	1916	
Henry	**Harris**		1899	Motorcycle mechanic
Paul	**Harris**		1888	Mechanic, worked for Arthur Harris
Molly	Harris	wife	1892	
Anna	Harris	daughter	1917	

continued on next page

Table 7.7. Continued.

Morris	**Harris**		1894		Worked for Arthur Harris
Hattie	Harris	wife	1897		
Sidney	Harris	son	1915		
Herbert	Harris	son	1917		
Sylvia	Harris	daughter	1918		
Benjamin	**Simon**		1857		Member Nassau Hebrew Assoc. 1913
Minnie	Simon	wife	1857		
Jacob	**Weinstein**		1880		Tailor
Mary	(Jaffe) Weinstein	wife	1885		
David	Weinstein	son	1907		
Morris	Weinstein	son	1910		
Arthur	Weinstein	son	1912		

Chapter 8

The Gold Coast

Including Great Neck, Manhasset, Port Washington, Roslyn,
Roslyn Harbor, Roslyn Heights, and Sands Point

The northern portion of Nassau County is made up of land with a coast-line that meanders along Long Island Sound. This property includes broad vistas with abundant water views and was ripe for real estate development in the early twentieth century. Titans of industry who made their fortunes during the industrial age following the Civil War purchased large swaths of land and created summer estates in this area within close proximity to New York City where their businesses were headquartered. Hundreds of mansions were built by a who's-who of wealthy businessmen during the era including J. P. Morgan, Alfred du Pont, F. W. Woolworth, Charles Pratt, and others.

Successful Jews on a similar financial level as these tycoons joined in the opulence of living on what became known as the Gold Coast. Merchants also inhabited the villages in this area stretching from Great Neck to Roslyn.

Great Neck

William Russell Grace was a successful businessman and philanthropist who served two terms as mayor of New York City in the 1880s. His tailor was a man named Abram Wolf who not only made suits for the mayor, but the two men had a social relationship and played pinochle together. Grace suggested to Wolf that he should consider moving out to Great Neck where Grace had a residence and many wealthy friends in need of tailoring. With no tailor available in town at the time, Wolf saw the opportunity and moved his wife Rose and five children out to Long Island in 1892. Abram and his family became the first Jews to live in Great Neck, taking up residence in a three-story house on Hicks Lane and rented out rooms for supplemental income. In addition to the Wolf family there were seven boarders living under the same roof in 1900.

Before long Abram gave up tailoring to become an assessor for the Town of North Hempstead, earning $35 a month. He gained valuable experience working for a public entity but decided to go into the private sector by establishing his own real estate and insurance company in 1908. Abram became a well-known citizen through his business and civic activities that included being a charter member of the Great Neck fire department. At this point there was no Jewish community in Great Neck to speak of; so in order to attend services at a synagogue Abram would walk to Flushing on the sabbath, but he also felt a need to associate with other Jews in social settings. To fill the void Abram organized the Nassau Hebrew Association in 1909 (a different organization than the Nassau County Hebrew Association of 1902 in Hempstead and 1906 in Rockville Centre) that brought Jews together from Great Neck, Roslyn, Manhasset, Port Washington, Glen Cove, Mineola, Hicksville, and other towns in the middle and northern portions of Nassau County. Another crucial function performed by the association, recognized at the time as a mutual benefit society by the American Jewish Committee, was to provide for the burial of its members. This was achieved within three years of the organization's inception by purchasing a plot at

Figure 43. Gated entrance for the Nassau Hebrew Association plot at Montefiore Cemetery. *Source*: Photo by Brad Kolodny.

Montefiore Cemetery in southern Queens just west of the Nassau County border. By 1912 the Nassau Hebrew Association had ninety-seven members.

In the 1920s, when Jews were moving to Great Neck in larger numbers, the desire to organize a congregation brought on the establishment of Temple Beth El by the end of the decade with Abram and his son-in-law Albert Antor as two of the founding members.

Port Washington

On a cold Friday morning in February of 1890, Harry Jacobs and his older brother Barney arrived in New York aboard *The Columbia* and were processed through Castle Garden, the immigration center used prior to the opening of Ellis Island. Within two days they were reunited with their brother Nathan who was a peddler living in Glen Cove and by Tuesday Harry was out on Long Island selling goods with a group of other young men. That first day was spent selling chair bottoms in Sea Cliff earning eighty cents while six times that amount went to the boss. After five days it was not difficult for Harry to see the benefits of being the boss leading the brash and motivated fifteen-year-old, who had been in America for all of one week, to go out on his own.

Monday morning Harry went to the peddlers supply market and purchased matches to sell. He boarded a boat that docked at Sands Point and made his first sale to the driver of the stagecoach that took him into Port Washington. A day's work brought a profit of two dollars and forty cents in addition to enjoying the people he met along the way. Harry continued to go back and forth between New York and Port Washington in order to replenish his stock and brought various items to sell. He also stayed over some nights in Port Washington with acquaintances or at a boarding house. This continued for two years until Harry opened his first store in a former billiard hall, paying fifteen dollars a month in rent.

Having success but not being content, young Harry asked his brother Nathan to join him in growing the business that became known as Jacobs Bros. Dry Goods and Notions. They rented a store on Carlton Avenue in 1893 with Nathan as the shopkeeper and Harry going out on the road with a horse and wagon selling goods to customers in Westbury, Hicksville, Sands Point, Locust Valley, and Oyster Bay. Before long the brothers amassed enough capital to invest in property buying an empty lot in town and constructing a two-story building at 283 Main Street in 1894. The ground level was used for a new modern store with a five-room residence above. The humble abode was large enough to house Harry and Nathan as well as their sister Rachel, her husband Max Israel and another sister Sarah who had come to America just a few months prior.

A quarrel arose between Harry and Nathan over the courtship of a young woman named Ida Gesas. The feud became irreconcilable causing Harry to separate himself from the business in favor of the woman he loved. Ida and Harry were married in Sea Cliff in 1896 where they made their home briefly before moving to Roslyn. Harry started over as a peddler out on his own again, until his ambitions became larger than Long Island could satisfy. He ended up heading west in 1900 with Ida and their three children, settling in Idaho. Meanwhile the Jacobs family footprint grew in Port Washington with Barney opening a grocery store on Main Street across from Nathan. Their parents Victor and Mollie Jacobs and their two youngest children, Norman and Rivki, also came to live in Port Washington upon their arrival in America in 1896.

There were not enough Jews in Port Washington to establish a congregation until the early 1930s; however, there is documentation that services for the High Holidays were organized in 1913 with thirty-five attendees.

Roslyn Harbor

Isaac, Louis, and Bernard Stern were the founders of Stern Brothers, a small dry goods store in Buffalo, New York, that would become Stern's Department Stores. They got their start in 1867 and a year later opened their first location in New York City on Sixth Avenue. Subsequently, the youngest of the four brothers, Benjamin, joined the partnership. As the Stern business grew so did the need for larger space, which led to construction of a six-floor facility on Twenty-Third Street in 1892, and twenty years later a nine-floor building was erected on Forty-Second Street. In 1905 Benjamin and his wife Madeleine purchased a nineteen-acre waterfront estate in the area today known as Roslyn Harbor as their country home and converted the existing mansion into a French-style chateau they called Claraben Court. Throughout their lives Benjamin and Madeleine were generous contributors to the Federation for the Support of Jewish Philanthropic Societies. This organization was one of a half-dozen Jewish charities named in Mrs. Stern's will, each receiving between $15,000 and $25,000 at the time of her death in 1933. The Sterns also answered the

Figures 44 and 45. Benjamin and Madeleine Stern. *Source*: National Archives and Records Administration accessed from familysearch.org.

call when approached to donate toward the construction of the synagogue for Congregation Tifereth Israel in Glen Cove. They made a contribution of $5,000 and Benjamin was given the honor of laying the cornerstone of the building that opened in 1928.

Sands Point

The name Guggenheim is perhaps most associated with the art museum on Fifth Avenue in New York City that bears the family name. Solomon Guggenheim, one of Meyer and Barbara Guggenheim's eleven children, created the foundation that established the museum. Meyer came to the United States in 1847 and created one of the wealthiest family legacies in the world through the mining and smelting industry. Solomon's brothers William, Isaac, and Daniel all owned estates used as summer residences in the ultra-exclusive area that served as the inspiration for East Egg, romanticized by F. Scott Fitzgerald in his novel *The Great Gatsby*.

William was the first of the Guggenheims to seek out property in Sands Point, the secluded Gold Coast community on the north tip of the

Figure 46. Castle Gould, the summer residence of Daniel and Florence Guggenheim. *Source:* Photo by Brad Kolodny.

Port Washington peninsula. He purchased 150 acres in 1900 and built an Italian-style villa called Waterside Farm. Isaac followed by building Villa Carola in 1916, which now functions as the Village Club of Sands Point. The following year Daniel purchased the estate of financier Howard Gould, including two mansions, Castle Gould, and Hempstead House. Today these mansions and other buildings are set on 216 acres that make up the Sands Point Preserve Conservancy.

Table 8.1. Residents of Great Neck

Albert	**Antor**		1884	1964	Jewelry store owner
Fannie	(Wolf) Antor	wife	1894		Daughter of Abram and Rose
Max	**Greenberg**		1881		Brother of Rose Jacoby
Julius	**Jacoby**		1873		
Rose	(Greenberg) Jacoby	wife	1881	1937	
Milton	Jacoby	son	1902		
Isaac	**Jaffe**		1889	1968	Son of Benjamin and Sarah from Roslyn
Lillian	(Moses) Jaffe	wife			
?	Jaffe	child			Born before 1918
Morris	**Lefkowitz**		1885		Son of Joseph and Ida from Port Washington
Jeanette	(Wolf) Lefkowitz	wife	1888		Daughter of Abram and Rose
Rosalind	Lefkowitz	daughter	1907		
Mortimer	Lefkowitz	son	1909		
Irene	Lefkowitz	daughter	1911		
Irving	Lefkowitz	son	1912		
Lawrence	Lefkowitz	son	1913		
Abram	**Wolf**		1861	1949	President Nassau Hebrew Assoc. 1909
Rose	(Scheich) Wolf	wife	1863	1922	
Lilly	Wolf	daughter	1883		
Isaac	Wolf	son	1886	1963	
William	Wolf	son	1886		
Jeanette	Wolf	daughter	1888		m. Morris Lefkowitz
Benjamin	Wolf	son	1890	1971	
Fannie	Wolf	daughter	1894		m. Albert Antor
Johanna	Wolf	daughter	1895	1895	
Louis	Wolf	son	1895		

Table 8.2. Residents of Manhasset

Michael	**Jaffe**		1889		Son of Benjamin and Sarah from Roslyn
Tillie	Jaffe	wife	1895		
Alfred	Jaffe	son	1915		
Herbert	Jaffe	son	1916		
Morris	**Manowitz**		1888	1930	Member Nassau Hebrew Assoc. 1913
Rose	(Hoffberg) Manowitz	wife	1889		

Table 8.2. Continued.

William	Manowitz	son	1912		
Samuel	Manowtiz	son	1914		
Edith	Manowitz	daughter	1917		
Morris	**Rosenstein**		1860		
Anna	(Goldman) Rosenstein	wife	1859		
Lily	**Woltenfelt**		1905		Niece of Morris Rosenstein

Table 8.3. Residents of Port Washington

Edward	**Belinson**		1882		Member Nassau Hebrew Assoc. 1913
Bessie	Belinson	wife	1884		
Louis	Belinson	son	1907		
May	Belinson	daughter	1911		
Max	**Israel**		1863	1928	Member Cong. Tifereth Israel in Glen Cove 1899
Rachel	(Jacobs) Israel	wife	1867	1938	Daughter of Victor and Mollie
Alexander	Israel	son	1889		
Ida	Israel	daughter	1891		
Louis	Israel	son	1897	1947	
Dora	Israel	daughter	1899	1988	
Nathan	Israel	son	1902		
Philip	Israel	son	1903		
Tessie	Israel	daughter	1905		
Samuel	Israel	son	1907		
Victor	**Jacobs**		1841	1919	
Mollie	(Tulin) Jacobs	wife	1845	1915	
Sarah	Jacobs	daughter			
Norman	Jacobs	son			
Rivki	Jacobs	daughter			
Barney	**Jacobs**		1870	1952	Member Nassau Hebrew Assoc. 1913, son of Victor and Mollie
Esther	Jacobs	wife	1876		
Philip	Jacobs	son	1900		
Hannah	Jacobs	daughter	1902		
Herman	Jacobs	son	1904		
Sadie	Jacobs	daughter	1906		

continued on next page

Table 8.3. Continued.

Raymond	Jacobs	son	1907		
Nathan	**Jacobs**		1872	1958	Member Cong. Tifereth Israel in Glen Cove 1899, son of Victor and Mollie
Annie	(Ellerstein) Jacobs	wife	1876	1917	
Lillian	Jacobs	daughter	1900		
Betram	Jacobs	son	1903		
Raymond	Jacobs	son	1904		
Samuel	Jacobs	son	1907		
Alexander	**Jaffe**		1875		Dry goods store owner
Rebecca	(Ryeck) Jaffe	wife	1881		
Israel	Jaffe	son	1904		
Sophie	Jaffe	daughter	1908		
Aaron	Jaffe	son	1912		
Joseph	**Lefkowitz**		1857	1942	Member Nassau Hebrew Assoc. 1913
Ida	(Rathowitz) Lefkowitz	wife	1857	1942	
Sarah	Lefkowitz	daughter	1879		
Morris	Lefkowitz	son	1883		m. Jeanette Wolf, lived in Great Neck
Fanny	Lefkowitz	daughter	1886		
Meyer	Lefkowitz	son	1891		
Elizabeth	Lefkowitz	daughter	1893		
Harry	Lefkowitz	son	1895		
George	Lefkowitz	son	1897		
Walter	**Levy**		1886	1916	Salesman
Julia	(Foise) Levy	wife	1892		
Evelyn	Levy	daughter	1918		
Max	**Raff**		1882	1912	Merchant
Minnie	Raff	wife	1885	1918	
Mildred	Raff	daughter	1908		
Morris	**Smith**		1877		Tailor
Hinde	Smith	wife	1882		
Louis	Smith	son	1900		

Table 8.4. Residents of Roslyn

Joseph	**Cooper**		1872		Member Nassau Hebrew Assoc. 1913

Table 8.4. Continued.

Fanny	Cooper	wife	1878		
Mary	**Isenburg**		1872		
Moses	Isenburg	son	1898		
Harry	**Jacobs**		1875	1957	Son of Victor and Mollie from Port Washington
Ida	(Gesas) Jacobs	wife	1876	1944	
Florence	Jacobs	daughter	1897	1986	
Joseph	Jacobs	son	1898	1969	
Bertha	Jacobs	daughter	1899	1953	
Benjamin	**Jaffe**		1858	1938	Dry goods merchant
Sarah	(Miller) Jaffe	wife	1852		
Samuel	Jaffe	son	1882	1948	
Isaac	Jaffe	son	1884		m. Lillian Moses lived in Great Neck
Michael	Jaffe	son	1889		m. Tillie lived in Manhasset
Ida	Jaffe	daughter	1892		
Elsie	Jaffe	daughter	1893		
Yetta	Jaffe	daughter	1896		
David	**Katz**		1877		Brother of Joseph from Mineola
Hyman	**Katz**		1881	1965	Jewelry store owner
Jennie	Katz	wife	1887	1974	
Rosie	Katz	daughter	1909		
Sarah	Katz	daughter	1911		
Isaac	**Kuby**		1878		Secretary Nassau Hebrew Assoc. 1913
Saul	**Kwart**		1882	1958	Variety store merchant
Jacob	**Rosenthal**		1870		Tea and coffee merchant
Fannie	(Cohen) Rosenthal	wife	1869		
Bertha	Rosenthal	daughter	1892		
Abraham	Rosenthal	son	1894		
Maurice	Rosenthal	son	1896		
Bessie	Rosenthal	daughter	1898		
Pearl	Rosenthal	daughter	1902		
Simon	**Steinberg**		1876		Driver of an ice cream car
Rosie	Steinberg	wife	1879		
Harold	Steinberg	son	1902		
Jessie	Steinberg	daughter	1906		
Clarence	Steinberg	son	1910		
Arthur	Steinberg	son	1915		

continued on next page

Table 8.4. Continued.

Nathan	**Zeifman**		1875	1960	Treasurer Nassau Hebrew Assoc. 1913
Anna	(Lefshitz) Zeifman	wife	1872		
Samuel	Zeifman	son	1897		

Table 8.5. Residents of Roslyn Harbor

Benjamin	**Stern**		1856	1933	Co-owner Stern's Dept. Store in NYC
Madeleine	(Schafer) Stern	wife	1873	1933	

Table 8.6. Residents of Roslyn Heights

Max	**Adelstein**		1883	1958	Stationery and newspaper store
Bessie	(Bassin) Adelstein	wife	1889		
Joshua	Adelstein	son	1911		
Benjamin	Adelstein	son	1915		
Rosalind	Adelstein	daughter	1918		

Table 8.7. Residents of Sands Point

Daniel	**Guggenheim**		1856	1930	Brother of Isaac and William
Florence	(Schloss) Guggenheim	wife	1863	1944	
Isaac	**Guggenheim**		1854	1922	Brother of Daniel and William
Carrie	(Sonneborn) Guggenheim	wife	1859	1933	
William	**Guggenheim**		1868	1941	Brother of Daniel and Isaac
Aimee	(Steinbergen) Guggenheim	wife	1875	1957	
William Jr	Guggenheim	son	1907	1947	

Part II
Suffolk County

Chapter 9

Bay Shore

*Including Central Islip, Deer Park,
East Islip, and Islip*

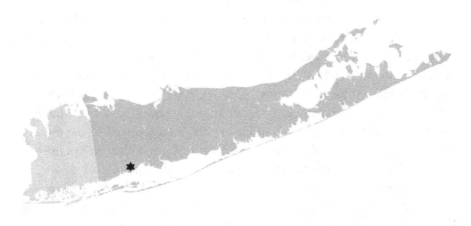

Michael Sachs, a thirty-year-old native of Russia, arrived on American
shores in 1880 and five years later was residing in Breslau (today Lindenhurst) when his wife Rachel gave birth to their second child. Michael was
earning a living as a junk dealer and moved the family to Bay Shore where
tragedy struck in 1893. Two of the Sachs's children, six-year-old Isaac and
their three-year-old daughter came down with smallpox, which forced the
family to live in quarantine and made it necessary for every school-age
child in Bay Shore to be vaccinated. Reporting from the day indicates the
illness did not spread to anyone else in the community but proved to be
fatal for the two infected Sachs children. Michael and Rachel's daughter

died on November 5 and was buried in nearby Oakwood Cemetery. Isaac succumbed to the disease on November 13.

In the fall of 1897 a movement was underway to formally organize the Jewish men of Bay Shore with the objective of establishing a cemetery. It is not difficult to imagine that the death of his children prompted Michael Sachs to be an active member of the group, offering his home as a location to hold meetings twice a month. Services for Yom Kippur that year were organized and took place on October 6 in the old schoolhouse led by two members, Cohen and Padlosky. By the end of the month, $75 had been raised, and twenty members joined from Bay Shore, Islip, and even as far away as Sayville and Kings Park. The necessary paperwork was filed with the Suffolk County clerk, and incorporation became official on December 10 for the Bay Shore United Hebrew Benevolent Cemetery Association.

It appeared the association had achieved its goal by purchasing property to dedicate a Jewish cemetery, but legal issues soon became apparent. Unbeknownst to the buyer and seller a local ordinance prohibited the use of any additional land in Bay Shore to be used for burials that was not already designated for said purpose. This rendered the transaction null and void, but the association was undeterred and pivoted to a new strategy. Since they could not use new land for burials, they approached the owners of the existing Oakwood Cemetery and worked out a deal to purchase a portion of that cemetery to be set aside for Jewish burials.

The greater Bay Shore Jewish community included men and women who lived in neighboring villages with their families including Morris and Rose Benstock from Central Islip and Akiva and Ida Goldstein from East Islip. Within the village of Islip several men made a living as merchants and peddlers while Jacob Morrison was a tailor and Max Schramm owned a barbershop. Schramm first lived in Babylon but moved to Islip in 1889. He was an active volunteer in associations both civic and religious becoming a trustee of the Islip Fire Department in 1890 and a director of Bay Shore United Hebrew Benevolent Cemetery Association when established in 1897. Max and his wife Tillie raised five children in Islip until moving to Westhampton Beach in 1912 where Max opened a stationery store.

Harry Freedman moved to Bay Shore as a sixteen-year-old young man in 1883 and established himself as a retail merchant. Around 1900 he opened his own department store that was located in a three-story building at the southeast corner of Main Street and Maple Avenue with the

Figure 47. The gravestone of Max and Tillie Schramm in Brooklyn. *Source:* Photo by Brad Kolodny.

top floor used as the residence for his family that included his wife Sadie and their daughters. Thanks to Harry's encouragement, his brother Morris moved into the village from Atlantic City, New Jersey, where he owned a bicycle shop. In 1914 Morris purchased a building on the north side of Main Street, located diagonally across from Harry's department store, and opened a hardware store that also sold bicycles. A year later Morris expanded his product line by selling Harley-Davidson motorcycles, Fisk automobile tires, and other parts and accessories.

Harry felt it was important to be a part of the local Jewish community by joining a synagogue, but in 1915 that meant becoming a member of the Lindenhurst Hebrew Congregation ten miles to the west. When a synagogue was in the works for Bay Shore toward the end of the decade, Harry showed his support by becoming a trustee.

In February 1917 a devastating fire destroyed Freedman's Department Store that took the life of Calista Cunnellan, a twenty-one-year-old saleswoman. Sadie and a daughter were rescued by a responding fireman who pulled them from an upper floor and took them down by ladder to

Figure 48. Morris Freedman and his wife Jennie in front of their store on Main Street in 1916. *Source*: Bay Shore Historical Society.

safety. Harry, who was away in Florida at the time, vowed to rebuild but suffered losses in excess of $80,000 with just $30,000 worth of insurance.

In addition to the villages of Bay Shore, Islip, and East Islip there were a large number of Jewish men and women, over a hundred at any given time, who lived in Central Islip but were confined to an institution known as Manhattan State Hospital (later renamed Central Islip State Hospital). The facility opened in 1889 to house the overflow of psychiatric patients from Manhattan that could not be accommodated within the borough. The rural area provided a setting where residents performed agricultural work as part of a prescription of rest and relaxation.

At the turn of the century Central Islip was not developed like other villages to the south. Shimon Leikach, an immigrant from eastern Europe who changed his name to Sam Clark, saw this as an opportunity to sell goods to employees at the State Hospital and residents along Carleton and Suffolk Avenues without much competition. He thought about opening a store given his experience as a peddler, having worked territory along

Figure 49. Department store owner Harry Freedman. *Source*: National Archives and Records Administration accessed from familysearch.org.

the north shore in Kings Park, Northport, Asharoken, and Eatons Neck. What Clark didn't have was enough capital for buying products to stock the shelves with, so he entered into a partnership with his friend Harry Bernstein, and they started out together in 1905. Business was good the first year, and over the long term Sam Clark was a successful merchant—but not without struggles. The partnership with Bernstein was dissolved after a few years over a dispute about opening the store during the High Holidays. In 1914 Clark fell on hard times and was not able to pay his bills, forcing the business into bankruptcy. All assets were put up for public auction and purchased by Sam's brother-in-law Jacob Glass who came to the rescue, enabling Sam to reestablish his store.

A formal congregation aimed at bringing the Jewish community together in Bay Shore for religious, educational, and social purposes was not established until 1919. That year a group of men had been meeting at the Knights of Columbus Hall on Second Avenue in a building that was constructed in 1895 as the town's firehouse. Benjamin Michnoff, a Torah

Figure 50. Inside Sam Clark's store in Central Islip. L to R: Sam's wife Bella, an unknown customer, Sam and Bella's son Isadore, and Sam. *Source*: Courtesy of Marcia Clark.

teacher who was a relatively new resident of Bay Shore having moved there from Brooklyn, led the group as their presiding officer. Benjamin and his wife Minnie had eight grown children with families of their own living on Long Island in Rockville Centre, Freeport, Babylon, and his daughter Pearl Schultz lived nearby in Bay Shore. On November 2, United Hebrew Congregation was incorporated, and the following year the old firehouse was purchased by the congregation for use as their synagogue. One of the trustees of United Hebrew Congregation was Benjimen Levy, the only individual to bridge the gap from being a director of the Bay Shore United Hebrew Benevolent Cemetery Association in 1897.

In the fifteen years following the creation of United Hebrew Congregation there were other organizations formed in Bay Shore filling the social and philanthropic needs of the Jewish residents. The Ladies Aid Society, the Junior League, and the Bay Shore Jewish Alliance all joined forces with the United Hebrew Congregation in September 1933 to form the Jewish Centre of Bay Shore, a conservative congregation that still exists today.

Table 9.1. Residents of Bay Shore

Marie	**Bromberg**		1835		Mother of Morris
Morris	**Bromberg**		1856		Merchant
Ida	Bromberg	wife	1866		
Harry	Bromberg	son	1899		
Philip	Bromberg	son	1910		
	Cohen				Co-leader of services Yom Kippur 1899
Henry	**Diamond**		1870	1927	Owned a bookstore
Ida	(Pollack) Diamond	wife	1868	1931	
Sarah	Diamond	daughter	1907	1936	
Samuel	Diamond	son	1909		
Jacob	**Finkelstein**		1875	1955	
Maude	(Epstein) Finkelstein	wife	1886	1917	Daughter of Isaac and Lena from Islip
Philip	Finkelstein	son	1908		
Harry	**Freedman**		1867	1932	Brother of Morris
Sadie	(Silberman) Freedman	wife	1883		
Lillian	Freedman	daughter	1907	1963	
Edith	Freedman	daughter	1911	1991	
Frances	Freedman	daughter	1918		
Morris	**Freedman**		1879		Brother of Harry
Jennie	Freedman	wife	1889		
Albert	Freedman	son	1909		
Yetta	Freedman	daughter	1912		
Leon	Freedman	son	1915		
Jacob	**Jublinsky**		1875		Tailor
Barne	Jublinsky	wife	1873		
Joseph	Jublinsky	son	1896		
Harry	Jublinsky	son	1902		
Ida	Jublinsky	daughter	1903		
Nate	Jublinsky	son	1905		
Esther	Jublinsky	daughter	1906		
Ezrah	Jublinsky	son	1907		
Harry	Jublinsky	son	1910		
Samuel	**Jublinsky**		1878		
Norma	Jublinsky	wife	1883		
Fannie	Jublinsky	daughter	1905		
?	**Kaplan**				

continued on next page

Table 9.1. Continued.

Bessie	(Rohlneck) Kaplan	wife	1887		Daughter of Louis and Jennie Rohlneck
Lillian	Kaplan	daughter	1913		
Louis	**Kapner**		1876	1973	Fruit and vegetable vendor
Lena	(Cohen) Kapner	wife	1878	1957	
Sarah	Kapner	daughter	1902		
Harry	Kapner	son	1904		
Rose	Kapner	daughter	1905		
Herman	Kapner	son	1907		
Elizabeth	Kapner	daughter	1909		
May	Kapner	daughter	1915		
Frances	Kapner	daughter	1916		
Benjimen	**Levy**		1852	1930	VP Hebrew Cemetery Assoc. 1898
Mary	(Stein) Levy	wife	1853	1934	Daughter of Rosie Stein
Louis	Levy	son	1878		
Henry	Levy	son	1881		
Joseph	Levy	son	1883	1950	m. Tessie Tennenberg, lived in Sayville
Matilda	Levy	daughter	1886		
Salvia	Lepetry	granddaughter	1908		daughter of Matilda
David	Levy	son	1892	1949	
Samuel	Levy	son	1894	1994	
Rose	Levy	daughter	1897		
Benjamin	**Michnoff**		1851		Bible teacher
Minnie	(Gilman) Michnoff	wife	1848		
Samuel	**Michnoff**		1881		Son of Benjamin and Minnie
Marion	(Wallach) Michnoff	wife	1886		
Ruth	Michnoff	daughter	1912		
Vivian	Michnoff	daughter	1915		
Mildred	Michnoff	daughter	1916		
Harry	**Miller**		1892		Dry goods peddler
Celia	Miller	wife	1892		
Minnie	Miller	daughter	1916		
Sadie	Miller	daughter	1917		
A	**Padlosky**				Trustee Hebrew Cemetery Assoc. 1897
Louis	**Posner**				Junk dealer
Eva	Posner	wife			

Table 9.1. Continued.

Bert	**Raskin**		1891	1954	Nephew of Jacob Finkelstein
Louis	**Rohlneck**		1862	1904	Trustee Hebrew Cemetery Assoc. 1897
Jennie	Rohlneck	wife	1866	1926	
Bessie	Rohlneck	daughter	1887		m. ? Kaplan
Isaac	Rohlneck	son	1896		
Harry	Rohlneck	son	1898		
Jacob	**Rosenthal**				Trustee Hebrew Cemetery Assoc. 1897
Michael	**Sachs**		1850	1917	Treasurer Hebrew Cemetery Assoc. 1898
Rachel	(Gold) Sachs	wife	1852	1921	
Maurice	Sachs	son	1882	1942	
Celia	Sachs	daughter	1885		
Isaac	Sachs	son	1887	1893	
?	Sachs	daughter	1890	1893	
Joseph	Sachs	son	1893		
Abraham	Sachs	son	1895		
Samuel	**Sacks**		1881	1960	Fruit dealer
Dora	Sacks	wife	1881	1946	
Charles	Sacks	son	1899		
Ethel	Sacks	daughter	1903		
Benjamin	Sacks	son	1906		
Mayer	**Schultz**		1872		Storekeeper
Pearl	(Michnoff) Schultz	wife	1878		Daughter of Benjamin and Minnie
Mathilde	Schultz	daughter	1910		
Marcella	Schultz	daughter	1912		
Sylvia	Schultz	daughter	1916		
Esther	Schultz	daughter	1918		
Leo	**Stockman**		1887		Tailor
Alice	Stockman	wife		1920	
Edmund	Stockman	son	1912	2003	
Cecilia	Stockman	daughter	1914		
Rosie	**Stein**		1820		Mother of Mary Levy
Moe	**Tobish**		1889	1943	Garbage remover
Sarah	Tobish	wife	1889	1936	
Abraham	Tobish	son	1907		
Arthur	Tobish	son	1908		

continued on next page

Table 9.1. Continued.

Robert	Tobish	son	1915		
Emanuel	**Underberger**				President Hebrew Cemetery Assoc. 1897
Arthur	**Watts**		1879	1954	Laborer in embroidery factory
Sophie	Watts	wife	1894	1957	
Samuel	Watts	son	1905		
Isador	Watts	son	1910		
Gladys	Watts	daughter	1914		

Table 9.2 Residents of Central Islip

Morris	**Benstock**		1874	1932	Dry goods merchant
Rose	Benstock	wife	1885		
David	Benstock	son	1906	1973	
George	Benstock	son	1911		
Sidney	Benstock	son	1913		
Harry	**Bernstein**		1880	1954	Dry goods merchant
Hannah	Bernstein	first wife	1881	1910	
Rose	Bernstein	daughter	1902		
Ida	Bernstein	daughter	1904		
Esther	Bernstein	daughter	1909		
Lena	(Dilbert) Bernstein	second wife	1883	1949	
Samuel	**Clark**		1881	1975	Last name originally was Leikach
Bella	(Okst) Clark	wife	1888	1969	Daughter of Jacob and Ida Okst from Kings Park
Isadore	Clark	son	1906	1951	
David	**Cohen**		1892	1936	Kitchen helper at State Hospital
Abraham	**Heller**		1874		Restaurant/hotel owner
Regina	Heller	wife	1882		
Herman	Heller	son	1913		

Table 9.3. Residents of Deer Park

Benjamin	**Katz**				
Annie	(Fenster) Katz	wife			
Harry	Katz	son	1885		m. Cecilia Kranzler, lived in Roosevelt

Table 9.4. Residents of East Islip

Charles	**Cohen**		1882		Brother of Jacob and Morris
Jacob	**Cohen**		1887		Brother of Charles and Morris
Morris	**Cohen**		1873		Brother of Charles and Jacob
Ida	Cohen	wife	1873		
Louis	Cohen	son	1897		
Ethel	Cohen	daughter	1899		
Annie	Cohen	daughter	1901		
Mary	Cohen	daughter	1903		
Jacob	**Follender**		1877	1921	Owned a doll factory
Ernestine	Follender	wife	1879	1954	
Otto	Follender	son	1904		
Norah	Follender	daughter	1913		
Akiva	**Goldstein**		1865	1950	Butcher
Ida	Goldstein	wife	1878	1953	
Harry	Goldstein	son	1898		
Bertha	Goldstein	daughter	1901		
Milton	Goldstein	son	1911	2001	
Ellsworth	Goldstein	son	1915		
Sidney	Goldstein	son	1915		

Table 9.5. Residents of Islip

Isaac	**Epstein**		1870	1942	Trustee Hebrew Cemetery Assoc. 1897
Lena	Epstein	wife	1867	1942	
Maude	Epstein	daughter	1886	1917	m. Jacob Finkelstein, lived in Bay Shore
Elsie	Epstein	daughter	1892	1966	m. Moses Serby
Ruth	Epstein	daughter	1896		
Ellsworth	Epstein	son	1897	1965	
Tessie	Epstein	daughter	1909		
Jacob	**Morrison**		1863	1939	Tailor
Mary	(Sininsky) Morrison	wife	1862	1951	
Frederick	Morrison	son	1899	1957	
Max	**Schramm**		1858	1935	Trustee Hebrew Cemetery Assoc. 1897
Tillie	(Thorman) Schramm	wife	1861	1924	

continued on next page

Table 9.5. Continued.

Nettie	Schramm	daughter	1881	1959	m. Joseph Schramm, lived in Fairground
Hattie	Schramm	daughter	1884	1941	
Belle	Schramm	daughter	1888	1977	
Jesse	Schramm	son	1893	1968	Fought in France during WWI
Frances	Schramm	daughter	1895	1948	
Isaac	**Segal**		1889		Metal dealer
Rebecca	Segal	wife	1892		
Morris	Segal	son	1915		
Rose	Segal	daughter	1918		
Moses	**Serby**		1888	1923	Stenographer at State Hospital
Elsie	(Epstein) Serby	wife	1892	1966	Daughter of Isaac and Lena
Abraham	**Skolnick**		1882	1971	Dry goods store owner
Ida	Skolnick	wife	1887	1958	
Rose	Skolnick	daughter	1908		
Anna	Skolnick	daughter	1913		
Louis	**Ulanowsky**		1886		Junk dealer
Celia	Ulanowsky	wife	1886		
Abraham	Ulanowsky	son	1910		
Etta	Ulanowsky	daughter	1913		
Jacob	Ulanowsky	son	1915		

Chapter 10

Greenport

Including Southold

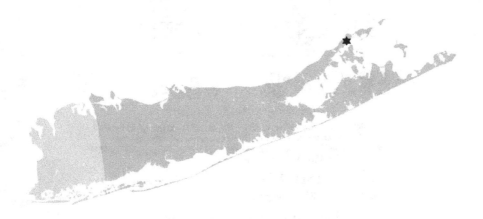

Situated on the north fork of eastern Long Island, the village of Greenport was a center for the whaling, shipbuilding, and fishing industries in the early 1800s. Adding further to the local economy was the arrival of the LIRR in 1844, but this was all before any Jews had arrived in town.

The first was Nathan Kaplan who opened a dry goods store on Front Street in 1862 but also had his hand in other business activities. Kaplan became one of the first to develop the oystering business in Peconic Bay and also bought and sold numerous plots of land as early as 1873. His wife, the former Sarah Bassarear, had a brother John who lived with the Kaplans in 1880 and worked for Nathan as a clerk in his store. By 1887

Kaplan decided to sell his business and found a buyer in his brother-in-law who entered into a partnership with Louis Jaeger. Before moving to Greenport Jaeger had been in retail for several years, working at well-known department stores in New York City including B. Altman and Co., Stern Brothers, and Bloomingdale Brothers.

Jaeger, a German immigrant, was thirty years old when he moved to Greenport in 1887 and was married the following year to Fannie Braunschweig from Switzerland. His partnership with John Bassarear lasted just five years when Louis decided to open his own store at 39 Main Street in 1892.

Another Kaplan to live in Greenport in the nineteenth century was Isaac but had no relation to Nathan. Isaac Kaplan and his wife Bryna were

GRAND OPENING.

JAEGER & BASSAREAR

(Successors to N. Kaplan.)

Having Purchased the Entire Stock of N. Kaplan, Consisting of Dry and Fancy Goods, Clothing, Carpets, Mattings and Oilcloths, Sewing Machines at one-half the cost price we are enabled to offer great inducements We have also added a Full and Complete line of

Fall and Winter Goods

at prices beyond competition, and you will find a full assortment of everything in our line.

SPECIAL ATTRACTIONS:

25 doz. English Derby Ribbed Children's Hose, all colors,	@ 25c
30 doz. Gents' Regular Made, Half Hose,	@ 10c
Extraordinary Bargains in all Linen Table Covers,	@ 50c
Linen Torshon Laces from 2c per yard up	
Linen Crash and Glass Toweling,	@ 4½c

Our Muslin sale the past few weeks was a grand success, we will repeat the same for 10 Days longer.

200 Pieces Continental O,	@ 6½c
100 Pieces Fruit of the Loom,	@ 8½c

We shall be pleased to have you call whether you purchase or not at the old stand,

Kaplan's Store,

Greenport, L. I

Figure 51. Advertisement announcing the transition of ownership from Nathan Kaplan to his brother-in-law John Bassarear and Louis Jaeger. *Source*: *Long Island Traveler*, November 18, 1887.

married in their native Russia and had five children before coming to the United States in 1889. Within a short time the family moved to Greenport where Isaac was a peddler and secondhand bottle dealer. Their oldest son, Zelig, was married to Hannah Weiner from Riverhead in 1891 and would go on to have four children who were all raised in Greenport. To support the family Zelig took on a variety of jobs including hauling coal for $1.50 a day, and for a time he raised cattle on Ram Island located in Gardiners Bay off the coast of Greenport, but for the majority of his life Zelig was a peddler like his father. This choice was made at the insistence of Hannah, who borrowed $25 to purchase a horse and wagon for her husband. While this was a large sum of money to a family with little means, the investment was just enough to buy a horse with a limp having only three good legs.

Isaac Kaplan was a religious man and a member of Congregation Tifereth Israel Anshei Greenport when the group was established in 1902, but the Jews of Greenport had been meeting for at least ten years prior. In

Figure 52. Zelig Kaplan with his family, c. 1906. *Source: And We're Still Here: 100 Years of Small Town Jewish Life* by Helene Gerard, courtesy of Lloyd Gerard.

1892 High Holiday services were held in the home of Lazar Kobre, and later more regular weekly gatherings were hosted by Morris and Fannie Levin before moving to Nathan Goldin's building in 1902. The first official meeting was held on October 5 that year when the name of the congregation was decided on, and plans for building a house of worship were initiated. Three weeks later fifteen voters cast their ballots and elected Joseph Brown, Samuel Blumenthal, and Samuel Levine as trustees of the congregation. In December 1903 a plot of land on Fourth Street was purchased for $300 with construction beginning immediately and opened just a month later with a dedication ceremony held on January 11, 1904. The synagogue is still in use today and is listed on the National Register of Historic Places.

Nathan Goldin was a partner with Maurice Beck, brother of his wife, Anna, from Patchogue. Goldin worked in the women's clothing business and owned stores in Greenport, Patchogue, and Sag Harbor. In 1910 Goldin bought out Beck's interest in the Greenport and Sag Harbor stores, which turned out to be an unwise business decision. Nathan was in debt to creditors and could not make his payments due to poor sales, which resulted in his declaring bankruptcy in 1911. Perhaps his decrease in business was the result of competition from another ladies' apparel shop in town called The Fashion, operated by Solomon Bush. Bush married Leah Rachlin in Russia; but shortly after the couple's first child was born, a daughter named Katie, Leah passed away. A not uncommon practice of the day when this situation presented itself was for the widowed husband to marry his deceased wife's sister. In about 1890 Solomon married Bessie Rachlin and went on to have seven of their own children together.

The synagogue in Greenport served its primary function as a place for members to gather and pray but also provided an opportunity for social interaction. In 1909 Anna Goldin organized a women's auxiliary consisting of fourteen members who raised funds for different charitable endeavors. The group was known as the Ladies Aid Society of Greenport and charged married women ten cents per meeting for dues, with unmarried women paying five cents. This financial commitment was in addition to the regular synagogue dues of $6 per year paid in monthly installments.

In December 1916 Tifereth Israel collected $14 in dues from twenty-one members and retained a total balance in the coffers of $29.91. One of the members contributing his fifty cents that month was Harry Katz, a tailor with a small shop on Front Street who was one of the newer members of

Figures 53 and 54. Solomon Bush and a Greenport street view with his store The Fashion visible on the left. *Source*: Courtesy of Ron Bush.

the congregation. Harry emigrated from Lodz, Poland, in 1904 settling down in New York City and was joined by his wife, Annie, and daughter Nettie a year later. The couple had another daughter, Rose, and a son named Max: both were born in New York before the Katz family moved to Greenport where their fourth child, Sam, was born in 1912. Katz was a full-service tailor making clothes and doing alterations on both men's and women's garments for customers in Greenport and neighboring communities. His dedication to the business was exemplified one winter day when a delivery needed to be made to a client on Shelter Island; however, Peconic Bay had frozen over, making the trip by boat impossible. Harry made the delivery on foot, walking across the ice from Greenport to Shelter Island and back. He later chose to focus more on women's fashions, opening Katz's Ladies Apparel Shop also on Front Street.

Figure 55. Harry Katz in front of his tailor shop on Front Street. *Source*: Courtesy of Gertrude Katz.

Table 10.1. Residents of Greenport

Benjamin	**Ballen**		1867	1935	Brother of Max
Rebecca	(Schless) Ballen	wife	1870		
Mollie	Ballen	daughter	1893		
Herman	Ballen	son	1895	1940	
Gussie	Ballen	daughter	1897		
Esther	Ballen	daughter	1898		
Fanny	Ballen	daughter	1902		
Maxwell	Ballen	son	1902		
Aaron	Ballen	son	1905		
Ruth	Ballen	daughter	1907		
Bessie	Ballen	daughter	1908		
Max	**Ballen**		1853		Brother of Benjamin
Philip	**Ballen**		1884		Nephew of Benjamin and Max
Samuel	**Blumenthal**		1867		Trustee of Tifereth Israel 1902
Rebecca	(Kaplan) Blumenthal	wife	1862		Second marriage, five children from her first marriage
Abraham	Kaplan	stepson	1887		
Mollie	Kaplan	stepdaughter	1890		
Barney	Kaplan	stepson	1893	1963	
Fanny	Kaplan	stepdaughter	1894		
Lizzie	Kaplan	stepdaughter	1897		
Aaron	**Brown**		1887		Son of Morris and Ethel
Bessie	(Cohn) Brown	wife	1884		
William	Brown	son	1909		
Morris	**Brown**		1862		Clothing merchant
Ethel	Brown	wife	1859		
Ida	Brown	daughter	1884		
Rachel	Brown	daughter	1889		
William	Brown	son	1891		
David	Brown	son	1896		
Abram	Brown	son	1897	1980	
Solomon	**Bush**		1864	1910	First wife Leah Rachlin died in Russia
Katie	Bush	daughter	1887	1960	m. Philip Gilman
Bessie	(Rachlin) Bush	second wife	1869	1938	Sister of Solomon's first wife Leah
Ida	Bush	daughter	1891		
Annie	Bush	daughter	1893		

continued on next page

Table 10.1. Continued.

Nathan	Bush	son	1895		
Ella	Bush	daughter	1897		
Samuel	Bush	son	1900		
Jacob	Bush	son	1903		
Jennie	Bush	daughter	1907		
Philip	**Gilman**		1882		
Katie	(Bush) Gilman	wife	1887	1960	Daughter of Solomon and Leah
Herman	Gilman	son	1912	2001	
Nathan	**Goldin**		1877	1932	Merchant
Anna	(Beck) Goldin	wife	1876	1943	Sister of Maurice and Benjamin from Patchogue
Ethel	Goldin	daughter	1896		
Ruby	Goldin	daughter	1898		
Leo	Goldin	son	1902		
Mervin	Goldin	son	1904		
Oscar	Goldin	son	1906		
Kenneth	Goldin	son	1907		
Arthur	Goldin	son	1909		
Harry	**Hirshfeld**		1877		Cousin of Herman Sandman
Louis	**Jaeger**		1857	1936	Dry goods store owner
Fannie	(Braunschweig) Jaeger	wife	1864		
Sidney	Jaeger	son	1890	1944	
William	Jaeger	son	1894		
Jeanette	Jaeger	daughter	1902		
Abraham	**Kaplan**		1871	1945	Son of Isaac and Bryna
Mollie	(Scheinberg) Kaplan	wife	1872	1944	
Maurice	Kaplan	son	1894		
Sarah	Kaplan	daughter	1898		
Minnie	Kaplan	daughter	1899		
Pauline	Kaplan	daughter	1902		
Philip	Kaplan	son	1904	1983	
Jacob	Kaplan	son	1906	1976	
Hyman	**Kaplan**		1884	1954	Son of Isaac and Bryna
Hannah	(Milsky) Kaplan	wife	1888	1979	
Louis	Kaplan	son	1909		
Maurice	Kaplan	son	1912		
Bernard	Kaplan	son	1917		

Table 10.1. Continued.

Isaac	**Kaplan**		1841		Peddler
Bryna	(Israel) Kaplan	wife	1841		
Zelig	Kaplan	son	1863	1940	m. Hannah Weiner
Ida	Kaplan	daughter	1868		
Abraham	Kaplan	son	1871	1945	m. Mollie Sheinberg
Fanny	Kaplan	daughter	1874		
Hyman	Kaplan	son	1884	1954	m. Hannah Milsky
Nathan	**Kaplan**		1845	1923	Married a non-Jewish woman
Zelig	**Kaplan**		1863	1940	Son of Isaac and Bryna
Hannah	(Weiner) Kaplan	wife	1873	1938	
Abraham	Kaplan	son	1894		
Samuel	Kaplan	son	1895		
Mollie	Kaplan	daughter	1897		
William	Kaplan	son	1905	1979	
Harry	**Katz**		1879	1946	Tailor
Annie	Katz	wife	1880	1942	
Nettie	Katz	daughter	1904	1953	
Rose	Katz	daughter	1906		
Max	Katz	son	1909	1998	
Samuel	Katz	son	1912	1987	
Lazar	**Kobre**		1873	1971	
Tillie	(Price) Kobre	wife	1874	1928	
Samuel	Kobre	son	1894	1967	
George	Kobre	son	1896	1969	
Bessie	Kobre	daughter	1897		
Benjamin	Kobre	son	1899	1993	
Helen	Kobre	daughter	1905		
Morris	**Levin**		1866		Owned a shoe store
Fannie	Levin	wife	1866		
Gussie	Levin	daughter	1888		
Jennie	Levin	daughter	1891		
Molly	Levin	daughter	1893		
Herman	Levin	son	1896		
Max	Levin	son	1901		
Aaron	Levin	son	1904		
Firna	**Levine**		1840	1913	Husband Abraham died in Russia
Julius	**Levine**		1878	1949	Son of Firna

continued on next page

Table 10.1. Continued.

Anna	(Willitskin) Levine	wife	1886		
Arthur	Levine	son	1907	2000	
Leo	Levine	son	1911		
Samuel	**Levine**		1881	1967	Son of Firna
Essie	Levine	wife	1891	1974	
Arthur	Levine	son	1910	1996	
Janet	Levine	daughter	1914	1998	
Lewis	**Levison**		1876		Peddler
Eva	(Puschkin) Levison	wife	1879	1973	Daughter of Joseph and Goldie
Isidor	Levison	son	1899		
Louis	**Levinson**		1880	1951	
Jennie	(Levine) Levinson	wife	1882	1969	Daughter of Firna Levine
Arthur	Levinson	son	1907		
Milton	Levinson	son	1908		
Harry	Levinson	son	1909		
Isaac	Levinson	son		1913	
Benjamin	**Lipman**		1883	1972	Son of Samuel and Miriam
Sarah	Lipman	wife	1894	1970	
Joseph	**Lipman**		1880	1947	Son of Samuel and Miriam
Fannie	(Schwartz) Lipman	wife	1891	1981	
Samuel	**Lipman**		1855	1938	
Miriam	(Kohn) Lipman	wife			
Ruby	Lipman	daughter	1880		m. Max Maizels, lived in in Bay Shore
Joseph	Lipman	son	1880	1947	m. Fannie
Benjamin	Lipman	son	1883	1972	m. Sarah
Mabel	Lipman	daughter	1891	1924	
Minnie	Lipman	daughter	1893		
Leopold	**Merzbach**		1850	1902	Owned a clothing and dry goods store
Joseph	**Puschkin**		1850	1917	First wife Goldie d. before 1900
Girly	Puschkin	second wife	1851		
Bernard	**Rosenthal**		1835		Owned a dry goods store
Ernestine	(Wittkowsky) Rosenthal	wife	1845		
Philip	Rosenthal	son	1863		
Julius	Rosenthal	son	1864	1931	
Florence	Rosenthal	daughter	1867	1929	

Table 10.1. Continued.

Viola	Rosenthal	daughter	1870		
Isaac	Rosenthal	son	1872		
Berdie	Rosenthal	daughter	1874		
Solomon	Rosenthal	son	1877		
Herman	**Sandman**		1859		
Nancy	(Haasz) Sandman	wife	1859		
Leo	Sandman	son	1882	1951	Married 3x, unlikely any were Jewish
Otto	Sandman	son	1887		
Edna	Sandman	daughter	1888		
Mervin	Sandman	son	1891	1990	
Israel	**Schlefstein**		1875		Tailor
Ella	(Tishler) Schlefstein	wife	1878	1932	
Esther	Schlefstein	daughter	1899		
Rose	Schlefstein	daughter	1904		
Morris	Schlefstein	son	1905	1982	
Daniel	Schlefstein	son	1909		
Minnie	Schlefstein	daugther	1913		
Leo	Schlefstein	son	1914		
Isaiah	Schlefstein	son	1915	1953	
Jacob	**Schless**				Member of Tifereth Israel 1902
William	**Smith**				
Sam	**Soloman**		1876		

Table 10.2. Residents of Southold

Arnold	**Sturmdorf**				
Regina	Sturmdorf	wife	1863	1951	

Chapter 11

Huntington

Including Fairground
(Now Huntington Station) and Halesite

In its early days Huntington consisted of the village centered at the inter-section of Main Street and New York Avenue, in close proximity to Hun-tington Harbor leading out to the Long Island Sound. Two miles south of the village the LIRR erected a station stop in 1867 that brought visitors from New York City and gave rise to the population of the area. Not far from the train station was a horseracing track and grounds where fairs were held that led to calling the vicinity Fairground. The name became official in 1890 with the opening of the post office. Today the area of Fairground is known as Huntington Station.

The first Jewish residents of Huntington arrived in the 1870s and all had businesses located on Main Street in the village. Among them were dry goods store owner Simon Hirschfeld and his wife Amalia, hotel and saloon keeper Bernard Friedman and his wife Johanna, and cabinet maker and upholsterer H. W. Stern and his wife Lena. While formalized Jewish gatherings had not yet been organized in the community, these merchants were dedicated to their religion and expressed a devotion of their faith by closing their stores on Rosh Hashanah.

Three generations of the Teich family were living in Fairground shortly after the turn of the century. Schloma and Bluma Teich were married in their homeland of Austria in 1863 and had five children who would all immigrate to the United States and make their way out to Long Island. Their oldest son William, a fruit merchant who became a dealer in cattle and operated

NEW STORE.

The Subscriber has opened and fitted up a NEW STORE on NEW ST., near MAIN, in the village of HUNTINGTON, where can be found a large and well assorted stock of

CLOTHING,

DRY GOODS,

GENT'S FURNISHING GOODS,

TRUNKS,

VALISES,

HOSIERY, FANCY GOODS,

&C., &C.,

☞ Call and examine.

SIMON HIRSCHFELD.

April 19th. 3m.

Figure 56. Advertisement for Simon Hirschfeld's store. *Source: The Long-Islander,* July 19, 1872.

Figures 57 and 58. Schloma and Bluma Teich, top. *Source*: Courtesy of the Teich family and the Huntington Historical Society; and their oldest son William with his wife Yetta. *Source*: Courtesy of Judy Leopold. The differences in style of dress and facial hair illustrate the contrast between older immigrants clinging to their traditions and the next generation who wanted to put life in the old country behind them to be American.

a dairy farm on Park Avenue, arrived in 1895 and was living in Fairground in 1904 when his wife Yetta gave birth to their second child, Ida. There was still no Jewish association in the area, but that would soon change with the formation of the Brotherhood of Jewish Men in Huntington in 1906. William, as one of the eight founding members, played a prominent role dedicating his time and resources to ensure their success. An early objective of the Brotherhood was to establish a cemetery, but they also conducted services regularly held at William and Yetta's home on Lowndes Avenue. When land for the cemetery became available on Old Country Road in Long Swamp (today South Huntington), the twenty-acre property could not be purchased by the Brotherhood. It was William who bought the land in February 1907 and deeded it to the Huntington Hebrew Congregation after they had been formally incorporated on March 6, 1907.

At the point of incorporation the congregation had ten directors who were split evenly living between the two central locations in the Huntington area. Max Abraham, Charles Bersohn, Louis Gottlieb, Max Klein, and Louis Weiss were from the village while Elle Aronson, Isaac Goldstein, Abraham Gross, Samuel Schwartz, and William Teich lived in Fairground. The Teich home was adequate for shabbat services, but larger facilities were needed for the High Holidays. Isaac Levenbron's clothing store on New York Ave-

Figure 59. Isaac Levenbron. *Source*: Courtesy of Lois Stern.

nue in Fairground was equipped with the latest technology—a telephone. But a phone had not yet been installed at the firehouse located next door. Whenever fire department assistance was needed local residents knew to call Levenbron, who would then ring the bell at the firehouse, sounding the alarm. For Levenbron's dedication to the community, the fire department was more than willing to make the space in their facility available to the Huntington Hebrew Congregation for Rosh Hashanah and Yom Kippur when they would draw larger-than-normal crowds from within Huntington as well as neighboring towns.

The next evolutionary step for the young Huntington Hebrew Congregation was to consider building a synagogue, an idea that was initiated by Samuel Schwartz in 1909. Schwartz, born in 1855, owned a grocery store on New York Avenue in Fairground and was an elder statesman of the congregation. In 1910 membership had grown to eighteen, and dues were $4 per year. Meetings were held in the home of I. Silverstein, one of a growing number who moved to Fairground rather than Huntington Village. It soon became apparent that when looking for a piece of land to build a synagogue, the location would be in Fairground. A search began in earnest in 1912, and by January 1913 the congregation purchased a plot on First Avenue (today Church Street) between New York Avenue and Hillside Avenue (today Academy Place) where a synagogue would soon be built.

Samuel Schwartz carried through on his vision for the synagogue by serving on the building committee along with Isaac Goldstein, Nathan Milrad, Abraham Gross, Max Kline, Charles Bersohn, and Samuel Lerner. Schwartz was also the master of ceremonies for the cornerstone-laying festivities that took place on Sunday afternoon July 20, 1913. The occasion was filled with all the pomp and circumstance appropriate for this moment of joy and accomplishment for the Jewish community of Huntington. The ceremony featured guest speakers including local dignitaries and a rabbi from Brooklyn, followed by the sale of stones to be used in the building as a fundraiser that brought in $1,500. The synagogue would be completed two months later in time for Rosh Hashanah at a cost of $7,500. At the time there were fifty members.

The design of the synagogue was a simple rectangular structure with the narrow end facing the street. An exterior staircase of six steps led up to the double door entrance flanked by a narrow vertical arched window on either side. Above the entrance near the peak of the roof was a large Star

Figure 60. Interior of the Huntington Hebrew Congregation synagogue that opened in 1913. The balcony is visible in the upper right and left corners of the photo. *Source*: Huntington Jewish Center.

of David, the unmistakable symbol identifying the edifice as a Jewish house of worship. The sanctuary made up the main level of the building and a basement level housed meeting space and classrooms for the children. In the Orthodox tradition, seating for women was relegated to a three-sided balcony overlooking the sanctuary.

Jewish communal life in Huntington extended beyond the synagogue with philanthropic organizations and causes being of paramount importance. In 1913 the Hebrew Ladies Aid Society was organized with twenty members, and in 1916 an effort was undertaken to raise funds to assist Jews in Europe during the war. Samuel Hirsch was the treasurer of the local Jewish Relief Committee and reported that over $300 had been raised in the first two weeks

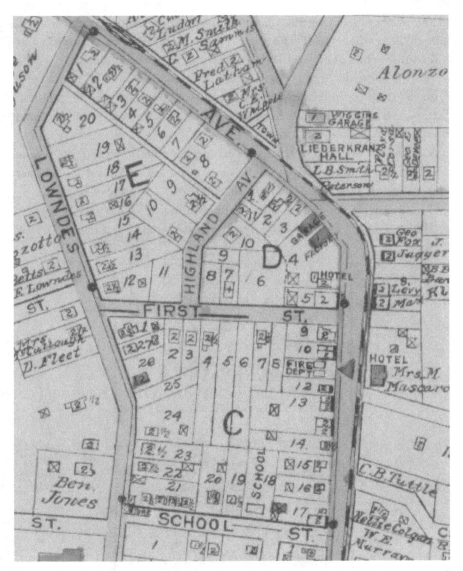

Figure 61. A 1915 map illustrates the most heavily populated Jewish area of Fairground. Bordered by School Street, Lowndes Avenue, and New York Avenue, one-quarter (fifteen of fifty-eight parcels) of the properties were Jewish owned. The synagogue was located on the map at D7 where the building still stands today but has been subdivided into residential housing. *Source*: 1915 *Atlas of a Part of Suffolk County, Long Island, New York* (Brooklyn: E. B. Hyde and Company).

of the pledge drive. Donations came in from over two-dozen men, women, and children who were affiliated with Huntington Hebrew Congregation as did contributions from several non-Jewish residents of Huntington.

One of the donors who contributed $5 to the cause was Sol Elkins, who ran a sporting goods business. His store was initially located in Huntington Station and sold everything from bicycles, thermoses, skates, and sleds to hunting gear, boasting "the biggest stock of shot guns, rifles, ammunition ever carried in town." In 1914 Elkins moved his store to New York Avenue and Elm Street in the village near the post office and expanded his product line to include motorcycles, automobile tires, parts, and repair services.

The Jewish community of Huntington was growing rapidly in the 1920s, and larger facilities for the congregation were in demand. A new

Figure 62. Advertisement for Sol Elkins who sold motorcycles out of his sporting goods store. *Source*: *The Long-Islander*, March 5, 1915.

synagogue was built just a few blocks away from the first at Woodhull and Nassau Roads in 1933, and twenty years later a third home was in the planning stage. A five-and-a-half-acre site was purchased in 1955 to build a synagogue accommodating the membership that had grown to nearly four hundred families. The land was located on Park Avenue and was the property of the former dairy farm run by the aforementioned William Teich, a founder of the Brotherhood of Jewish Men in Huntington fifty years prior.

⋘⚬⋙

One Family, Seven Generations in Huntington

There are a variety of reasons why someone would choose to move to a certain community and equally as many reasons why someone would decide to leave. It is not uncommon to find young married couples putting down roots in the same town as their parents and perhaps their grandparents—beyond that, however, this practice becomes increasingly rare. The Teich (pronounced *teach*) family has stood the test of time in Huntington for over 120 years.

Schloma and Bluma Teich, both born in 1847, left their hometown of Podhoridishch, Austria, and came to the United States in 1898. It is not known exactly when they moved to Huntington, but they had definitely settled there by 1910. Perhaps their arrival in the United States was planned in order to attend their daughter Selia's wedding when she married Abraham Gross, also in 1898. Selia had come to America three years before, and the newlyweds were living in Huntington by 1900.

William Teich, the second of Schloma and Bluma's children, immigrated to the United States in 1895. He and his wife Yetta lived in Greenlawn when their daughter Fanny was born in 1903. They moved to Fairground in 1904 and went on to have three more daughters: Ida, Esther, and Belma. Belma, the youngest, born in 1916, is named after her grandmother Bluma, who died in 1913. The family lineage in Huntington continues as follows:

Fanny Teich, a bookkeeper at her father's dairy farm, married Benjamin Mankin and had two children, Leah and David.
Leah Mankin married Norman Greenstein who changed his last name to Greene. They had two children, William and Judy.

Judy Greene married Michael Leopold and had two sons, Saul and Daniel. Judy is currently married to Alan Orloff.

Saul Leopold married Jacqueline Rose. Their three children, Joseph, Luke, and Violet have attended services at Huntington Jewish Center for many years on Rosh Hashanah and Yom Kippur.

Max Teich, another child of Schloma and Bluma, also leaves a legacy that lives on in Huntington Station today and will continue for years to come.

Figures 63 and 64. Judy Leopold admiring historical documents and artifacts at the Huntington Jewish Center Museum organized by her mother Leah in 1989. One of the items on display is a wood groger that was hand carved by Judy's great-grandfather William Teich in 1915. *Source*: Photos by Brad Kolodny.

In 1921 Max and his wife Rosie purchased a home situated on more than an acre of land for their dairy farm on Hillside Avenue (today Academy Place). Continuously occupied by the family until 2012, the house was sold to the Town of Huntington by Max and Rosie's grandchildren. In 2018 it was designated a historic landmark and the Max and Rosie Teich Homestead is now a museum for Huntington Station.

Table 11.1. Residents of Huntington

Max	**Abrahm**		1866		Member Huntington Hebrew Cong. 1907
Selma	Abrahm	wife	1878		
Bertha	Abrahm	daughter	1899		
Jerome	Abrahm	son	1901		
Ruth	Abrahm	daughter	1902		
Hazel	Abrahm	daughter	1910		
Jacob	**Ahrens**		1857		Brother of Johanna Friedman
Charles	**Bersohn**		1869	1949	Member Huntington Hebrew Cong. 1907
Esther	Bersohn	wife	1879	1952	
Harry	Bersohn	son	1902	1985	
Sarah	Bersohn	daughter	1905	2000	
Joseph	**Fiegerman**		1894		Tailor
Sarah	(Cooper) Fiegerman	wife	1895		
Augusta	Fiegerman	daughter	1918		
Joseph	**Fleischman**		1870		Member Huntington Hebrew Cong. 1913
Bernard	**Friedman**		1835	1895	Hotel and saloon owner
Johanna	(Ahrens) Friedman	wife	1854	1903	Sister of Jacob Ahrens and Rosetta Ollendorf
Herman	**Friedman**		1866	1918	Shoe store owner
Carrie	(Schwarz) Friedman	wife	1870		
Martin	Friedman	son	1886		
Lillian	Friedman	daughter	1896		
Minnie	Friedman	daughter	1900		
Leo	**Friedman**		1892		Son of Herman and Carrie
?	Friedman	wife			
?	Friedman	child			
Benjamin	**Goldstein**		1882	1943	Son of Harris and Annie
Minnie	(Ashman) Goldstein	wife	1890		
Mortimer	Goldstein	son	1913		
Annette	Goldstein	daughter	1917		
Harris	**Goldstein**		1844	1926	Brotherhood of Jewish Men 1906
Annie	(Bloomburg) Goldstein	wife	1854	1906	

Table 11.1. Continued.

Adele	Goldstein	daughter	1872		m. Lewis Gottlieb
Henriette	Goldstein	daughter	1875	1906	m. Joseph Bernstein, lived in Glen Cove
Benjamin	Goldstein	son	1882	1943	m. Minnie Ashman
Jesse	Goldstein	son	1890		
Lillian	Goldstein	daughter	1894		m. Irving Whitestone
Isaac	**Goldstein**		1867	1934	Brotherhood of Jewish Men 1906
Dora	Goldstein	wife	1871	1951	
Sadie	Goldstein	daughter	1894		
Max	Goldstein	son	1896		
Pearl	Goldstein	daughter	1898		
Louis	Goldstein	son	1902		
Ida	Goldstein	daughter	1904		
Gussie	Goldstein	daughter	1907		
Morris	Goldstein	son	1909		
Lewis	**Gottlieb**		1864	1937	Member Huntington Hebrew Cong. 1907
Adele	(Goldstein) Gottlieb	wife	1872	1924	Daughter of Harris and Annie
Florence	Gottlieb	daughter	1896		
Bertram	Gottlieb	son	1898		
Emanuel	Gottlieb	son	1902		
Dorothy	Gottlieb	daughter	1905		
Annette	Gottlieb	daughter	1912		
Jacob	**Hirschfeld**		1886	1965	Son of Simon and Amalia
Elsie	(Popper) Hirschfeld	wife	1889		
Dorothy	Hirschfeld	daughter	1910	2001	
Shirley	Hirschfeld	daughter	1917		
Michael	**Hirschfeld**		1846	1908	Brother of Simon
Simon	**Hirschfeld**		1842	1908	Clothing and dry goods store owner
Amalia	(Cohen) Hirschfeld	wife	1849	1925	
David	Hirschfeld	son	1873	1891	
Bessie	Hirschfeld	daughter	1875		m. Samuel Nemlich
Hattie	Hirschfeld	daughter	1878		m. Joseph Levy
Joel	Hirschfeld	son	1880		Liquor store owner
Jacob	Hirschfeld	son	1886	1965	m. Elsie Popper
Helen	Hirschfeld	daughter	1891		

continued on next page

Table 11.1. Continued.

Max	**Kline**		1881	1958	Brotherhood of Jewish Men 1906
Rose	(Atlas) Kline	wife	1885	1955	
Jacob	Kline	son	1901	1963	
Bertha	Kline	daughter	1904		
Esther	Kline	daughter	1908	1989	
Samuel	Kline	son	1910		
Sara	Kline	daughter	1911	1999	
Paul	Kline	son	1918	1982	
Solly	**Lefkowitz**		1869		A saloon keeper
Minnie	(Henschel) Lefkowitz	wife	1874		
Vincent	Lefkowitz	son	1901		
Albert	Lefkowitz	son	1906	1907	
Samuel	**Lerner**				Financial secretary Huntington HC 1914
?	Lerner	wife			
?	Lerner	daughter	1916		
Joseph	**Levy**		1830		Farmer
Fannie	(Schwartz) Levy	wife	1833		
Abram	Levy	son	1854		
Isadore	Levy	son	1856		
Solomon	Levy	son	1857		
Barbara	Levy	daughter	1858		
Jacob	Levy	son	1862		
Delia	Levy	daughter	1864		
Sophia	Levy	daughter	1866		
Joseph	**Levy**		1877		Son of William and Jennie
Hattie	(Hirschfeld) Levy	wife	1878		Daughter of Simon and Amalia
Samuel	**Levy**				Lived in Huntington in 1758
William	**Levy**		1850		Brick manufacturer in West Neck
Jennie	(Kahn) Levy	wife	1849		
Joseph	Levy	son	1877		m. Hattie Hirschfeld
Judah	**Mears**				Owned a house in Huntington 1734
Jochabed	(Michaels) Mears	wife			
Echiel	**Millman**		1875		Farmer
Ella	Millman	wife	1880		

Table 11.1. Continued.

Rebecca	Millman	daughter	1904		
Rose	Millman	daughter	1906		
Nathan	**Milrad**		1883		Real estate broker
Samuel	**Nemlich**		1880		Wholesale cigar dealer
Bessie	(Hirschfeld) Nemlich	wife	1875		Daughter of Simon and Amalia
Bernard	Nemlich	son	1907		
Seaman	Nemlich	son	1915		
Rosetta	**(Ahrens) Ollendorf**		1859		Sister of Johanna Friedman
Isidor	**Raymon**		1887	1974	Brother of Samuel
Bella	(Tamor) Raymon	wife	1887	1974	
Sylvia	Raymon	daughter	1915		
Vivian	Raymon	daughter	1917		
Samuel	**Raymon**		1882	1967	Brother of Isidor
Etta	Raymon	wife	1891	1966	
Sidney	Raymon	son	1913	1994	
Harold	Raymon	son	1918		
Isaac	**Shapiro**		1876	1943	Brother of Benjamin from Hempstead
Daniel	**Shear**		1877	1939	Secretary Huntington HC 1913
Yetta	(Klar) Shear	wife	1883	1950	
Irving	Shear	son	1903	1972	
Minnie	Shear	daughter	1905		
Frances	Shear	daughter	1909		
Morris	Shear	son	1912		
Hannah	Shear	daughter	1918		
Mayer	**Siegel**		1869	1944	
Rachel	(Marcus) Siegel	wife	1873	1949	
Hyman	Siegel	son	1907	1965	
Celia	Siegel	daughter	1912	1994	
H. W.	**Stern**		1866		In the furniture business, cabinet maker
Lena	Stern	wife	1871	1902	
Flora	Stern	daughter	1891		
Michael	Stern	son	1892		
Moses	Stern	son	1893		
Solomon	Stern	son	1897		
Milton	Stern	son	1899		

continued on next page

Table 11.1. Continued.

Isadore	**Weiss**		1887	1953	Tailor
Dora	Weiss	wife	1892	1973	
Harry	Weiss	son	1914		
Jacob	Weiss	son	1917		
Joseph	**Weiss**		1881	1976	Tailor
Molly	(Drescher) Weiss	wife	1885	1973	
Jean	Weiss	daughter	1908	2008	
Dorothy	Weiss	daughter	1910	1996	
Martin	Weiss	son	1915	2004	
Louis	**Weiss**		1874		Brother of Harry from Hicksville
Celia	(Weiss) Weiss	wife	1877		Maiden name was Weiss
Thelma	Weiss	daughter	1899		
Arthur	Weiss	son	1903		
Irving	**Whitestone**		1891		Manager of Palace Theatre
Lillian	(Goldstein) Whitestone	wife	1894		Daughter of Harris and Annie
Bertram	Whitestone	son	1918		

Table 11.2. Residents of Fairground (Now Huntington Station)

Elija	**Aaronson**		1881		Fruit peddler
Fanny	Aaronson	wife	1883		
Harry	Aaronson	son	1905		
Nathan	Aaronson	son	1907		
Morris	Aaronson	son	1909		
Bernat	**Adelman**		1888	1964	Automobile driver
Sylvia	Adelman	wife	1891	1960	
Sarah	Adelman	daughter	1914		
Dorothy	Adelman	daughter	1915		
Bessie	Adelman	daughter	1918		
Louis	**Adelman**		1888	1965	Auto supply store owner
Rose	(Levenbron) Adelman	wife	1892	1971	Daughter of Isaac and his first wife
Arthur	Adelman	son	1914	1976	
Mildred	Adelman	daughter	1916	1966	
Howard	Adelman	son	1917	1952	
Elle	**Aronson**		1882	1945	Member Huntington Hebrew Cong. 1907
Fannie	(Press) Aronson	wife	1880	1928	
Harry	Aronson	son	1905		

Table 11.2. Continued.

Nathan	Aronson	son	1908		
Morris	Aronson	son	1909	1915	
Samuel	Aronson	son	1912	1962	
Bernard	Aronson	son	1918		
Joseph	**Aronson**		1878	1967	Owned Aronson's Furniture
Rebecca	(Elkins) Aronson	wife	1878	1939	Daughter of Pauline
Sadie	Aronson	daughter	1902		
Anne	Aronson	daughter	1905		
Ida	Aronson	daughter	1908		
Betty	Aronson	daughter	1910		
Jack	Aronson	son	1913		
Bernard	Aronson	son	1915		
Jacob	**Axelrod**		1876		Brother of Esther Halbreich
Charles	**Brenner**		1884	1936	Trustee Huntington Hebrew Cong. 1914
Sarah	Brenner	wife	1889	1973	
Harry	Brenner	son	1908		
Abraham	Brenner	son	1909	1924	
Herman	Brenner	son	1915		
Charles Jr.	Brenner	son	1915		
Morris	**Cohen**		1873		Fruit peddler
Ida	Cohen	wife	1873		
Louis	Cohen	son	1897		
Ethel	Cohen	daughter	1899		
Annie	Cohen	daughter	1901		
Mary	Cohen	daughter	1903		
Abraham	**Cohn**		1872		Bread merchant
Fanny	Cohn	wife	1882		
Sadie	Cohn	daughter	1904		
Isador	Cohn	son	1905		
Lewis	Cohn	son	1906		
Harry	Cohn	son	1909		
Bella	Cohn	daughter	1910		
William	Cohn	son	1913		
Ada	Cohn	daughter	1915		
Kate	Cohn	daughter	1917		
Robert	**Dans**		1887		Carpenter
Sarah	(Schaffer) Dans	wife	1886	1968	
Joseph	Dans	son	1910		
Harold	Dans	son	1914	1949	

continued on next page

Table 11.2. Continued.

Wolf	**Elkin**		1875		Glazier
Esther	(Ritman) Elkin	wife	1878		
Jacob	Elkin	son	1896		
Philip	Elkin	son	1899		
Israel	Elkin	son	1901		
Joseph	Elkin	son	1904		
Aaron	Elkin	son	1905		
Fannie	Elkin	daughter	1906		
Benjamin	Elkin	son	1909		
Ida	Elkin	daughter	1911		
Edna	Elkin	daughter	1914		
Pauline	**Elkins**		1845		Mother of Rebecca Aronson
Sol	**Elkins**		1888		Sporting goods store owner
Rosie	(Stearn) Elkins	wife	1894		
Bessie	Elkins	daughter	1912		
Nathan	Elkins	son	1914		
Charles	**Gold**		1882	1964	Sewing machine store owner
Fanny	(Lefkowitz) Gold	wife	1887		
Loretta	Gold	daughter	1903		Born in Glen Cove
Edward	Gold	son	1905		
Dorothy	Gold	daughter	1907		Born in Hempstead
Marion	Gold	daughter	1911		
Samuel	**Goldblum**		1871	1943	Owned a bakery
Rose	(Schreck) Goldblum	wife	1895	1947	
Morris	Goldblum	son	1918		
Julius	**Gordon**		1876		
Yettie	Gordon	wife	1879		
Minnie	Gordon	daughter	1904		
Eva	Gordon	daughter	1905		
Max	**Greenwald**		1881		Dentist
Sadie	Greenwald	wife	1885		
Ruth	Greenwald	daughter	1907		
Morton	Greenwald	son	1909		
Abraham	**Gross**		1868		Brotherhood of Jewish Men 1906
Selia	(Teich) Gross	wife	1872		Daughter of Schloma and Bluma
Morris	**Grossman**		1886	1914	Furrier

Table 11.2. Continued.

?	Grossman	wife			
Rose	Grossman	daughter	1908		
Jacob	Grossman	son	1912		
Ber	**Halbreich**		1883	1952	
Esther	(Axelrod) Halbreich	wife	1885	1960	Sister of Jacob Axelrod
Blanche	**Hall**		1902		Niece of Max Greenwald
Samuel	**Hirsch**		1891		Treasurer Jewish War Fund 1916
David	**Hollander**		1885		Dry goods merchant
Kate	(Ehrlich) Hollander	wife	1888		
Dorie	Hollander	daughter	1912		
Julius	Hollander	son	1915		
Philip	Hollander	son	1917		
Lillian	Hollander	daughter	1918		
Judah	**Hollander**		1844		Father of David and Lena who married Jacob Patiky
Bernard	**Kaplan**		1881	1943	
Frances	(Schwartz) Kaplan	wife	1883	1971	Daughter of Samuel and Rose
Milton	Kaplan	son	1912		
Samuel	**Klaristenfeld**		1882	1928	
Dora	(Teich) Klaristenfeld	wife	1888	1947	Daughter of Schloma and Bluma
Nathan	Klaristenfeld	son	1911		
Belma	Klaristenfeld	daughter	1916		
Isadore	**Klein**				Son of Samuel and Sophia
Becky	Klein	wife			
Bennert	Klein	son	1907		
Samuel	**Klein**		1856		Harness maker
Sophia	Klein	wife	1862		
Isadore	Klein	son			m. Becky
Josephine	Klein	daughter	1891	1944	m. Joseph Wolf
Helen	Klein	daughter	1899		
William	Klein	son	1900		
Isaac	**Levenbron**		1872	1940	Brotherhood of Jewish Men 1906
?	Levenbron	first wife			
Rose	Levenbron	daughter	1892	1971	m. Louis Adelman
Jacob	Levenbron	son	1894	1941	
Bertha	Levenbron	daughter	1899	1995	

continued on next page

Table 11.2. Continued.

Sylvia	Levenbron	daughter			
Rebecca	Levenbron	second wife	1887	1943	Married Isaac in 1908
Blanche	Levenbron	daughter	1909	2001	
Maurice	Levenbron	son	1914	2018	
Benjamin	**Levine**		1884		Rabbi
Annie	Levine	wife	1884		
Ruben	Levine	son	1908		
Israel	Levine	son	1910		
Rose	Levine	daughter	1912		
Philip	Levine	son	1914		
Harry	Levine	son	1916		
Morris	**Levine**		1891		VP Huntington Hebrew Cong. 1914
Ray	Levine	wife	1892		
Benjamin	Levine	son	1914		
Samuel	**Levy**		1883	1965	Butcher
Celia	Levy	first wife	1889	1917	
Samuel	Levy	son	1911		
Sylvia	Levy	daughter	1914		
Bertha	Levy	daughter	1916		
Sophie	Levy	second wife	1893	1970	
Max	**Littman**		1867		Dry goods peddler
Beckie	Littman	wife	1876		
Eva	Littman	daughter	1896		
Fanny	Littman	daughter	1901		
Annie	Littman	daughter	1904		
Charles	Littman	son	1908		
Samuel	**Mittelman**		1877		Pres. Huntington Hebrew Cong. 1918
Ida	(Cohen) Mittelman	wife	1879		
Isadore	Mittelman	son	1898		
Etta	Mittelman	daughter	1906		
Milton	Mittelman	son	1914		
Richard	Mittelman	son	1916		
Benjamin	**Raskin**		1880		Merchant
Rosa	Raskin	wife	1882		
Ida	Raskin	daughter	1902		
Bessie	Raskin	daughter	1906		
Abraham	**Resnicoff**		1893		Tailor
Sadie	Resnicoff	wife	1896		

Table 11.2. Continued.

?	Rooschwarg				Rabbi
Philip	Rosen		1882		Grocery store owner
Molly	Rosen	wife	1882		
Sarah	Rosen	daughter	1907		
Jennie	Rosen	daughter	1911		
Joseph	Schramm		1872	1921	A bayman in oystering
Nettie	(Schramm) Schramm	wife	1873	1959	Daughter of Max and Tillie from Islip
Grace	Schramm	daughter	1895		
Allen	Schramm	son	1900		
John	Schwartz		1890		Son of Samuel and Rose
Anna	(Okst) Schwartz	wife	1900		Daughter of Jacob and Ida from Kings Park
Samuel	Schwartz		1855	1926	Brotherhood of Jewish Men 1906
Rose	Schwartz	wife	1859	1942	
Frances	Schwartz	daughter	1883	1971	m. Bernard Kaplan
John	Schwartz	son	1890		m. Anna Okst
Esther	Schwartz	daughter	1891		
William	Schwartz	son	1900	1983	
David	Schwartz	son	1902	1968	
I.	Silverstein				Hosted meetings of HHC 1910
Morris	Somer		1875		Cooper in a pickle factory
Lena	Somer	wife	1881		
Isadore	Somer	son	1914		
David	Somer	son	1918		
William	Sragow		1883		Furniture store owner
Rose	(Halbreich) Sragow	wife	1878	1945	
Milton	Sragow	son	1909		
Bernard	Sragow	son	1911		
Max	Teich		1879	1934	Son of Schloma and Bluma
Rose	(Schreiber) Teich	wife	1883	1961	
Samuel	Teich	son	1907	1995	
Fannie	Teich	daughter	1910		Born in Mineola
Annie	Teich	daughter	1911	1917	
Schloma	Teich		1847		
Bluma	(Milrad) Teich	wife	1845	1913	
Selia	Teich	daughter	1872		m. Abe Gross

continued on next page

Table 11.2. Continued.

William	Teich	son	1877	1947	m. Yetta
Max	Teich	son	1879	1934	m. Rose Schreiber
Dora	Teich	daughter	1888	1947	m. Samuel Klaristenfeld
Joseph	Teich	son	1889	1970	
William	**Teich**		1877	1947	Son of Schloma and Bluma
Yetta	Teich	wife	1880	1947	
Fannie	Teich	daughter	1903	1993	
Ida	Teich	daughter	1904		
Esther	Teich	daughter	1911		
Belma	Teich	daughter	1915	2000	
William	**Thaler**				VP Huntington Hebrew Cong. 1913
?	Thaler	wife			
Tillie	Thaler	daughter			
Joseph	**Wolf**		1875		
Josephine	(Klein) Wolf	wife	1891	1944	Daughter of Samuel and Sophia
?	Wolf	daughter	1908		

Table 11.3. Resident of Halesite

Isaac	**Solomonoff**		1894	1918	Worked for August Heckscher

Chapter 12

Kings Park

Including Commack, East Northport, Elwood,
Northport, and Smithtown

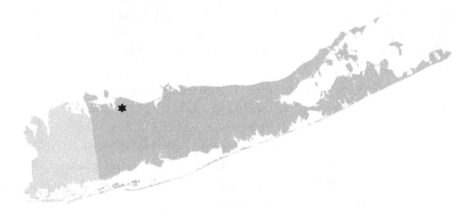

Every Jewish community on Long Island has its roots in a handful of people who lived in close proximity to each other and came together with the intent of religious observance. Such is the case with Kings Park where the origins of Jewish communal gathering and the growth of Judaism in this area can be largely attributed to the Patiky family.

The Abraham and Sarah of the Kings Park Jewish community were Gershon and Rachel Patiky, immigrants from Russia who came to America in 1887 and lived in New York City. The impetus for moving out to Long Island came as the result of an illness in the family that prompted Gershon to become a farmer in Elwood beginning in 1889. He was a husky man with red cheeks and a gray beard; he always greeted people with a warm and hearty handshake. His wife Rachel, a small but not frail woman, opened her home not just for family and friends but those traveling through town, peddlers, and others in need of a place to rest and a kosher meal. It is not surprising that Gershon and Rachel would welcome the community to their home as the location for High Holiday gatherings. Jews who came from Kings Park, Huntington, Northport, East Northport, Greenlawn, and Central Islip, some walking seven miles each way, would be treated to a kiddush following services prepared by Rachel that included kreplach, cakes, and other delicacies. Gershon would pour the liquor, mixing a combination of schnapps, honey, and pepper.

Acquiring kosher provisions in a rural and remote area on Long Island was no easy task in the late 1800s. Trips would need to be taken into New York City where kosher butchers were plentiful but required an arduous journey from Long Island. A member of the Patiky family would ride on horseback from the farm in Elwood to Huntington Harbor and board a boat to Long Island City. From there travel continued by ferry into Manhattan where the kosher food would be purchased, and the route would be repeated in reverse to get back home. This necessary pattern continued until about 1908 when Gershon and Leah's son Jacob bought a farm in Elwood entering into business with his niece Rose's husband Charlie Johnson. The two became dealers of horses and cattle with a butchering operation under the supervision of a shochet (ritual slaughterer of cattle and poultry), Mr. Rutfarg, enabling them to sell kosher meat locally with demand coming from Kings Park, Lindenhurst, and Huntington.

When Gershon and Rachel arrived in the United States they were in their late forties and had six children in Russia, some who were already married and had children of their own. All immigrated to America with Ida, Elias, Max, Jacob, and Samuel, settling in Suffolk County and making a substantial contribution to the growth of the Jewish community in Kings Park. In 1923, when Gershon and Rachel both passed away, they had forty-two direct descendants and their spouses living locally in Kings Park and neighboring towns, including twenty grandchildren and nine great-grandchildren. In addition, the Patikys were blessed with an even larger extended family of grandchildren and great-grandchildren who did not live on Long Island.

Elias Patiky was Gershon and Rachel's oldest son. He immigrated to America with his wife, Jennie, in 1887 and initially lived in New York City and worked in a mill that processed raw wool. Following a bout with anthrax,

Elias decided to leave the city and move east, growing and harvesting crops alongside his father. However, the farmer's life for Elias was not meant to be, and instead he became a merchant, opening a dry goods store in 1897. It is believed that Elias selected Kings Park because of the opportunities that existed in doing business with the nearby psychiatric hospital. Opened in 1885, the Kings County Asylum was rapidly expanding and was taken over by New York State, becoming Kings Park State Hospital in 1895. To garner additional revenue Elias regularly took a selection of his merchandise via horse and wagon for sale in neighboring villages, leaving Jennie to run the store. Over time he would establish relationships and sell his wares to regular clientele, which enabled him to open additional stores in Northport and Huntington with his brother Samuel as a business partner.

LOOK
For Your Own Benefit

When buying always look for the place where you can get your money's worth.

¶We are here to serve the people with the best merchandise at the lowest prices. We can well afford to do this as we buy merchandise in large quantities to supply our two stores and traveling wagon. Our stock consists of an

—Up-to-date Line of—

CLOTHING
Ladies' & Gent's Furnishings
Hats, Caps, Shoes, etc.

Tickets will be given with every purchase. For each $25 worth of tickets the customer will be entitled to $1.50 worth of merchandise.

E. Patiky & Bro.

Adams Block.   Corner Main and New Streets
HUNTINGTON, L. I.
Kings Park, L. I.   -   -   -   -   E. PATIKY

Figure 65. Ad for the new Patiky store in Huntington, 1909. *Source: The Long-Islander*, May 14, 1909.

Figure 66. Sam Patiky with his horse Doc. *Source*: Courtesy of Susan Field.

FATHER

אליהו ב"ר גרשון
נפ' כ"ד אלול תש"ד

BELOVED HUSBAND

ELIAS

1868 — 1944

ת נ צ ב "ה

Figure 67. The grave of Elias Patiky in the Kings Park Jewish cemetery. *Source*: Photo by Brad Kolodny.

Not only was Elias a successful merchant, but he was also a dedicated family man and an instrumental figure in growing the Jewish community in Suffolk County. Both he and Jennie played a crucial role taking in relatives when they first arrived from Europe, helping to establish them in business and providing guidance on places to live and other necessary adjustments to life in the new country. While Elias was part of the Jewish gatherings at his parents' home he was also one of the original eight members of the Brotherhood of Jews in Huntington when organized in March 1906. Inspired by their formalization Elias brought that enthusiasm closer to home as president of the Jewish Brotherhood of Kings Park, leading them to be incorporated in July that same year. With his father Gershon and brothers Max and Sam, the Patiky men were four of the seven directors of the congregation at its inception. Elias continued to support the growth of Judaism on Long Island, making a contribution toward having a synagogue built on the south shore of western Suffolk County. For his generosity Elias was given the honor of placing one of three Torahs into the ark during the dedication ceremony for the Lindenhurst Hebrew Congregation synagogue on August 29, 1915.

As a newly formed official corporation the Jewish Brotherhood was able to establish a cemetery as was customary for new congregations formed in Suffolk County in the early twentieth century. The land for burials was acquired from the Jewish Agricultural and Industrial Aid Society that operated the five-hundred-acre Indian Head Farm. It was funded by the Baron de Hirsch Foundation, an organization that supported teaching agriculture to new Jewish immigrants and used the farm in King's Park as a testing ground from 1905 to 1908. By this time Gershon had retired from farming, moved to Kings Park, and opened a feed store. Services were now more centrally located in Gershon and Rachel's new home in the village of Kings Park. With space limited inside their house, Gershon decided to build an extension specifically to be used for services to accommodate the growing community. Before long even this enlarged clubhouse became inadequate, and plans for building a synagogue were put into motion.

In 1908 a campaign began that raised $800 toward materials and labor for constructing the synagogue that would be located right next door to Gershon and Rachel's home. It was agreed the architectural style would be a simple design in the Orthodox tradition that included a balcony with seating for women. But a point of contention arose about whether or not to include a mikveh (ritual bath) as part of the structure. Most felt it was

Figure 68. The synagogue for the Jewish Brotherhood of Kings Park, 1923. Gershon and Rachel Patiky's home is visible on the left. *Source*: Courtesy of Susan Field.

a superfluous expense for a ritual exercise associated with the Old World left behind in Europe. A small faction of traditionalists won out, and the mikveh was included, much to the delight of Jacob Okst.

Ida Patiky, Elias's older sister, married Jacob Okst in their homeland of Russia in 1883 and immigrated to the United States in 1902 with their children Bella, Rose, Etta, Israel, Dora, and Anna. Following their arrival in America the couple added two more children, Bess and George. Jacob was a religious man who helped organize the Jewish Brother of Kings Park serving as secretary in 1906. He owned multiple properties within the business district on Broadway (now route 25A) known as the flats that housed a hardware store, a grocery, and a stationery/cigar/candy store with the Okst family residence on the second floor. A fourth store that Jacob rented out as a barbershop and billiard parlor caught fire on the afternoon of May 15, 1917, when an oil stove was overturned. The flames spread to other buildings, destroying an entire block of nine stores. Damages included a $50,000 loss to Elias from the two buildings he owned across the street that were ignited by flying embers and burned to the ground. The devastation from that fateful day was extensive, but no deaths or injuries occurred. The Okst family persevered, continued to be fruitful and multiplied through

Figure 69. The family of Jacob Okst, including his mother and his wife's parents, c. 1908. *Source*: Courtesy of Susan Field.

their two sons and six daughters who married into the Clark, Johnson, Glass, Meyers, Schwartz, and Raskin families.

Another Jewish family that lived in Elwood was the Silbersteins. The father Victor and George Patiky had much in common being from the same generation, they came to America the same year 1887, and both were farmers. Victor and his wife Yetta moved there with three sons Max, Morris, and Isaac in 1893 and had two more boys born in Elwood, Charles, and Harry. Isaac went into the family business and started his own small-scale dairy farm in 1910 that would grow to become Oak Tree Dairy Farm. The enterprise included his brothers Charles and Harry as partners and at its peak boasted 250 cows on 400 acres producing about 3,700 quarts of milk a day.

The original synagogue in Kings Park no longer stands, having been destroyed in a fire on May 28, 1962. A new Kings Park Jewish Center was built on the south side of Route 25A in the mid-1960s and is still in use today carrying on the legacy of the founders whose memory can also be found elsewhere in town. Upon exiting the synagogue parking lot and heading west, the first block on the left is Okst Street, and on the right you will find Elias and Jennie's home still standing on the northeast corner of 25A and Patiky Street.

L'dor v'dor . . . from Generation to Generation

Jennie Patiky lived a full life of ninety-eight years. She was born in Russia and came to America with her husband Elias, lived in New York City for a few years, moved to Elwood, and finally settled in Kings Park before the turn of the century. The oldest of their five children, Bertha, was born in 1891 and is known in the family as Birdie. In 1913 Birdie married Louis Pastor from Bangor, Maine. The wedding ceremony took place in Kings Park followed by the couple making their home in Bangor. A year later the Pastors had their first of three children, a son named Sewall, and by 1920 the family had moved to Philadelphia. Sewall married Louise Bartok in 1938 and opened his doctor's office in Farmingdale in 1940, the same year their first child Jamie was born. Sewall later worked at Huntington Hospital and joined a medical practice in Huntington established by his uncle Joseph Patiky. In 1972 Jamie married Ronald Bolnick and had their first child, a daughter named Britt.

The photo below was taken in October 1972, a week after Britt was born and just a few weeks before Jennie passed away. It is rare to see five generations in one family photograph that exemplifies the passage of time and links the generations one to another.

Figure 70. L to R: Britt, Jamie, Jennie, Sewall, and Birdie. *Source:* Courtesy of Jamie Pastor.

Table 12.1. Residents of Kings Park

Harry	**Brown**		1881		
Ida	Brown	wife	1886		
David	**Cohen**		1880		Brother of Solomon
Annie	Cohen	wife	1885		
Sidney	Cohen	son	1907		
Bernard	Cohen	son	1909		
Leon	Cohen	son	1915		
Rosalind	Cohen	daughter	1918		
Solomon	**Cohen**		1869		Brother of David
Ida	Cohen	wife	1867		
Sarah	Cohen	daughter	1894		
Rosa	Cohen	daughter	1899		
Minnie	Cohen	daughter	1903		
Harry	Cohen	son	1905		
Jennie	Cohen	daughter	1906		
Jacob	**Glass**		1882	1951	Candy merchant
Etta	(Okst) Glass	wife	1891	1984	Daughter of Jacob and Ida
Evelyn	Glass	daughter	1913	2015	
Bernard	Glass	son	1916	1988	
Harris	**Henschel**		1863	1931	Son of Morris and Rachel from Amityville, named for his uncle killed in the Civil War at Gettysburg in July 1863
Maude	(Basford) Henschel	wife	1872		
Elsie	Henschel	daughter	1893	1986	m. Joseph Shuffleton
Mildred	Henschel	daughter	1897		m. Leo Perry, lived in Northport
Howard	Henschel	son	1901		
Morris	**Herman**		1866		Dry goods peddler
Ida	Herman	wife	1871		
Sarah	Herman	daughter	1901		
Sophia	Herman	daughter	1902		
Jacob	Herman	son	1904		
Nathan	**Kass**		1857	1930	
Libby	Kass	wife	1857	1932	
Annie	Kass	daughter	1880	1972	m. Abraham Pheffer
Julius	**Levy**		1859		Cigar maker
Minnie	(Henschel) Levy	wife	1861		Daughter of Morris and Rachel from Amityville

continued on next page

Table 12.1. Continued.

Rose	Levy	daughter	1887		
Esther	Levy	daughter	1893		
Chawe	**Okst**		1840	1909	Mother of Jacob
Jacob	**Okst**		1864	1935	Owned grocery and hardware stores
Ida	(Patiky) Okst	wife	1864	1947	Daughter of Gershon and Rachel
Bella	Okst	daughter	1888	1969	m. Sam Clark, lived in Central Islip
Etta	Okst	daughter	1891	1984	m. Jacob Glass
Israel	Okst	son	1893	1981	
Dora	Okst	daughter	1897	1974	
Rose	Okst	daughter	1899		m. Charles Johnson, lived in East Northport
Anna	Okst	daughter	1899	1942	m. John Schwartz, lived in Huntington
Bess	Okst	daughter	1903		
George	Okst	son	1906	1942	
James	**Pastor**		1873	1926	Jewish Brotherhood of Kings Park 1906
Louis	**Pastor**		1883	1942	Brother of James
Bertha	(Patiky) Pastor	wife	1891	1981	Daughter of Elias and Jennie
Elias	**Patiky**		1868	1944	Son of George and Rachel
Jennie	(Kalika) Patiky	wife	1874	1972	
Bertha	Patiky	daughter	1891	1981	m. Louis Pastor
Joseph	Patiky	son	1893	1954	
Rebecca	Patiky	daughter	1899	1900	
Doris	Patiky	daughter	1901	1993	
Jacob	Patiky	son	1905	1999	
Gershon	**Patiky**		1839	1923	Farmer
Rachel	(Knobel) Patiky	wife	1840	1923	
Ida	Patiky	daughter	1864	1947	m. Jacob Okst
Elias	Patiky	son	1868	1944	m. Jennie Kalika
Max	Patiky	son	1872	1947	m. Hattie Miller
Jacob	Patiky	son	1878	1950	m. Lena Hollander, lived in East Northport
Samuel	Patiky	son	1883	1971	Jewish Brotherhood of Kings Park 1906
Max	**Patiky**		1872	1947	Son of Gershon and Rachel
Hattie	(Miller) Patiky	wife	1874	1937	
Mamie	Patiky	daughter	1892		

Table 12.1. Continued.

Rebecca	Patiky	daughter	1896		
Sadie	Patiky	daughter	1898		
Goldie	Patiky	daughter	1900		
Maurice	Patiky	son	1902	1954	
George	Patiky	son	1904	1985	
Albert	Patiky	son	1909		
Michael	**Patiky**		1879	1941	Nephew of Gershon Patiky and brother of Abraham from East Northport
Fanny	(Bronstein) Patiky	wife	1884	1941	
Belle	Patiky	daughter	1907	1991	
Alida	Patiky	daughter	1911	2000	
Abraham	**Pheffer**		1870	1936	Farmer
Annie	(Kass) Pheffer	wife	1880	1972	Daughter of Nathan and Libby
Fred	**Schmidt**				Jewish Brotherhood of Kings Park 1906
Ely	**Shanis**		1877		
Bunya	(Leikach) Shanis	wife			Sister of Sam Clark from Central Islip
Itta	Shanis	daughter	1903		
Ruchel	Shanis	daughter	1905		
Joseph	**Shuffleton**		1885	1969	Doctor at Kings Park Hospital
Elsie	(Henschel) Shuffleton	wife	1893	1986	Daughter of Harris and Maude
Jacob	**Stein**		1884		Extractor at a laundry
Sadie	Stein	wife	1884		
Harry	Stein	son	1908		
Eva	Stein	daughter	1910		

Table 12.2. Residents of Commack

Simon	**Koff**		1873	1953	Farmer
Rosie	Koff	wife	1875	1955	
Sarah	Koff	daughter	1899		
Lottie	Koff	daughter	1900		
William	Koff	son	1903		
James	Koff	son	1905		
Mary	Koff	daughter	1916		
Morris	**Glass**		1895	1955	Painter
Charles	**Johnson**		1882	1959	Cow and horse dealer

continued on next page

Table 12.3. Residents of East Northport

Rose	(Okst) Johnson	wife	1884	1964	Daughter of Jacob and Ida from Kings Park
Bessie	Johnson	daughter	1905		
Abraham	Johnson	son	1906		
Max	Johnson	son	1907	1943	
Harry	Johnson	son	1910		
Harris	**Lichtenberg**		1866	1937	
Rebecca	Lichtenberg	wife	1870	1943	
Abraham	**Patiky**		1880	1961	Nephew of Gershon Patiky and brother of Michael from Kings Park
Minnie	Patiky	wife	1880		
Sarah	Patiky	daughter	1907		
Ida	Patiky	daughter	1912		
Bella	Patiky	daughter	1915		
Jacob	**Patiky**		1878	1950	Son of Gershon and Rachel from Kings Park
Lena	(Hollander) Patiky	wife	1874	1959	Daughter of Judah from Huntington
Julius	Patiky	son	1905	1978	
Mollie	Patiky	daughter	1908		
Jeanette	**(Eisemann) Schloss**		1839	1901	Mother of Celia Wollman
Julius	**Wollman**		1866	1945	Farmer
Celia	(Schloss) Wollman	wife	1872	1944	
William	Wollman	son	1900	1977	
Jeanette	Wollman	daughter	1902	2002	
Daniel	Wollman	son	1910	1990	

Table 12.4. Residents of Elwood

Victor	**Silberstein**		1852	1921	
Yetta	(Fischer) Silberstein	wife	1863	1929	
Marcus	Silberstein	son	1889		
Morris	Silberstein	son	1890		
Isaac	Silberstein	son	1892	1968	Dairy farmer started Oak Tree Dairy
Charles	Silberstein	son	1895	1951	Worked with brother Isaac
Harry	Silberstein	son	1901		Worked with brother Isaac

Table 12.5. Residents of Northport

Louis	**Alter**		1879	1962	Co-owner Saltz and Alter dept. store

Table 12.5. Continued.

Anna	(Apsel) Alter	wife	1885	1971	Sister of Reuben and Martha Saltz
Clarice	Alter	daughter	1906		
Reuben	Alter	son	1908	1916	
Selma	Alter	daughter	1915		
Reuben	**Apsel**		1890	1907	Brother of Anna Alter and Martha Saltz
Max	**Bernstein**		1881	1935	Proprietor of Beach Hotel
Julia	(Friedman) Bernstein	wife	1887	1947	
Wilfred	Bernstein	son	1916	1919	
David	**Cohen**		1866	1936	Clothing merchant
Ida	(Balterman) Cohen	wife	1867		
Charles	Cohen	son	1888		
Roy	Cohen	son	1890		
Murray	Cohen	son	1891		
Louis	Cohen	son	1892		
Samuel	Cohen	son	1896		
Annie	Cohen	daughter	1898	1939	
Isaac	**Cohen**		1868		Clothing merchant
Emma	(Klauber) Cohen	wife	1867		
Jacob	Cohen	son	1899		
Joel	Cohen	son	1903		
Sol	**Greenberg**		1867	1937	Shoe store owner
Jennie	Greenberg	wife	1875	1944	
Fanny	Greenberg	daughter	1897	1977	
Louis	Greenberg	son	1902		
Harry	Greenberg	son	1904		
Zelick	**Greenberg**				Jewish Brotherhood of Kings Park 1906
Abraham	**Ingerman**		1885	1956	Dry goods store owner
Sarah	(Kahn) Ingerman	wife	1886	1941	
Rose	Ingerman	daughter	1912		
Percy	Ingerman	son	1913	1994	
Ethel	Ingerman	daughter	1915		
Leo	**Perry**		1894		Worked for the IRS
Mildred	(Henschel) Perry	wife	1899		Daughter of Harris and Maude from Kings Park
Charles	Perry	son	1917		
Max	**Saltz**		1882	1957	Co-owner Saltz and Alter dept. store

continued on next page

Table 12.5. Continued.

Martha	(Apsel) Saltz	wife	1882	1953	Sister of Reuben and Anna Alter
Irving	Saltz	son	1905	1910	
Herman	Saltz	son	1912		
Alida	Saltz	daughter			

Table 12.6. Residents of Smithtown

Lazarus	**Bearman**		1881		Tailor
Eva	(Kaufman) Bearman	wife	1883		
Charles	Bearman	son	1906		
Freda	Bearman	daughter	1908		
Sarah	Bearman	daughter	1909		
Samuel	Bearman	son	1910		
Rosie	Bearman	daughter	1914		
Ida	Bearman	daughter	1916		
Heime	Bearman	son	1918		
Joseph	**Brown**		1872	1938	Fruit merchant
Rebecca	Brown	wife	1870	1957	
Abraham	Brown	son	1899	1919	
David	Brown	son	1916		
Joseph	**Forman**		1889	1954	Dry goods merchant
Gussie	Forman	wife	1889	1969	
Percy	Forman	son	1918	1945	
Isaac	**Henschel**		1876		Son of Morris and Rachel from Amityville
Bertha	(Kressley) Henschel	wife	1885		
Raymond	Henschel	son	1904		
Rachel	Henschel	daughter	1907		
Louis	**Levitt**		1876		Dentist
Tillie	(Rosenberg) Levitt	wife	1885		
Virginia	Levitt	daughter	1911		
Beatrice	Levitt	daughter	1912		
Jerome	**Schechter**		1885	1961	Dry goods merchant
Esther	(Braaf) Schechter	wife	1887	1951	
Harry	Schechter	son	1912	1969	
Eva	Schechter	daughter	1913	1989	
Edith	Schechter	daughter	1916		
Herman	Schechter	son	1917		
Irving	Schechter	son	1917		

Chapter 13

Lindenhurst

Including Amityville, Babylon, and Copiague

Rural areas along the south shore of western Suffolk County did not develop into notable communities until the arrival of the South Side Railroad, a competitor of the LIRR, in 1867. German immigrants left New York City to establish themselves and their families in the city of Breslau that was incorporated in 1870 (the name was changed to Lindenhurst in 1891). Some of the early Germans to make the move eastward were Jewish, and before too long a congregation was established. They called themselves Neta Szarschea, meaning "planting of thy seed," an appropriate name for a group that was the first Jewish congregation formed on Long Island. On November 23, 1874, ten men gathered in the home of Herman Rosenstein at 7 p.m. to formalize their organization. Rosenstein was elected president,

Simon Spitz secretary, and Louis Perlmann treasurer. In October 1876 Neta Szarschea purchased a portion of land in the northeast section of Breslau Cemetery for $135, which was set apart for Jewish burials only.

Sadly, there is no further information known to exist about Neta Szarschea. The paper trail of available records runs out with no information about what became of this seminal congregation. Speculation would suggest the group disbanded by 1887 because it was in that year articles of incorporation were filed with the Suffolk County Clerk's Office for an organization called the Breslau Hebrew Cemetery Association. As the name indicates, this group was founded to serve as the administration for and care of the Jewish cemetery, presumably in the absence of the congregation that originally purchased the land. The membership of this new association also indicates the Jewish community centered in Breslau extended to neighboring villages. Six trustees were voted in, plus two officers: Jacob Hartmann as president and Nathan Cohen as secretary. Both men lived in Amityville.

Figure 71. Entrance gate to the Jewish section of the Breslau Cemetery. *Source*: Photo by Brad Kolodny.

What is a German community without a distributor for supplying beer? Jacob Hartmann identified this need on the south shore and was able to fill it by starting his own bottling company. The Hartmann family moved to Amityville in 1877 when Jacob's father Samuel, born in Germany in 1802, purchased a four-and-a-half-acre property bordered on the west by the county line road that divided Queens and Suffolk (Nassau County was not established until 1899). At the age of eighty-one Samuel deeded his property to Jacob, and five years later it was sold, perhaps giving Jacob the necessary capital to start the Suffolk County Bottling Company in 1890, which was later renamed the Amityville Bottling Company. Welz & Zerweck Brewery in Brooklyn would ship kegs of High Ground Lager, Export Lager, and Gambrinus Brau by freight train to Amityville to be bottled and sold to saloons by Hartmann's company. He had a similar arrangement with the Schaefer Company and also branched out to bottling seltzer and high-grade mineral waters.

Figure 72. A relic from Jacob Hartmann's bottling company. It is thought the interlocking letters "SH" on the bottle are a tribute to his father, Samuel Hartmann. *Source*: From the collection of the author.

It is not known why George Barasch came to settle in Lindenhurst. The father of five came to the United States by himself in 1893 followed by his wife Hilda and four sons who arrived in 1898. In between, George and Hilda's oldest child, Rose, came to New York in 1895 and within a year was married to Louis Edelman, a dry goods peddler. By 1900 Louis, Rose, and their son Herman, as well as George, Hilda, and sons Michael, Max, Harry, and Louis all lived in Lindenhurst.

George started out as a peripatetic merchant selling goods out of his horse-drawn wagon. By 1905 he had established a store in Lindenhurst specializing in crockery and by 1910 owned a two-story building at the corner of Hoffman Avenue and Nostrand Avenue (today First Street). In the decade that followed, the Barasch building would become a center of growth for two important developments in Lindenhurst: the rise of the embroidery industry and the construction of a synagogue.

Figure 73. George (with beard) and Hilda (wearing glasses), the patriarch and matriarch of the Barasch family, c. 1927. *Source*: Courtesy of Betsy Plevan.

The Jewish community made another attempt to organize into a more cohesive and lasting group than Neta Szarschea with the formation of the First Lindenhurst Hebrew Society in 1908. Without a synagogue located within twenty-five miles it was a goal for this society to erect a place where Jews from Lindenhurst and the surrounding areas could gather for worship and other activities. The neighboring communities were well represented by the group's president, Charles Siegel, a tailor who had a shop on Deer Park Avenue in Babylon beginning in 1894. Other officers of the fledgling organization included Louis S. Barasch (not the son of George and Hilda) as vice president, Louis Alter as secretary, and M. Friedman as treasurer.

Lindenhurst was an industrious village during the early twentieth century with several manufacturing facilities providing hundreds of job opportunities. According to the New York State Register of Factories for 1912 there were 34 factories in Lindenhurst, the largest employing 131 people. Some were used to manufacture shoes, buttons, brass pins, clasps, and other items, but the majority were for silk and cotton embroidery. Various branches of the Barasch family wanted to capitalize on the growing trend and decided to enter the embroidery business. Max and Louis opened a factory utilizing a 35' × 40' space in the rear of their father George's building at Hoffman and Nostrand Avenues with machinery shipped over from Switzerland. Max and Louis's brother Harry, who was married with two children at the time and living in Freeport, also started an embroidery business, manufacturing handkerchiefs with Swiss machinery. Their brother-in-law Louis Edelman entered the business, too. He was already established in the village with a department store at the northeast corner of Wellwood Avenue and Humboldt Avenue (today East John Street). Behind his store Edelman had a two-story building erected and installed four new embroidery machines. These three new enterprises all commenced in 1913 and carried on for years to come, offering employment to local citizens who could expect to make seven dollars per week. Edelman expanded his operation by purchasing the embroidery plant owned by Louis Liehl in 1916. By 1920 there were at least twenty-nine documented Jewish residents of Lindenhurst who worked as stitchers, spanners, or in other jobs at the many embroidery shops in the village.

On October 26, 1913, a meeting took place at the Barasch building that would set the course for building a synagogue in Lindenhurst. A new society was formed known as the Lindenhurst Hebrew Congregation, and temporary officers were elected including George Barasch as president.

Figure 74. Looking north up Wellwood Avenue, with Louis Edelman's Department Store at right. *Source*: Lindenhurst Historical Society.

Real action was taken that evening as $200 was pledged and a committee established to find a suitable site to build a synagogue. The congregation was officially incorporated on January 19, 1914, and a month later Barasch purchased two lots on West Broadway (today North Fourth Street) north of Palmer Avenue (today West John Street) with the hopes of having the synagogue erected in the spring of 1914. Alas, it wasn't until May 1915 when plans had been prepared for the building. During this period, services were taking place in the home of Rabbi Hyman Benjamin Diamond on Bismark Avenue (today North Eighth Street).

The cornerstone for the synagogue was laid during festive ceremonies on June 20 with over three hundred people in attendance. Seven hundred dollars was raised through the auction of bricks to be installed in the build-ing. Nathan Freedman, a resident of Lindenhurst since the early 1880s, was the highest bidder for the first brick, donating $80. Construction would take place over the next two months and be nearly completed in time for the formal opening on August 29. In addition to speeches from local dig-nitaries and additional funds being raised there was a procession of three Torahs that were carried from Rabbi Diamond's home to the synagogue. The six members of the building committee who were most instrumental in seeing this vision become a reality were Abraham Weinstein, Rabbi

Diamond, Nathan Freedman, Elias Klapper, Louis Edelman, and George Barasch. Forty years after the first congregation had been established, the Jews of Lindenhurst finally had their own synagogue.

In November 1915 Charles Siegel, former president of the First Lindenhurst Hebrew Society, decided to take a vacation from his tailoring business for the first time in eleven years and spent a couple of weeks in the town of Mountaindale, New York. The bucolic setting in the Catskill Mountains of upstate New York may have been an antidote for Charles who was in failing health. His physician was Dr. Solomon Weingrad, a resident of Mountaindale, who was introduced to Charles's oldest daughter Ruth. A courtship ensued, and the two were married on Sunday afternoon, May 19, 1916 (note: the photo on the cover and at the end of this chapter is from the wedding). It was the first wedding ceremony performed in the new synagogue, with over two hundred people in attendance from Lindenhurst, Babylon, Amityville, Bay Shore, Patchogue, Freeport, New York City, including Ruth's uncle Isaac Siegel who came all the way from California. Not in attendance was the father of the bride who had passed away two months previously on March 25.

Less than twenty years later Lindenhurst Hebrew Congregation outgrew their synagogue and built a larger one in the early 1930s located on North Fourth Street just south of the original. The postwar generation brought new Jewish families to Lindenhurst, and a third synagogue was built at the corner of West John Street and North Fourth Street in 1959.

Neta Szarschea, established in 1874, is remembered as the first Jewish congregation on Long Island; however, there is no synagogue in Lindenhurst today. Young Jewish families were not moving to Lindenhurst in the 1990s as they had in prior decades. And with a significant decline in membership, drastic measures had to be taken. In 2006 Lindenhurst Hebrew Congregation merged with Congregation Beth-El in nearby Massapequa and sold their building to the Holy Family Ukrainian Catholic Church.

An Amityville Haberdashery for over One Hundred Years

Many of the world's finest tailors have received their training at the famed clothing shops on Savile Row in London. Among them was Louis Cohn, an immigrant from Poland who learned his craft as an apprentice prior to arriving in the United States in 1907. Cohn opened the Amityville Men's Shop in 1911, offering a full line of men's clothing and accessories in addition to custom tailoring and dry-cleaning services.

Louis and his bride Fannie were married in 1912 and went on to have six children—three girls and three boys—the youngest named Irving, who was born in 1925. At an early age Irving worked in his father's store from time to time and was also a runner for the Gutowitz jewelry store, owned by another Jewish merchant in Amityville, at 174 Park Avenue. Irving would deliver items from Amityville to the Gutowitz branch location in Hempstead via the LIRR. After the war Irving went to work for his father full time in 1946.

Irving's son Warren took an interest in the family business as a young boy and can remember watching his grandfather at work in the back room

Figure 75. Louis Cohn in front of his store, 1913. *Source*: Amityville Historical Society.

Figure 76. Father and daughter, Warren and Alexa Cohn, at the Amityville Men's Shop. *Source*: Photo by Brad Kolodny.

of the shop. Warren observed Louis's intricate stitching and handiwork, visible through the haze of smoke rising from a cigarette teetering at the edge of his desk. Upon graduating college in 1978 Warren went to work for his father in the shop. Fast forward forty years and Warren's daughter Alexa became involved as part of the fourth generation of Cohns to work in the Amityville Men's Shop. She has her own ideas on how to appeal to the next generation of customers but has great respect for the past and those who came before her to make the store what it is today.

Six Generations in the Town of Babylon

Joseph and Gertrude Felcher were born in Germany and had moved to England by the time their first child, Rachael, was born in 1875. Rachael was married to Charles Siegel, a native of Vienna who was an apprentice in London in 1883 where he learned to be a tailor. Charles came to the United States in 1886, settling in Newark, New Jersey, spent two years living in New York City, married Rachael in 1891, and by 1894 had a tailor shop on Deer Park Avenue in Babylon. Two years later Rachael's parents came to America from England and settled in Lindenhurst.

The Siegels started their family with the birth of Solomon in 1895 followed by Morris, Ruth, Ralph, Sidney, Walter, and Sylvia. Ruth, who was known within the family by her middle name, Esther, married Dr. Solomon Weingrad in 1916. A photo from the joyous occasion is shown below. Ralph Siegel was the best man and is standing next to the groom with Sidney, another of Esther's brothers, poking his head between the bride and groom. Presumably Esther's mother Rachael is wearing white and standing next to the bride, and a further presumption is that Rachael's parents Joseph and Gertrude are standing in front of her. Esther's father Charles had passed away two months before the wedding.

Figure 77. Wedding of Ruth Esther Siegel and Dr. Solomon Weingrad, 1916. *Source*: From the collections of the Town of Babylon, Office of Historic Services.

In 1927 Sidney Siegel joined the Babylon firm Snedecor & Norton, which sold real estate and insurance. After six years with the company the name was changed to Norton & Siegel, as it is still known today. Sidney's daughter Marjorie, who married Peter Stein, worked for Norton & Siegel for thirty-five years. Peter and Marjorie's son Aaron Stein is the current owner of the business, and Aaron's son Ben is following in his father's, grandmother's, and great grandfather's footsteps by selling insurance for Norton & Siegel at their office on Main Street in Babylon.

Figure 78. Father and son, Aaron and Ben Stein, at the office of the family insurance business. *Source*: Photo by Brad Kolodny.

Table 13.1. Residents of Lindenhurst

George	**Barasch**		1854	1933	Dry goods merchant
Hilda	Barasch	wife	1858	1936	
Rose	Barasch	daughter	1877		m. Louis Edelman
Harry	Barasch	son	1877	1937	m. Regina Rattner, lived in Freeport
Michael	Barasch	son	1884		m. Eva, lived in Rockville Centre
Max	Barasch	son	1887		m. Cecilia Hepner
Louis	Barasch	son	1889		Manufacture and sale of handkerchiefs
Louis S.	**Barasch**		1882	1936	Owned a candy store
Celia	Barasch	wife	1891	1986	
Stella	Barasch	daughter	1912		
Dorothy	Barasch	daughter	1917		
Max	**Barasch**		1887		Son of George and Hilda
Cecilia	(Hepner) Barasch	wife	1895	1949	Daughter of Sophie from Rockville Centre
Jack	Barasch	son	1918		Changed name to Jack Barry and became a television game show host
David	**Bendheim**				Member of Lindenhurst Hebrew Cong.
Max	**Bergman**		1890	1942	Stitcher in an embroidery shop
Eva	(Warshawsky) Bergman	wife	1891	1969	
Harry	Bergman	son	1918	1968	
Joseph	**Berman**		1870	1927	Tailor
Anna	Berman	wife	1863		
Joseph	**Bibro**				Member of Neta Szarschea 1874
Abe	**Blum**		1894		Stitcher in an embroidery shop
Mary	Blum	wife	1897		
Mildred	Blum	daughter	1916		
Florence	Blum	daughter			
Samuel	**Cohen**		1890		Trustee Lindenhurst Hebrew Cong. 1913
Annie	(Brower) Cohen	wife	1893	1918	Daughter of Harris and Sarah from Farmingdale
Evelyn	Cohen	daughter	1913		
Ruth	Cohen	daughter	1916		
Milton	Cohen	son	1917		

Table 13.1. Continued.

Anna	Cohen	daughter	1918		
Max	**Datomski**					Member of Neta Szarschea 1874
Hyman	**Diamond**		1872	1927	Rabbi
Ida	(Gutowitz) Diamond	wife	1868	1931	
Isidor	Diamond	son	1892		Embroiderer
Solomon	Diamond	son	1895	1967	Embroiderer
Rose	Diamond	daughter	1898	1928	
Dora	Diamond	daughter	1900		
Pauline	Diamond	daughter	1902		
Louis	**Edelman**		1876		Dept store and embroidery shop owner
Rose	(Barasch) Edelman	wife	1877		Daughter of George and Hilda
Herman	Edelman	son	1898		
Harry	Edelman	son	1902		
Reuben	Edelman	son	1907		
George	**Feinberg**		1870	1918	
Annie	Feinberg	wife	1871		
Ida	Feinberg	daughter	1897		
Bella	Feinberg	daughter	1902		
Max	Feinberg	son	1903		
Norman	Feinberg	son	1905		
Robert	Feinberg	son	1910		
George	**Feinberg**		1887		
Jennie	Feinberg	wife	1888		
Sidney	Feinberg	son	1912		
Herbert	Feinberg	son	1913	1984	
Leo	Feinberg	son	1916	1997	
Joseph	**Felcher**		1851	1933	Trustee Lindenhurst Hebrew Cong. 1913
Gertrude	Felcher	wife	1856	1940	
Rachael	Felcher	daughter	1875	1959	m. Charles Siegel, lived in Babylon
Nellie	Felcher	daughter	1882	1968	m. Alter Berman, lived in Babylon
Isaac	Felcher	son	1884	1916	m. ?
Louis	Felcher	son	1885		

continued on next page

Table 13.1. Continued.

Solomon	Felcher	son	1888	1976	m. Rose Siegel
Isaac	**Felcher**		1884	1916	
?	Felcher	wife			
Regina	Felcher	daughter	1912		
Solomon	**Felcher**		1888	1976	Son of Joseph and Gertrude
Rose	(Siegel) Felcher	wife	1887	1961	Sister of Charles, Harris and Isaac from Babylon
Eva	**Freedman**		1840		Sister-in-law of Nathan Freedman
Nathan	**Freedman**		1855		VP Lindenhurst Hebrew Cong. 1913
Lena	Freedman	wife	1855		
Samuel	Freedman	son	1879		m. Minnie Fine
Louis	Freedman	son	1882		
Jennie	Freedman	daughter	1891		
Samuel	**Freedman**		1879		Son of Nathan and Lena
Minnie	(Fine) Freedman	wife	1888		
Isidor	**Friedman**		1884		Stitcher at an embroidery shop
Mary	(Mirlich) Friedman	wife	1890		
Fanny	Friedman	daughter	1911		
Morris	**Friedman**				Trustee Breslau Hebrew Cemetery 1887
?	Friedman	wife			
?	Friedman	daughter			
Samuel	**Friedman**		1878		Trustee Lindenhurst Hebrew Cong. 1913
Minnie	Friedman	wife	1888		
Irwin	Friedman	son	1913		
Herman	**Goldberg**		1864		Trustee Lindenhurst Hebrew Cong. 1913
?	Goldberg	first wife			
Ralph	Goldberg	son	1890		
Katie	Goldberg	daughter	1892		Spanner in an embroidery factory
Mary	Goldberg	daughter	1895		Spanner in an embroidery factory
Sophie	Goldberg	daughter	1900		
Gussie	(Blume) Goldberg	second wife	1868		First husband ? Blume
Rose	Goldberg	daughter	1902		Daughter of Gussie and ? Blume
Samuel	Block	son	1910		Adopted by Herman and Gussie

Table 13.1. Continued.

Simeon	**Hartmann**				Trustee Hebrew Cemetery Assoc. 1887
Frieda	Hartmann	wife			
Davis	**Hillman**		1866		Trustee Lindenhurst Hebrew Cong. 1913
Bertha	Hillman	wife	1867		
Izzie	**Jaffe**		1887		Butcher
Kate	Jaffe	wife	1894		
Teddy	Jaffe	son	1914		
Edward	Jaffe	son	1915		
Ruth	Jaffe	daughter	1917		
Rosie	**Jaffe**		1883		Niece of Joseph Berman
E.	**Kaufman**		1905		Fruit dealer
Philip	**Kaufman**		1883		Stitcher in an embroidery shop
Minnie	(Rothenberg) Kaufman	wife	1892	1936	
Benjamin	Kaufman	son	1911		
Harry	Kaufman	son	1917		
Elias	**Klapper**		1883	1946	Recording secretary Lindenhurst Hebrew Cong. 1913
Ida	Klapper	wife	1890	1940	
Walter	Klapper	son	1916		
Max	**Kochman**		1887	1980	Owned an embroidery shop
Lena	Kochman	wife	1888		
Mollie	Kochman	daughter	1911		
Philip	Kochman	son	1913		
Harry	Kochman	son	1917		
Abraham	**Kreitzman**		1882	1942	Son of Samuel and Lena
Jennie	(Studhren) Kreitzman	wife	1890		
Max	**Kreitzman**		1887		Junk peddler
Fannie	Kreitzman	wife	1886		
Dorothy	Kreitzman	daughter	1909		
Samuel	**Kreitzman**		1859	1931	
Lena	Kreitzman	wife	1862		
Isidor	**Landau**		1892	1931	Worked at Landau Bros. embroidery
Beckie	(Stein) Landau	wife	1894		
Martha	Landau	daughter	1916		

continued on next page

Table 13.1. Continued.

Ruth	Landau	daughter	1918		
Max	**Landau**		1892		Stitcher in an embroidery shop
Minnie	Landau	wife	1886		
Fanny	Landau	daughter	1914		
Annie	Landau	daughter	1916		
B.	**Levine**				Rabbi at Lindenhurst synagogue 1916
?	Levine	wife			
?	Levine	child			
?	Levine	child			
?	Levine	child			
?	Levine	child			
?	Levine	child			
Jacob	**Lewis**		1825		Worked in a factory
Hanna	Lewis	wife	1825		
Jacob	Lewis	son	1851		
Abraham	Lewis	son	1858		
Lazarus	Lewis	son	1860		
Reuben	**Lewis**		1845	1946	Manufacturer
Jennette	Lewis	wife	1853		
Esther	Lewis	daughter	1874		
Fannie	Lewis	daughter	1877		
Julius	**Litvin**		1885		Worked in a fur factory
Bertha	Litvin	wife	1886		
Isadore	Litvin	son	1911		
Robert	Litvin	son	1914		
Frank	**Miller**		1882		A filler at Lindenhurst Manufacturing Co.
Anna	Miller	wife	1890		
Herman	Miller	son	1908		
Molly	Miller	daughter	1909		
Max	Miller	son	1911		
David	Miller	son	1916		
Samuel	**Miller**		1885		Button maker
Anna	Miller	wife	1890		
Morris	Miller	son	1909		
David	Miller	son	1913		
Louis	Miller	son	1915		
Bertha	Miller	daughter	1917		

Table 13.1. Continued.

Louis	**Perlmann**			Treasurer of Neta Szarschea 1874
Jacob	**Rosenberg**			Member of Neta Szarschea 1874
Felix	**Rosenfeld**		1886	Worked in Max Kochman's embroidery
Helen	Rosenfeld	wife	1902	
Herman	**Rosenstein**			President of Neta Szarschea 1874
Abraham	**Rosenthal**			Member of Neta Szarschea 1874
Jacob	**Rosenthal**			Member of Neta Szarschea 1874
Marcus	**Rosenthal**			Member of Neta Szarschea 1874
Harry	**Rothenberg**		1877	Stitcher in an embroidery shop
Fanny	Rothenberg	wife	1892	
Gertrude	Rothenberg	daughter	1916	
Max	Rothenberg	son	1918	
Samuel	**Schotzsky**		1862	
Clara	Schotzsky	wife	1865	
Pauline	Schotzsky	daughter	1895	
Sarah	Schotzsky	daughter	1897	
Samuel	**Simon**		1883	Stitcher in an embroidery shop
Rachel	Simon	wife	1896	
Alice	Simon	daughter	1914	
Lillian	Simon	daughter	1916	
Bernard	Simon	son	1918	
Jacob	**Sobel**		1880	Worked in Louis Edelman's embroidery
Rebecca	Sobel	wife	1880	
Lillian	Sobel	daughter	1904	
Harry	Sobel	son	1907	
Samuel	Sobel	son	1909	
William	Sobel	son	1912	
Jessie	Sobel	daughter	1914	
Jacob	**Spitz**			Member of Neta Szarschea 1874
Simon	**Spitz**			Secretary of Neta Szarschea 1874

continued on next page

Table 13.1. Continued.

Isaac	**Taylor**				Trustee Hebrew Cemetery Assoc. 1887
Abraham	**Tarush**		1877		Shoemaker
Sarah	Tarush	wife	1885		
Ida	Tarush	daughter	1904		
Jacob	Tarush	son	1909		
Rose	Tarush	daughter	1913		
Julius	**Wachtel**		1882		Stitcher in an embroidery shop
Fanny	Wachtel	wife	1886		
Mary	Wachtel	daughter	1908		
Minnie	Wachtel	daughter	1910		
Samuel	Wachtel	son	1916		
Abraham	**Weinstein**		1867		President Lindenhurst HC 1914, '15, '17
Berna	Weinstein	wife	1873		
Mollie	Weinstein	daughter	1885	1966	m. Abraham Katzenbogen, lived in Babylon
Nathan	Weinstein	son			
Pauline	Weinstein	daughter			
Michael	Weinstein	son	1896	1987	m. Francis
Ruth	Weinstein	daughter	1901		
Harry	Weinstein	son	1903		
Ralph	Weinstein	son	1905		
Norman	Weinstein	son	1909		
Michael	**Weinstein**		1896	1987	Son of Abraham and Berna
Francis	Weinstein	wife	1897		
Leonard	Weinstein	son	1918		
Sadie	**Zenner**		1892		Niece of George Barasch

Table 13.2. Residents of Amityville

Carl	**Cedar**		1886	1931	Cousin of Philip Cedar from Babylon
Rose	(Glanz) Cedar	wife	1891	1978	
Estelle	Cedar	daughter	1915	2001	
Joseph	Cedar	son	1916	2011	
Isabel	Cedar	daughter	1918		
Gertie	**Cohen**		1892		Niece of Nathan Cohen
Nathan	**Cohen**		1849	1939	
Yetta	(Rothchild) Cohen	wife	1850	1925	

Table 13.2. Continued.

Isidor	**Cohn**		1855	1940	
Rachel	Cohn	wife	1865	1946	
Louis	**Cohn**		1887	1963	Son of Isidor and Rachel
Fannie	Cohn	wife	1888	1950	
Sarah	Cohn	daughter	1914		
David	Cohn	son	1915		
Belle	Cohn	daughter	1916		
Israel	**Edelman**		1878	1937	Hardware merchant
Lena	Edelman	wife	1883	1952	
Sadie	Edelman	daughter	1900		
Annie	Edelman	daughter	1902		
Julius	Edelman	son	1904		
Morris	**Gutowitz**		1865	1931	Jeweler
Anna	(Alasotsky) Gutowitz	first wife	1864	1897	
Rosie	Gutowitz	daughter	1889	1895	
Katherine	Gutowitz	daughter	1891	1911	
Benjamin	Gutowitz	son	1893	1967	
Esther	Gutowitz	daughter	1895		
Rose	(Savitt) Gutowitz	second wife	1870	1940	
Louis	Gutowitz	son	1900	1956	
Herman	Gutowitz	son	1907	1960	
Harry	**Hartmann**		1872	1902	Son of Jacob and Caroline
Julia	(Dubowitz) Hartmann	wife	1874		
Jacob	**Hartmann**		1842	1922	Pres. Hebrew Cemetery Assoc. 1887
Darrah	(Henschel) Hartmann	first wife		1869	
Samuel	Hartmann	son			Died at age 31
Freda	Hartmann	daughter			Died at age 4
Caroline	(Schwan) Hartmann	second wife	1845	1911	
Harry	Hartmann	son	1872		m. Julia Dubowitz
Rose	Hartmann	daughter	1876		
Bella	Hartmann	daughter	1877		m. Louis Kohen
Samuel	**Hartmann**		1802	1891	Trustee Hebrew Cemetery Assoc. 1887
Freda	(Wulf) Hartmann				Died before 1883

continued on next page

Table 13.2. Continued.

Jacob	Hartmann	son	1842	1922	m. Darrah Henschel, m. Caroline Schwan
Hannah	Hartmann	daughter			
Morris	**Henschel**		1835	1917	Tin and stove store owner
Rachel	Henschel	first wife	1841		Died before 1898
Samuel	Henschel	son	1859	1936	m. Martha Wolheim, lived in Port Jefferson
Minnie	Henschel	daughter	1861		m. Julius Levy, lived in Kings Park
Harris	Henschel	son	1863	1931	m. Maude Basford, lived in Kings Park
Jennie	Henschel	daughter	1866		
Emily	Henschel	daughter	1868	1961	m. Louis Lefkowitz
Esther	Henschel	daughter	1870		m. Julius Mayer
Aaron	Henschel	son	1872		m. Rose Davison, lived in Freeport
Dora	Henschel	daughter	1874	1963	m. Robert Freedman, lived in Glen Cove
Isaac	Henschel	son	1876		m. Bertha Kressley, lived in Smithtown
Rachel	Henschel	daughter	1880		
Montifiore	Henschel	son	1884		
David	Henschel	son	1885		
Amelia	Henschel	second wife	1847	1917	Married to Morris in 1898
Morris	**Karp**		1874		Dry goods merchant
Celia	(Resnick) Karp	wife	1875		
Alexander	Karp	son	1895		
Mandel	Karp	son	1897		
Eva	Karp	daughter	1899		
Jacob	Karp	son	1901	1939	
David	Karp	son	1903		
Rosie	Karp	daughter	1904		
Annie	Karp	daughter	1906		
Sylvia	Karp	daughter	1909		
Harry	Karp	son	1912		
Louis	**Kohen**	son	1874	1929	Dir. Amityville Merchants Assoc. 1906
Bella	(Hartmann) Kohen	wife	1877	1962	Daughter of Jacob and Caroline
Willard	Kohen	son	1900		
Carol	Kohen	daughter	1915		

Table 13.2. Continued.

Alexander	**Leifert**		1876		Trustee Lindenhurst Hebrew Cong. 1913
Annie	Leifert	wife	1878		
Louis	**Lefkowitz**		1864	1944	Had a tea, coffee, and spice business
Emily	(Henschel) Lefkowitz	wife	1868	1961	Daughter of Morris and Rachel
Dora	Lefkowitz	daughter	1890	1967	
Tressie	**Marks**		1884		Niece of Nathan Cohen
Jacob	**Mayer**		1855	1929	Barber
Eliza	(Kahn) Mayer	wife	1857		
Morris	Mayer	son	1878		
Julius	**Mayer**		1869	1946	
Esther	(Henschel) Mayer	wife	1870		Daughter of Morris and Rachel
Benno	**Rieser**		1888	1968	Trustee Lindenhurst Hebrew Cong. 1913
Margaret	(Falk) Rieser	wife	1890		
Bernard	Rieser	son	1918		
Morris	**Weiss**		1882		Dry goods merchant
Ida	(Hirsch) Weiss	wife	1879		Morris was her second husband
Abraham	Weiss	son	1908		
Emanuel	Hirsch		1899		Son of Ida and ? Hirsch
Frank	Hirsch		1900		Son of Ida and ? Hirsch

Table 13.3 Residents of Babylon

Alter	**Berman**		1881	1918	Had a confectionery store
Nellie	(Felcher) Berman	wife	1882	1967	Daughter of Joseph and Gertrude from Lindenhurst
Harry	Berman	son	1904		
David	Berman	son	1907	1991	
Harry	**Breitbard**		1881		Foreman at a clothing factory
Sadie	Breitbard	wife	1893		
Earl	Breitbard	son	1917		
Philip	**Cedar**		1890		Cousin of Carl Cedar from Amityville
Eva	Cedar	wife	1896		
Sidney	Cedar	son	1918		

continued on next page

Table 13.3. Continued.

Israel	**Charles**		1889		Brother-in-law of Fannie Kaufman
Max	**Cohen**		1880		Trustee Lindenhurst Hebrew Cong. 1913
Sara	Cohen	wife	1882		
Samuel	Cohen	son	1912		
Ethel	Cohen	daughter	1914		
Rosie	Cohen	daughter	1916		
Evelyn	Cohen	daughter	1917		
Harry	**Edelman**		1885		Dry goods merchant
Clara	Edelman	wife	1886	1921	
Rubin	Edelman	son	1909		
Isadore	Edelman	son	1915		
Leopold	**Fishel**		1838	1913	Brother of Andrew from Patchogue and Jonas from Riverhead
Therese	(Schott) Fishel	wife	1835	1902	Leopold was her second husband, first was Ephraim Fishel a cousin of Leopold, from Patchogue
Lillian	Fishel	daughter	1868	1948	
Lulu	Fishel	daughter	1869	1960	
Harry	Fishel	son	1872	1919	
Leo	Fishel	son	1877	1960	m. Laura Duerstein, lived in Freeport
Jacob	**Glass**		1884		Candy and cigar store owner
Katie	Glass	wife	1890		
Martin	Glass	son	1916		
Isidor	**Goldberger**		1877		Owned a restaurant
Rose	Goldberger	wife	1889		
Leon	Goldberger	son	1910		
Sidney	Goldberger	son	1913		
Esther	Goldberger	daughter	1917		
Moses	**Greenberg**		1871	1932	Second-hand furniture dealer
Rose	Greenberg	wife	1885		
Benjamin	Greenberg	son			
Caroline	Greenberg	daughter			
Abraham	**Katzenbogen**		1886	1948	
Mollie	(Weinstein) Katzenbogen	wife	1885	1966	Daughter of Abraham and Berna from Lindenhurst

Table 13.3. Continued.

Edward	Katzenbogen	son	1909		
Beatrice	Katzenbogen	daughter	1910	2008	m. Samuel Teich, lived in Huntington
John	**Kaufman**		1874		Fruit peddler
Fannie	Kaufman	wife	1870		
Samuel	Kaufman	son	1896		
Ruben	Kaufman	son	1900		
Harry	Kaufman	son	1901		
Louis	Kaufman	son	1903		
Rannie	Kaufman	daughter	1906		
Blanche	Kaufman	daughter	1907	1978	
Lester	Kaufman	son	1909		
Martin	Kaufman	son	1917		
Samuel	**Molbegat**		1881		Dry goods merchant
Sarah	(Jacobi) Molbegat	wife	1887		
Bertha	Molbegat	daughter	1906		
Abner	Molbegat	son	1908		
Rose	Molbegat	daughter	1915		
David	**Sandman**		1872		Son of Michael and Caroline from Glen Cove
Cecelia	(Thorman) Sandman	wife	1877		
Mabel	Sandman	daughter	1898		
Bernard	Sandman	son	1903		
Charles	**Siegel**		1868	1916	Brother of Harris, Isaac and Rose Felcher from Lindenhurst
Rachael	(Felcher) Siegel	wife	1875	1959	Daughter of Joseph and Gertrude from Lindenhurst
Solomon	Siegel	son	1895		
Morris	Siegel	son	1896		
Ruth	Siegel	daughter	1897	1979	
Ralph	Siegel	son	1899		
Sidney	Siegel	son	1903	1984	
Walter	Siegel	son	1907		
Sylvia	Siegel	daughter	1914		
Harris	**Siegel**		1871	1933	Brother of Charles, Isaac and Rose Felcher from Lindenhurst
Annie	(Levy) Siegel	wife	1883		
Ruth	Siegel	daughter	1903		

continued on next page

Table 13.3. Continued.

Solomon	Siegel	son	1907		
Isadore	Siegel	son	1914	1935	
Isaac	**Siegel**				Brother of Charles, Harris and Rose Felcher from Lindenhurst
Abraham	**Weinberg**		1868		Dry goods merchant
Hannah	Weinberg	wife	1884		
Herman	Weinberg	son	1899		
Jessie	Weinberg	son	1901		
Morton	Weinberg	son	1907		
Ruth	Weinberg	daughter	1911		
Eleanor	Weinberg	daughter	1916		

Table 13.4. Residents of Copiague

Isadore	**Smith**		1891		Plumber
Sophia	Smith	wife	1891		
Elsie	Smith	daughter	1918		

Chapter 14

Patchogue

*Including Bellport, Brookhaven, Medford, Sayville,
South Haven, and West Sayville*

In the mid-nineteenth century, Patchogue was a typical village visited by traveling merchants and others crossing the south shore of Long Island from west to east and vice versa. The first Jew in town was Andrew Fishel, a peddler who had opened his own store by 1860. Two years prior he married a Christian woman named Julia Ketcham with ancestral roots in America going back to 1635. He was drafted for military service during the Civil War but did not see any active duty. Andrew went on to be a successful merchant much like his brothers Jonas in Riverhead and Leopold in Babylon. Fishel was also involved in starting many important institutions in Patchogue, including the Suffolk Insurance Company in 1882, the Patchogue

Figure 79. Andrew Fishel's store in 1894 after it was sold to two of his clerks, Arthur Swezey and Fred Newins, and later became known as Swezey's. The building featured the unique architectural element known around town as Fishel tower. *Source*: Greater Patchogue Historical Museum.

Bank in 1885, and the Board of Trade in 1887, which was formed with the objective of bringing manufacturing to the village.

One such company lured to Patchogue in 1889 was the American Lace and Manufacturing Company. Their factory provided job opportunities for existing residents with steady employment giving out of towners a good reason to move to Patchogue rather than other villages. The production of lace curtains and tablecloths grew over the years, enabling the company to expand and hire more workers. By 1912 American Lace was renamed Patchogue Manufacturing Company and had 650 employees.

The arrival of new residents in town brought a higher demand for everyday goods and services that gave rise to new businesses. Merchants set up shop and raised families as the village grew to new heights in the 1890s. Enough Jews had moved to Patchogue for a Hebrew Society to

Figures 80. Lace mill, c. 1906. *Source*: Greater Patchogue Historical Museum.

be formed by 1900 with services held at multiple locations including the United Methodist Church and the Lyceum building on Lake Street. A formal congregation known as the Patchogue Hebrew Congregational Church was incorporated in February 1904 with eight trustees: Maurice Beck, Samuel Cohn, Joseph Drue, Lewis Feynman, Louis Laikin, Harold Lichenstein, Samuel Perkal, and Abraham Ratchick. Seven of the eight were merchants, and some had their own stores in the center of the village on Main Street and Ocean Avenue.

One of the trustees, Maurice Beck, opened a women's clothing store in 1892. His sister Annie married Nathan Goldin in 1896 and lived in Greenport. By 1905 Maurice and Nathan were in partnership owning three stores, one in Patchogue, one in Greenport, and another in Sag Harbor. Another trustee, Samuel Cohn, was the proprietor of a men's clothing store on South Ocean Avenue in 1879, and later his wife Emma ran her own clothing business at 39 West Main Street.

Lewis Feynman had a dry goods and furnishings store on Ocean Avenue. Abraham Ratchick and his partner Louis Monnies established the Star Furniture Company and expanded the business in 1914, buying out Feynman to create R & M Department Store.

Figures 81 and 82. Advertisements for stores owned by Abraham Ratchick and Louis Monnies. *Source*: *Suffolk County News*, July 3, 1908, and November 13, 1914.

Another early member of the Jewish community in Patchogue was Duvid Verchaglad, who changed his name to Daniel Davidow shortly after his arrival in America in 1890. He and his wife Ethel were married in their small village of Zvenigorodka in Ukraine and had three children with one on the way when Daniel immigrated to the United States by himself. Two years later the family was reunited when Ethel, Edward, Minnie, Harry, and Louis joined with Daniel to make their home in Bay Shore where they lived for six years. Daniel became active in Jewish affairs as a director of the Bay Shore United Hebrew Benevolent Cemetery Association when it was formed in 1897. The following year the Davidows, now a family of seven with the birth of Israel in 1895, moved to Patchogue where Daniel operated a dry goods store and later a grocery. The couple had two more children, Laura and Samuel, both born in Patchogue.

Daniel and Ethel arrived in Patchogue just as the dozen or so Jewish families were beginning to organize. Both would play a prominent role with Daniel as a trustee of the synagogue in 1905 and vice president two years later while Ethel was a vice president of the Daughters of Israel, a

Figure 83. Daniel and Ethel Davidow, seated in center, surrounded by their seven children, spouses, and grandchildren, c. 1929. *Source*: Courtesy of Lawrence Davidow.

philanthropic organization giving to those in need regardless of their religious affiliation.

Not all businesses run by residents of Patchogue were located in the heart of the village. Others such as Israel Katz had to ride out of town to work at the farm he owned in Holtsville. Katz came to the United States from Russia in 1906 and started out as a cow and horse dealer. He later established a wholesale dairy business on his farm that also had a slaughterhouse on the premises. Smaller villages near Patchogue also attracted Jews, some only on a seasonal basis. Francis Gerber was a peddler living in Sayville by 1870 who owned $600 worth of property in town. Two years later he opened a department store bearing his surname at Main and Smith Streets that Francis would operate for fifty years until his death in 1921.

Herman Leblang was a cattle dealer from Budapest who immigrated to the United States in 1885. He and his wife Theresa were Manhattanites living on First Avenue in 1892 as were Jonas and Rosa Hecht who resided

Figure 84. Gerber's Department Store on Main Street in Sayville, c. 1907. *Source*: From the collection of the author.

on Clinton Street. On April 20 Herman and Theresa purchased two plots of land in Bellport, 100' × 25' each, from the New York and Brooklyn Suburban Investment Company of New York. In November Leblang and Hecht were two of the ten men who founded an Orthodox congregation called Agidath Achim Ansche Bellport. The Leblangs were not year-round residents of Bellport, nor was their son Joseph, who also owned property there. Joseph Leblang achieved some notoriety originating the idea of selling discounted tickets to the masses for Broadway shows beginning in the 1890s. "Joe Broadway," as he became known, established the Central and Public Service Theatre Ticket Office in Times Square and built a Broadway empire worth $20 million at the time of his death in 1931 (a value of $342 million in 2021 dollars). It is not known how long Agidath Achim lasted as no records exist, but it is noteworthy for being just the third Jewish congregation to be established on Long Island. As for Herman and Theresa Leblang, they made the unusual decision to leave the United States and went back to Budapest in 1895. Whatever their intention was, it must not have panned out because they stayed in Budapest for just two years before returning to New York.

In the years following the establishment of the Patchogue Hebrew Congregational Church in 1904 Jewish life thrived within a very accepting community. The congregation erected a synagogue on the north side of Oak Street just east of Jayne Avenue opening that year with the first service held on September 9. The following year the Jewish women formed the Daughters of Israel in Patchogue led by Caroline Manus as president, Ethel Davidow as vice president, Haska Tellman as recording and financial secretary, Jennie Monnies as treasurer, and three trustees Rose Marganoff, Rebecca Charach, and Sarah Simon. The Patchogue Hebrew Mutual Aid Society was chartered in 1906, and in 1911 the Patchogue Hebrew Cemetery Association was established with grounds located north of the village.

Figure 85. The Leblang family, c. 1889. L to R, back row: Joe and Minnie; front row: Rudolph, Theresa, Hugh, Herman, and Jennie. *Source*: Courtesy of Nancy Leblang.

A growing community through the 1920s necessitated plans to expand resulting in a new synagogue at the same location as the first. Once the old synagogue was torn down a new larger modern structure was erected in its place opening in time for Rosh Hashanah in 1931. Not just a synagogue for ritual purposes, the new building was designed to serve the social, educational, and recreational needs of its members reflected in their new name Patchogue Jewish Center. In the 1950s the congregation adopted the name Temple Beth El as it is known today.

~~~~~~~~

A Family Law Practice for over One Hundred Years

While the majority of Jewish residents on Long Island in the late nineteenth and early twentieth centuries made a living as merchants or craftsmen, there were some who broke the mold and established themselves in professional careers that required a postgraduate degree. Harry Davidow, son of Daniel and Ethel, studied law at New York University and upon being admitted to the New York State Bar Association in March 1913, he opened his law practice in Patchogue.

In the early days Harry handled all matters requiring legal expertise out of his second-floor office on West Main Street in Patchogue. He was always reliable, confidential, and served his clients with the highest level of excellence, key attributes Harry passed down to future generations and the hallmark qualities of the firm today. Harry married Rae Kirshberg in 1918 and had two sons, Sanford and Wallace, who both became lawyers. Sanford joined his father in 1948, leading to a name change for the firm to Davidow & Davidow. Four years later Wallace entered the family business.

Sanford and Wallace had differing personalities but made a great team, carrying on the legacy of the firm together after their father died in 1954. Sanford was a strong litigator who enjoyed spending time in court while Wallace was happy to work behind the scenes on contractual matters and doing research. Success enabled the brothers to build their own new office space in 1961 at 110 North Ocean Avenue.

The third generation of the Davidow family became part of the firm when Wallace's son Lawrence got his law degree in 1986. By that time

Figures 86 and 87. Harry Davidow's New York State Bar Association certification from 1913, and his grandson Lawrence, who currently runs the firm. *Source*: Courtesy of Lawrence Davidow.

Sanford had retired, and the father-son duo was ready to take their business in a new direction. With Lawrence asserting some new ideas, they decided to focus on a specialty area rather than practicing general law and became the first full-service elder law firm in Suffolk County. Wallace eased into retirement in the early 1990s, giving full control to Lawrence who moved the office to Islandia in 1992. Since then the firm has opened two additional branch offices located in Garden City and Mattituck.

᎓᎒᎐

Keeping the Heritage of Farming Alive in Brookhaven

Upon entering the property at 2948 Montauk Highway in Brookhaven a seasonal farm stand offers a bounty of local produce and flowers for sale. Meghan Bush has gathered much of the harvest from the land cultivated by her and her father. Just beyond the neatly displayed eggplant, cauliflower, squash, and tomatoes is a building that is barren on the inside except for some empty crates. On the outside hangs a variety of sickles and scythes, not to be used but rather on display. They are the first indication that this property is not just an ordinary farm, rather it is a historical preservation of the way rural Long Islanders made their living more than a century ago.

Meghan's father, Ronald Bush, grew up in his grandfather's farmhouse in Holtsville until moving to Patchogue in 1941. He owned a real estate business for over thirty-five years; however, farming has always been in his blood. On a cool September morning Ron spryly climbs up on a tractor, starting the engine for his visitor and proudly mentions that the newest of his fleet of tractors used on the farm is from 1953. In his spare time Ron assembles and displays thousands of items he has amassed over the decades from purchasing farm equipment and tools at auctions and bankruptcy sales. His vast and varied collection includes large wagons and carriages used in the nineteenth century, small hand tools and implements found in a carpenter's shop, oyster rakes and whaling harpoons, knives and blades in all shapes and sizes, everything needed to run a dairy business, and much more. Of all these artifacts his most prized possessions are the many noteworthy pieces that have a personal connection for Ron coming from the farms owned and operated by his uncle and grandfather.

Ron's grandparents, Israel and Anna Katz, made their home on West Avenue in Patchogue. Israel, referred to as "Pop" by his grandson, earned a living as a cattle dealer working a forty-acre farm in Holtsville. Pop's daily routine began at 5 a.m. with a shot of whisky before going out to the barn to milk the cows. At 8 a.m. he would have a breakfast consisting of eggs fried in schmaltz (chicken fat) and another shot of whisky. Work on the farm commenced until noon with a break for lunch, a third shot of whisky, and back out to tend the cattle. A late afternoon cold beer was enjoyed before completing his twelve-hour workday at 5 p.m.

Israel and Anna had six children, the oldest being Sarah who married Jacob Bush from Greenport in 1930. Jacob had a successful dental practice in Patchogue, while the Katzes' second child, Abraham, took up the family business. Abe learned to work the farm under his father's tutelage and started out on his own in 1933, leasing the Dune Alpin dairy farm in East Hampton. Three years later Abe purchased the farm for $10,000 and operated his dairy business until selling the land to a real estate developer in 1974.

Today Ron still does real estate appraisals, maintains a farm stand on Fire Island, and shares his firsthand knowledge of the history of agriculture and farming on Long Island with those visiting his personal museum. Ron overcame coronavirus in the spring of 2020 and at eighty-seven shows no signs of slowing down.

Figure 88. Ron Bush in the attic of a cow barn on his property, one of a half-dozen buildings that house his collection of antique farm equipment, tools, and much more. *Source*: Photo by Brad Kolodny.

Table 14.1. Residents of Patchogue

Samuel	**Backomitch**		1880		Ladies tailor
Lena	(Mathien) Backomitch	wife	1884		Sister of Fannie Mathien
Lewis	Backomitch	son	1904		
Herman	Backomitch	son	1906		
Harry	Backomitch	son	1908		
Benjamin	**Beck**		1860	1940	Brother of Maurice and Annie Goldin from Greenport
Sarah	(Malbin) Beck	wife	1869	1944	
Sidney	Beck	son	1885	1912	
Libby	Beck	daughter	1890		
Leo	Beck	son	1893	1919	
Sadie	Beck	daughter			
Olga	Beck	daughter	1899	1968	
Norman	Beck	son	1903	1967	
Maurice	**Beck**		1875	1953	Treasurer Patchogue Hebrew Assn. 1903
Samuel	**Berkowitz**		1879	1935	Tailor
Lena	Berkowitz	wife	1883	1942	
Louis	Berkowitz	son	1903	1963	
Herman	Berkowitz	son	1905	1974	
Harry	Berkowitz	son	1907	1982	
Martin	Berkowitz	son	1912	1977	
Lewis	**Cantor**		1884	1967	Merchant
Annie	(Polansky) Cantor	wife	1895		
Louis	**Cantor**		1884		Worked at lace factory
Nathan	Cantor	son	1906		
Morris	Cantor	son	1908		
Benjamin	**Charach**		1874		Dir. Patchogue Hebrew Cemetery 1911
Rebecca	Charach	wife	1880		Trustee Daughters of Israel 1905
Charles	Charach	son	1904		
Judith	Charach	daughter	1908		
Bernard	Charach	son	1915		
Benjamin	**Cohn**		1858		Peddler
Louis	**Cohn**		1873	1928	Trustee Hebrew Mutual Aid Assn. 1906
Bessie	Cohn	wife	1880	1946	Member Daughters of Israel 1915

Table 14.1. Continued.

Benjamin	Cohn	son	1899	1980	
Ida	Cohn	daughter	1900		
Herman	Cohn	son	1902		
Henry	Cohn	son	1905		
Samuel	**Cohn**		1854	1938	Men's clothing store owner
Emma	(Seylon) Cohn	wife	1855	1951	
Etta	Cohn	daughter	1879	1964	
Mabel	Cohn	daughter	1884	1953	m. Abraham Goldstein lived in Southampton
Dewitt	Cohn	son	1888	1968	
Leonard	Cohn	son	1891		
Lucille	Cohn	daughter	1893		
Chaim	**Cooper**		1850		Dir. Patchogue Hebrew Cemetery 1911
Dora	Cooper	wife	1851		
Stephen	**Croker**		1887		Factory laborer
Daniel	**Davidow**		1858	1936	Trustee Patchogue Hebrew Cong. 1905
Ethel	(Pinkovsky) Davidow	wife	1860	1941	VP Daughters of Israel
Edward	Davidow	son	1884	1964	
Minnie	Davidow	daughter	1888	1966	m. Samuel Girshoff
Harry	Davidow	son	1889	1954	m. Rae Kirshberg
Louis	Davidow	son	1890	1968	
Isidore	Davidow	son	1895	1982	
Laura	Davidow	daughter	1899	1974	
Samuel	Davidow	son	1900	1952	
Harry	**Davidow**		1889	1954	Son of Daniel and Ethel
Rae	(Kirshberg) Davidow	wife	1897	1973	
Joseph	**Drue**		1871		Member Patchogue Hebrew Cong. 1904
Heddy	Drue	wife	1880		
Harry	**Eisenburgh**		1883		
Sarah	Eisenburgh	wife	1879		
Beccy	Eisenburgh	daughter	1904		
Simon	**Feinberg**		1897		Son of Isaac and Mary from East Quogue
Francis	(Tarnopol) Feinberg	wife	1898		Sister of Pauline Greenfield

continued on next page

Table 14.1. Continued.

Lewis	**Feynman**		1862		President Patchogue Hebrew Assn. 1903
Annie	Feynman	wife	1862		
Laura	Feynman	daughter	1888		
Melville	Feynman	son	1890	1946	
Addie	Feynman	daughter	1894		
Arthur	Feynman	son	1896		
Bessie	Feynman	daughter	1898		
Andrew	**Fishel**		1828	1902	Wife was not Jewish
Ephraim	**Fishel**		1827	1866	Cousin of Andrew
Therese	(Schott) Fishel	wife	1835	1902	m. Second husband Leopold Fishel, lived in Babylon
Anna	Fishel	daughter	1855		
Fanny	Fishel	daughter	1858		
Eugene	Fishel	son	1859	1907	Attorney
Gustave	Fishel	son	1861		
Nathan	**Fuss**		1873	1952	
Rose	Fuss	wife	1873	1952	
Louis	Fuss	son	1897		
Julius	Fuss	son	1898		
Cecilia	Fuss	daughter	1900		
Fannie	Fuss	daughter	1901		
Achiel	**Gelfer**		1858	1907	Father of Adolph
Adolph	**Gelfer**		1875	1951	
Dora	Gelfer	wife	1877	1969	
Samuel	Gelfer	son	1901		
May	Gelfer	daughter	1903		
Francis	Gelfer	daughter	1907	1937	
George	Gelfer	son	1908	1992	
Maurice	Gelfer	son	1911	1986	
Meyer	**Gersowit**		1880	1949	Tailor
Pauline	Gersowit	wife	1884	1960	
Victoria	Gersowit	daughter	1909		
Sarah	Gersowit	daughter	1910		
Martha	Gersowit	daughter	1918		
Samuel	**Ginsberg**		1876		Fruit dealer
Annie	Ginsberg	wife	1872		
Minnie	Ginsberg	daughter	1898		
Herman	Ginsberg	son	1900		
Martha	Ginsberg	daughter	1904		
Rosie	Ginsberg	daughter	1906		

Table 14.1. Continued.

Jennie	Ginsberg	daughter	1910		
Samuel	**Girshoff**		1880	1967	Merchant
Minnie	(Davidow) Girshoff	wife	1890	1966	Daughter of Daniel and Ethel
Paul	Girshoff	son	1912	2003	
Dorothy	Girshoff	daughter	1916		
William	**Goldin**		1868	1926	
Fannie	Goldin	wife	1875	1939	
Ida	Goldin	daughter	1897		
Max	Goldin	son	1899		
Harry	Goldin	son	1900	1945	
Bertha	Goldin	daughter	1903		
Harry	**Goldstein**		1872		
Annie	Goldstein	wife	1880		
Ellie	Goldstein	son	1901		
Herman	Goldstein	son	1903		
Sidney	Goldstein	son	1906		
J.	**Goldstein**		1864		
Beccy	Goldstein	wife	1876		
Bennie	Goldstein	son	1897		
Goldi	Goldstein	daughter	1899		
Abie	**Gordon**		1890		
Harry	**Gordon**		1888		
Freida	Gordon	wife	1889		
Nathan	Gordon	son	1914	1982	
Samuel	**Gordon**		1880	1950	
Minnie	Gordon	wife	1884	1961	
Dorothy	Gordon	daughter	1912		
Nathan	Gordon	son	1915		
Wolf	**Greenberg**		1868	1935	Dry goods merchant
David	**Greenfield**		1882		Brother of Majer
Helen	Greenfield	wife	1893		
Majer	**Greenfield**		1880		Brother of David
Pauline	(Tarnopol) Greenfield	wife	1894		Sister of Francis Feinberg
Frederick	Greenfield	son	1913		
Amelia	Greenfield	daughter	1914		
Estella	Greenfield	daughter	1915		
Manuel	Greenfield	son	1917		
Isidore	**Hochheiser**		1888	1960	Brother of Joseph

continued on next page

Table 14.1. Continued.

Joseph	**Hochheiser**		1874	1955	Brother of Isidore
Lena	(Hardstein) Hochheiser	wife	1873	1929	
Samuel	Hochheiser	son	1908	1995	
Jacob	Hochheiser	son	1912	1990	
Henry	Hochheiser	son	1913	1983	
Morris	**Hodkin**		1866	1933	Trustee Hebrew Mutual Aid Assn. 1906
Ada	Hodkin	wife	1862	1962	
Lawrence	Hodkin	son	1898	1955	
Sara	Hodkin	daughter	1898	1985	
Louis	Hodkin	son	1902		
Anna	Hodkin	daughter	1904		
Max	**Isaacs**		1885		Laborer in a factory
Jennie	(Levin) Isaacs	wife	1889		
Dinah	Isaacs	daughter	1910		
Samuel	**Jacoby**		1873		Secretary Patchogue Hebrew Con. 1910
Bessie	Jacoby	wife	1881		
Abraham	**Katz**		1870	1914	
Sarah	Katz	wife	1875	1934	
Esther	Katz	daughter	1897	1959	
Isidore	Katz	son	1899		
Joseph	Katz	son	1904		
Israel	**Katz**		1881	1973	Wholesale milk and cattle dealer
Anna	(Cohen) Katz	wife	1886	1944	
Sarah	Katz	daughter	1909		
Abraham	Katz	son	1910	1978	
Ida	Katz	daughter	1912	1914	
Beth	Katz	daughter	1915		
William	**Katz**		1876		
Ada	(Belkowitz) Katz	wife	1880		
Esther	Katz	daughter	1897		
Betty	Katz	daughter	1901	1986	
Anna	Katz	daughter	1903		
Rose	Katz	daughter	1908		
Henry	Katz	son	1910		
Samuel	**Kramer**		1875		
?	Kramer	wife			

Table 14.1. Continued.

Minnie	Kramer	daughter	1899		m. Simon Brown, lived in East Quogue
Herman	Kramer	son	1900		
Martha	Kramer	daughter	1904		
Rose	Kramer	daughter	1906		
Morris	**Kremen**		1886		
Herman	**Kremer**		1890		Nephew of Jacob Kremer
Jacob	**Kremer**		1872		Trustee Patchogue Hebrew Cong. 1907
Bessie	Kremer	wife	1885		Member Daughters of Israel 1915
Tonnie	**Kueyk**		1834		
Louis	**Laikin**			1921	Member Patchogue Hebrew Cong. 1904
Jacob	**Levy**		1862		Trustee Hebrew Mutual Aid Assn. 1906
Eva	Levy	wife	1868		
Pearl	Levy	daughter	1890		
Max	Levy	son	1891		Factory laborer
Frieda	Levy	daughter	1895		
Aron	Levy	son	1897		
Frank	Levy	son	1899		
?	Levy	son	1901		
Sarah	Levy	daughter	1903		
Mary	Levy	daughter	1906		
Harold	**Lichenstein**		1863	1914	Member Patchogue Hebrew Cong. 1904
Lillian	Lichenstein	wife	1862	1946	
Isaac	Lichenstein	son	1889		Confectionery store owner
Emily	Lichenstein	daughter	1891		Factory laborer
Rose	Lichenstein	daughter	1893		Factory laborer
Louis	Lichenstein	son	1894		
Etta	Lichenstein	daughter	1899		
H.	**Luchinski**				President Patchogue Hebrew Con. 1905
Mayer	**Liffshitz**		1871		
Celia	Liffshitz	wife	1882		
Milton	Liffshitz	son	1899		
Israel	Liffshitz	son	1901		
Joshua	Liffshitz	son	1907		

continued on next page

Table 14.1. Continued.

Isaac	**Manus**		1845		Cigar store owner
Caroline	Manus	wife	1852		President Daughters of Israel 1905
Bernard	**Marganoff**		1884	1932	Hardware store owner
Rose	Marganoff	wife	1884	1964	Trustee Daughters of Israel 1905
Harry	Marganoff	son	1908	1980	
Daniel	Marganoff	son	1912		
Fannie	**Mathien**		1888		Sister of Lena Backomitch
Abraham	**Mendelson**		1858	1935	
Sarah	Mendelson	wife	1858	1942	
Mark	Mendelson	son	1888		
Mary	Mendelson	daughter	1892		
Hattie	Mendelson	daughter	1894		
Frieda	Mendelson	daughter	1896		
Nathan	**Mendelson**		1855	1928	
Rose	Mendelson	wife	1856	1932	
Sadie	Mendelson	daughter	1886		
Abraham	Mendelson	son	1891		
Hattie	Mendelson	daughter	1894		
Ella	Mendelson	daughter	1896		
Louis	**Monnies**				Trustee Hebrew Mutual Aid Assn. 1906
Jennie	Monnies	wife			Treasurer Daughters of Israel 1905
Max	**Peltz**		1886	1966	Son of Morris and Annie from Riverhead
Nellie	Peltz	wife	1892		
Esther	Peltz	daughter	1916		
Samuel	**Perkal**		1864	1934	Member Patchogue Hebrew Cong. 1904
Mildred	Perkal	wife	1862		
Ida	Perkal	daughter	1887	1952	
Emma	Perkal	daughter	1889		
Reuben	Perkal	son	1891		
Lena	Perkal	daughter	1893		
Anna	Perkal	daughter	1895	1948	
Fannie	Perkal	daughter	1897		
Eleanor	Perkal	daughter		1985	
Daniel	**Platt**		1853		Trustee Patchogue Hebrew Cong. 1905

Table 14.1. Continued.

Bertha	Platt	wife	1854		
Henrietta	Platt	daughter	1879		
Emma	Platt	daughter	1882		
Martha	Platt	daughter	1885		
Albert	Platt	son	1887		
Lillie	Platt	daughter	1889		
Sidney	Platt	son	1897		
Henry	**Platt**		1869		Brother of Daniel
Freidel	**Rabinovitz**		1881		Son of Morris and Minnie
Lena	Rabinovitz	wife	1883		
Ida	Rabinovitz	daughter	1904		
Samuel	Rabinovitz	son	1905		
Morris	**Rabinovitz**		1861		Cabinet maker
Minnie	Rabinovitz	wife	1861		
Freidel	Rabinovitz	son	1881		m. Lena
Jacob	**Raffe**		1890		
Jennie	Raffe	wife	1892		
Esther	Raffe	daughter	1908		
Rosie	Raffe	daughter	1910		
Barney	**Raffie**		1880		Laborer in a factory
Lena	Raffie	wife	1880		
Sammy	Raffie	son	1902	1980	
Teddy	Raffie	son	1907		
Henry	Raffie	son	1910		
Solomon	Raffie	son	1910		
Abraham	**Ratchick**		1877	1928	VP Patchogue Hebrew Cong. 1904
Sarah	(Peltz) Ratchick	wife	1883	1947	Daughter of Morris and Annie from Riverhead
Leon	Ratchick	son	1904	1965	
Rae	Ratchick	daughter	1908		
Milton	Ratchick	son	1911		
Irving	Ratchick	son	1913	2001	
Sylvia	Ratchick	daughter	1916	2004	
Mendel	**Rubin**		1879	1919	
Rose	(Melnick) Rubin	wife	1880	1973	
Shlomo	Rubin	son	1904	1906	
Samuel	Rubin	son	1907		
Mildred	Rubin	daughter	1908	1991	

continued on next page

Table 14.1. Continued.

Philip	**Rubin**		1883	1964	Chauffer
Rose	Rubin	wife	1883		
Lillian	Rubin	daughter	1909		
May	Rubin	daughter	1913		
Max	**Ryana**		1878		Fruit peddler
Sarah	Ryana	wife	1880		
Bella	Ryana	wife	1898		
Joseph	Ryana	son	1900		
Louis	Ryana	son	1902		
Michael	Ryana	son	1907		
Mattie	Ryana	daughter	1909		
Joseph	**Schneider**		1887		Salesman for a paper company
Alice	(Siegel) Schneider	wife	1892		
Elie	**Schwartz**		1872		
Fanny	Schwartz	wife	1880		
Rosie	Schwartz	daughter	1902		
Charles	Schwartz	son	1906		
Jennie	Schwartz	daughter	1907		
Dora	Schwartz	daughter	1910		
Jacob	Schwartz	son	1914		
Harris	**Seltzer**		1865	1943	Peddler
Annie	(Greenberg) Seltzer	wife	1869	1934	
Samuel	Seltzer	son	1888		
Sarah	Seltzer	daughter	1889		
Isaac	Seltzer	son	1890		
Sallie	Seltzer	daughter	1891		
Solomon	Seltzer	son	1894	1946	
Jacob	Seltzer	son	1898		
Abie	Seltzer	son	1901		
Minnie	Seltzer	daughter	1903		
Mildred	Seltzer	daughter	1905		
Herman	Seltzer	son	1906		
Achiel	**Shapiro**		1842	1918	Trustee Hebrew Mutual Aid Assn. 1906
Annie	Shapiro	wife	1863		
Ida	Shapiro	daughter	1892		
Louis	Shapiro	son	1894		
Mary	Shapiro	daughter	1896		
Samuel	**Siegel**		1871		Trustee Patchogue Hebrew Cong. 1910

Table 14.1. Continued.

Mary	Siegel	wife	1872		
Samuel J.	Siegel	son	1892		
Morris	Siegel	son	1896		
Tillie	Siegel	daughter	1894		
Annie	Siegel	daughter	1908		
Max	**Simon**				Trustee Patchogue Hebrew Cong. 1907
Meyer	**Simon**		1879	1947	Brother of Morris from Sag Harbor
Sarah	Simon	wife	1882		Trustee Daughters of Israel 1915
Arthur	Simon	son	1903		
Edith	Simon	daughter	1905		
Beatrice	Simon	daughter	1907		
Alex	**Sinkoff**		1860		Dry goods peddler
Sarah	Sinkoff	wife	1862		
Samuel	Sinkoff	son	1882	1959	
Max	Sinkoff	son	1888		
Mary	Sinkoff	daughter	1898		
Libbie	Sinkoff	daughter	1898		
Louis	**Sinkoff**		1857	1914	Dir. Patchogue Hebrew Cemetery 1911
Max	**Sinkoff**		1885	1975	Wholesale produce business
Bessie	Sinkoff	wife	1893		
Sidney	Sinkoff	son	1914		
Herbert	Sinkoff	son	1917		
Joseph	**Snider**		1885		
Samuel	**Souvener**		1883		
Ida	Souvener	wife	1885		
Harry	Souvener	son	1904		
Jennie	Souvener	daughter	1906		
Ruth	Souvener	daughter	1910		
Jette	**Stern**		1853		Sister-in-law of Isaac Manus
Samuel	**Stockman**		1871		Shoemaker
Celia	Stockman	wife	1878		
Alex	Stockman	son	1903		
Abraham	Stockman	son	1904		
Sarah	Stockman	daughter	1905		
Wolff	**Sugal**		1879	1941	Shoemaker
Lena	(Miller) Sugal	wife	1877	1960	

continued on next page

Table 14.1. Continued.

Philip	Sugal	son	1906		
Michael	Sugal	son	1908		
Julius	Sugal	son	1910	1983	
Jennie	Sugal	daughter	1915		
Hyman	**Tellman**		1877	1957	Factory laborer
Haska	(Silverman) Tellman	wife	1884	1930	Secretary Daughters of Israel 1905
Daniel	Tellman	son	1902	1943	
Gertrude	Tellman	daughter	1906		
Mayer	**Tellman**		1877	1932	
Sofia	Tellman	wife	1887	1942	
Dinah	Tellman	daughter	1907		
Esther	Tellman	daughter	1910		
Ida	Tellman	daughter	1916		
Bennie	**Treniski**		1876		
Gertrude	Treniski	wife	1882		
Paul	Treniski	son	1900		
Jacob	Treniski	son	1902		
Sarah	Treniski	daughter	1906		
Willie	Treniski	son	1908		
Samuel	**Udeskin**		1884		Laborer in lace mill
Mary	Udeskin	wife	1883		
Jacob	**Umeski**		1882		House painter
Libbie	Umeski	wife	1884		
Mollie	Umeski	daughter	1908		
Uddie	Umeski	son	1910		
Max	**Weiner**		1877		Fruit peddler
Sarah	(Shapiro) Weiner	wife	1878		
Bertha	Weiner	daughter	1899		
Joseph	Weiner	son	1900		
Lewis	Weiner	son	1903		
Myer	Weiner	son	1908		
Mary	Weiner	daughter	1910		
Jacob	Weiner	son	1912		
Abraham	Weiner	son	1917		
Edward	**Wilson**		1895		Mechanic
Josephine	(Terrell) Wilson	wife	1896		
Solomon	**Wolfson**				Trustee Hebrew Mutual Aid Assn. 1906
Alexander	**Zickerman**		1877	1969	Son of Martin and Fannie

Table 14.1. Continued.

Mary	Zickerman	wife	1889	1953	
Ruth	Zickerman	daughter	1913		
Elisia	Zickerman	daughter	1916		
Martin	**Zickerman**		1852	1915	
Fannie	Zickerman	wife	1857	1923	
Alexander	Zickerman	son	1877	1969	m. Mary
Celia	Zickerman	daughter			
Emma	Zickerman	daughter			
Samuel	Zickerman	son	1889		
Grace	Zickerman	daughter	1891	1934	
Emil	Zickerman	son	1893	1961	
Julius	Zickerman	son	1895		
Helen	Zickerman	daughter	1900		
Louis	Zickerman	son	1904		
Max	**Zucker**		1852	1915	Rabbi
Jennie	Zucker	wife	1863		
Maurice	Zucker	son			
Sarah	Zucker	daughter			
Esther	Zucker	daughter			
Ida	Zucker	daughter	1894		

Table 14.2. Residents of Bellport

Jacob	**Amoschefsky**				Second Trustee Agidath Achim 1892
Barnet	**Blaustein**				VP Agidath Achim 1892
Pincus	**Goldstein**				Third Trustee Agidath Achim 1892
Moses	**Gotlieb**				Treasurer Agidath Achim 1892
Elias	**Gotlieb**				First Trustee Agidath Achim 1892
Barnet	**Grieser**				Secretary Agidath Achim 1892
Jonas	**Hecht**		1847		Member Agidath Achim 1892
Rosa	(Kodziesen) Hecht	wife	1849		
Lora	Hecht	daughter	1887		
Gisela	Hecht	daughter	1891		
Herman	**Leblang**		1846	1922	Member Agidath Achim 1892
Theresa	(Brust) Leblang	wife	1847	1929	

continued on next page

Table 14.2. Continued.

Joseph	Leblang	son	1874	1931	Broadway discount ticket empire
Hermina	Leblang	daughter	1876	1936	
Rudolf	Leblang	son	1882		
Jennie	Leblang	daughter	1883	1952	
Hugh	Leblang	son	1885		
Herman	**Lerner**				Sgt. At Arms Agidath Achim 1892
Israel	**Levy**		1865		Cousin of Samuel
Anna	Levy	wife	1874		
Harry	Levy	son	1889		
Jacob	Levy	son	1893		
Susan	Levy	daughter	1896		
Samuel	**Levy**		1866		Cousin of Israel
Sarah	(Chiese) Levy	wife	1870		
Samuel	Levy	son	1884		
Pauline	Levy	daughter	1889		
Marion	Levy	daughter	1891		
Barney	Levy	son	1893		
Meier	**Meisels**				President Agidath Achim 1892

Table 14.3. Residents of Brookhaven

Hillel	**Shapiro**		1882	1974	Farm worker
Tillie	Shapiro	wife	1889	1958	
Nathan	Simson				May have been a shopkeeper in 1705

Table 14.4. Residents of Medford

Harry	**Weiss**		1870		Milkman
Esther	(Wachtel) Weiss	wife	1870		
Rebecca	Weiss	daughter	1892		
Martha	Weiss	daughter	1894		
Joseph	Weiss	son	1899		

Table 14.5. Residents of Sayville

Edward	**Cohen**		1857	1898	Clothing merchant

Table 14.5. Continued.

Sarah	(Hecht) Cohen	wife	1862	1946	First husband was Edward's brother
Estelle	Cohen	daughter	1884		
?	Cohen	son			
?	Cohen	daughter			
Bennet	**Cohn**		1864		Clothing merchant
?	Cohn	first wife			
Leon	Cohn	son	1883		
Donald	Cohn	son	1891	1981	
Barbara	(Schwartz) Cohn	second wife	1868	1931	
Etta	Cohn	daughter	1896		
Florence	**Denise**		1907		Niece of Solomon Engle
Solomon	**Engle**		1863		
Minnie	Engle	wife	1866		
Francis	**Gerber**		1842	1921	Department store owner
Fannie	(Hirsch) Gerber	first wife	1854	1904	Sister of Clara and Gilbert Hirsch
Estella	Gerber	daughter	1877	1921	
Clara	(Hirsch) Gerber	second wife	1862	1938	Sister of Fannie and Gilbert Hirsch
Gilbert	**Hirsch**		1865	1933	Brother of Fannie and Clara
Joseph	**Levy**		1883		Son of Benjimen and Mary from Bay Shore
Tessie	(Tennenberg) Levy	wife	1885		Daughter of Max and Annie
Ira	Levy	son	1911		
Ruth	Levy	daughter	1912	1976	
Norma	Levy	daughter	1917		
Max	**Maizels**		1876	1952	Jewelry store owner
Ruby	(Lipman) Maizels	wife	1880		Daughter of Samuel and Miriam from Greenport
Evelyn	Maizels	daughter	1907		
Natalie	Maizels	daughter	1912		
Irma	Maizels	daughter	1916		
E.	**Schapiro**				
Max	**Sherman**		1883	1911	Fruit store owner
?	(Sherman) Sherman	wife			
?	Sherman	child	1907		
?	Sherman	child			
?	Sherman	child	1911		

continued on next page

Table 14.5. Continued.

?	Sherman	child	1911		
S.	**Sherman**				Brother of Max Sherman's wife
Max	**Tennenberg**		1861		Manager Lyceum Theatre in Riverhead
Annie	(Rosenwasser) Tennenberg	wife	1862		
Tessie	Tennenberg	daughter	1885		m. Joseph Levy
Cecilia	Tennenberg	daughter	1886	1890	
Harold	Tennenberg	son	1894		
Max	**Wolff**		1884		
Sarah	(Segal) Wolff	wife	1890		
Lillian	Wolff	daughter	1909		
Anna	Wolff	daughter	1910		

Table 14.6. Residents of South Haven

Levy	**Michaels**				
?	Michaels	wife			
Myer	Michaels	son	1760		

Table 14.7. Residents of West Sayville

Cornelius	**De Ruiter**		1865		Oysterman
Bella	De Ruiter	wife	1868		
William	De Ruiter	son	1892		
Johanna	De Ruiter	daughter	1896		
Andrew	De Ruiter	son	1898		
Bessie	De Ruiter	daughter	1900		
Frederick	De Ruiter	son	1902	1981	
Cornelius	De Ruiter	son	1906		
John	De Ruiter	son	1908		
Abraham	**Glostein**		1876	1899	Peddler

Chapter 15

Riverhead

Including Calverton, Center Moriches, Eastport, East Quogue, Good Ground (Now Hampton Bays), Quogue, and Westhampton Beach

Simon Leavitt found his way out to Riverhead as a wandering peddler in 1883 and grew his business over the next two decades to the point where he was able to open his own clothing store in 1906 on Peconic Avenue. Leavitt's experience was typical of an immigrant merchant who worked hard and enjoyed success, but after several years he also diversified his business portfolio. Simon became involved in the entertainment industry by purchasing a theater that would feature a performance created by the greatest inventor of the day.

Figure 89. Simon Leavitt. *Source: And We're Still Here: 100 Years of Small Town Jewish Life* by Helene Gerard, courtesy of Lloyd Gerard.

Leavitt was not the first Jew to arrive in Riverhead. That distinction belongs to Jonas Fishel who settled in the village in 1855 and owned a store selling clothing, including popular outerwear at the time such as cloaks and dolmans. Over the years Jonas became an active citizen in the financial community as a charter member of the Riverhead Savings Bank and later a director of Suffolk County National Bank. Jonas lived in Riverhead for more than fifty years, raised four children there with his wife Betsy, and was a treasurer for the Odd Fellows, but he never had the opportunity to join a synagogue in his village before his passing in 1909 at the age of seventy-six.

The Brotherhood of Jews of Riverhead was incorporated in 1911 with services for Rosh Hashanah held that year in Odd Fellows Hall. There are 18 men identified as founders of the Brotherhood but in reality it was likely only 11 or 12 original members. The first president was Samuel Saxstein, and other early members included Samuel Alper, Joseph Brown, Harry Cohn, Louis Frank, Samuel Goldman, Shepard Goldman, Max Harding, Samuel Harding, Jacob Hochheiser, Simon Leavitt, Reuben Lipetz, Morris Katz,

Sam Peltz, Joseph Pushkin, Nathan Reed, Alex Weiss, and George Wiesen.

With his clothing store doing well, Simon Leavitt was able to pursue a real estate investment and purchased a building in the heart of Riverhead's business district in 1908. The two-story structure was built by David Vail in 1881 and would provide an excellent location for Leavitt's store at the street level. On the second floor was a theater, previously known as Music Hall but by 1908 was called the Lyceum Theatre, which would attract patrons for theatrical performances, music recitals, vaudeville shows, and the like. It also provided a convenient space for the Brotherhood of Jews of Riverhead to hold services and would play host to a seminal moment in the history of the motion picture industry.

Among Thomas Edison's numerous inventions were the phonograph that played sound and the kinetoscope that displayed moving pictures.

Figure 90. Edison's kinetophone was used at Simon Leavitt's Lyceum Theatre in 1914 to show the first moving pictures with synchronized sound. *Source*: *County Review*, May 8, 1914.

While both of these technologies were available in the 1890s, the synchronization of sound with visual motion on film to be projected for audiences did not occur until twenty years later. Beginning in 1913 Edison took his new kinetophone on the road sharing his latest innovation with audiences around the country. On May 8, 1914, the tour made a stop on eastern Long Island at Simon Leavitt's Lyceum Theatre. Thirteen years before *The Jazz Singer* starring Al Jolson (considered the first "talkie"), Riverhead

Figure 91. Jacob Meyer promoted his department store by running chic advertisements in local newspapers. *Source*: *County Review*, May 22, 1914.

residents would be among the first to witness this latest development in entertainment by spending a night out at the movies.

Following his retirement in 1896, Jonas Fishel's store was rented out to Jacob Meyer. Originally from Germany, Meyer came to the United States as a ten-year-old boy in 1875 and was in business with his brother Morris beginning in 1883. Their initial store located in Sag Harbor offered dry goods and men's clothing under the appropriate name of Meyer Brothers. It is not known why the partnership of Jacob and Morris dissolved in 1888, but Jacob kept the store and the company name, bringing in another brother, David, as his new partner. In 1892 they opened a second branch location in East Hampton, which was managed by a fourth Meyer brother, Isaac. And when the opportunity came up to take over the Fishel store, a third Meyer Brothers location was established. The store in Riverhead would be managed by Jacob and became the largest of the three, offering apparel for men, women, and children; household furnishings; linens; kitchen accessories; luggage; rugs; and more within a three-floor department store.

Figure 92. Jacob Meyer. *Source*: *County Review*, March 14, 1924.

Jacob was a risk taker, a man not satisfied to rest on his laurels and someone who believed in marketing and promotion in order to grow his retail establishments. Meyer Brothers advertisements appeared regularly in the *Sag Harbor Express, East Hampton Star, Southampton Press*, and *County Review* newspapers with boastful tag lines such as "The Largest Clothiers on Long Island" and "Suffolk's Leading Store." Jacob held contests and installed plate-glass windows with attractive displays to draw customers into his stores. He was also civic minded and maintained his ties to the Jewish community in Sag Harbor. For the dedication of the Sag Harbor synagogue on October 28, 1900, Jacob attended the ceremony and was given the honor of opening the new building. When a Merchants Association was formed in Riverhead in 1902 Meyer was installed as a vice president. In later years he became a director of the Suffolk County Trust Company and a trustee of Riverhead Savings Bank.

To the south of Riverhead there is a string of several smaller towns dotting the landscape from the Shinnecock Canal to Moriches. Anyone traveling along the Montauk Highway would pass through the central area of each of these villages, encountering Jewish-owned businesses and residents along the way. On Main Street in Good Ground (today Hampton Bays) in 1901 there was a dry goods, clothing, and furniture store run by Charles Frank. East Quogue featured the Seaside Market opened by Moses Weixelbaum and August (Gus) Mainzer in 1917. Weixelbaum was a butcher in Quogue during the summers beginning in 1898 and went into business on a year-round basis with his friend Gus, a German immigrant from Nievern Bad Ems, as his partner. The Wimpfheimer brothers were in business together and owned two markets with Irving running their location in Quogue and Herbert in charge of the market in Westhampton Beach. Continuing west and entering the village of Eastport, one would find Harry Goldstein's general merchandise store on the south side of Montauk Highway that opened in 1892. Thirty-one years later the store expanded into a newly constructed larger location across the street under the name Harry Goldstein & Sons Department Store. This same store would remain in the family until 2018 operating as Lloyd's Antiques, run by Harry's grandson Lloyd and great-granddaughter Terry. Harry and Annie Bernstein moved to Center Moriches in 1903 and started a duck farm there in 1909. At its peak the farm was able to raise as many as two hundred thousand ducks in a single year. Bernstein also operated a pocketbook manufacturing

Figures 93 and 94. Gus Mainzer in front of his market in East Quogue and the Goldstein family from Eastport in 1911. L to R: Esther, Jeanette, Harry, Raymond, Lawrence, and Herbert. *Source*: Courtesy of Harry Mainzer.

operation out of his home and expanded the business by purchasing a hotel on Frowein Road and converting it into a factory in 1918.

Finding a spouse to start a family could not have been easy with a limited number of Jews living in the vicinity, but things seemed to have worked out for Harry Sacks and his family. Harry and his wife Jennie had moved to East Quogue by 1905. Their daughter Sarah married Frank Crowitz from Sag Harbor. Harry's sister Sarah, who was married to Max Brown, lived next door in East Quogue then later in Riverhead. Max and Sarah's son Simon married Minnie Kramer from Patchogue, their older daughter Mary married Louis Frank and lived in Riverhead, and their youngest child, Fannie, married Morris Harding and also made Riverhead their home.

In 1924 when Riverhead's first synagogue was built there were nearly a hundred Jews living in the village. Twenty years later the congregation was ready to build another synagogue and changed their name from the Brotherhood of Jews of Riverhead to Temple Israel of Riverhead. The congregation's second and current synagogue on Northville Turnpike was dedicated on August 10, 1947.

Table 15.1. Residents of Riverhead

Samuel	**Alper**		1875	1953	Brotherhood of Jews in Riverhead 1911
Sarah	(Kodosh) Alper	wife	1882	1963	
Eva	Alper	daughter	1910	1977	
Joseph	**Brown**		1874		Brotherhood of Jews in Riverhead 1911
Sarah	(Beck) Brown	wife	1873		
Ethel	Brown	daughter	1896		
Rose	Brown	daughter	1899		
Fannie	Brown	daughter	1905		
Isabelle	Brown	daughter	1908	1934	
Irving	Brown	son	1912		
Max	**Cloven**		1898		Nephew of Morris Segal
Simon	**Cohn**		1852		
Clara	**Edinson**		1872		Sister-in-law of Morris Segal
Jonas	**Fishel**		1833	1909	Dry goods merchant
Betsy	(Cohn) Fishel	wife	1844	1897	
Gilbert	Fishel	son	1863	1957	
Edwin	Fishel	son	1865	1942	
Arthur	Fishel	son	1868	1945	
Jenny	Fishel	daughter	1873		
Sygmond	**Fishel**		1853		
Louis	**Frank**		1894	1976	Brotherhood of Jews in Riverhead 1911
Mary	(Brown) Frank	wife	1898	1987	Daughter of Max and Sarah from East Quogue
Hymen	**Goldberg**		1862		Dry goods peddler
Nellie	(Weiner) Goldberg	wife	1861		
Harry	Goldberg	son	1891		
Leon	Goldberg	son	1893		
Samuel	Goldberg	son	1895		
William	Goldberg	son	1899		
Lewis	**Goldberg**		1834		Dry goods peddler
Julia	Goldberg	wife	1857		
Bertha	Goldberg	daughter	1880		
Emma	Goldberg	daughter	1881		
Freddie	Goldberg	son	1891		
Sheppard	**Goldman**		1873	1960	Brotherhood of Jews in Riverhead 1911
Rose	Goldman	wife	1879	1973	

continued on next page

Table 15.1. Continued.

Ida	Goldman	daughter	1900		
Samuel	Goldman	son	1904	1954	
Israel	Goldman	son	1907	2002	
Louis	Goldman	son	1909		
Isadore	Goldman	son	1912		
Benjamin	**Gutstadt**		1865		
Celia	(Jacobson) Gutstadt	wife	1870		Sister of Anna Meyer
Jerome	Gutstadt	son	1899		
Max	**Harding**		1874	1961	Brother of Samuel
Dora	Harding	wife	1875	1950	
Morris	Harding	son	1902	1965	
Bessie	Harding	daughter	1908	1960	
Samuel	**Harding**		1875	1972	Brother of Max
Rose	(Polich) Harding	wife	1882	1975	
Louis	Harding	son	1905	1994	
Jacob	Harding	son	1908	1999	
Maurice	Harding	son	1909	1999	
Florence	Harding	daughter	1915		
Jacob	**Hochheiser**		1882	1949	Brotherhood of Jews in Riverhead 1911
Hannah	Hochheiser	wife	1886	1968	
Sidney	Hochheiser	son	1912		
Harold	Hochheiser	son	1915	1990	
Morris	**Kaplan**		1895		Son of Abraham and Mollie from Greenport
?	(Stone) Kaplan	wife			
Rene	Kaplan	daughter			
Morris	**Katz**		1883		Brotherhood of Jews in Riverhead 1911
Mary	Katz	wife	1887		
Solomon	**Klein**		1843		Cigar maker
Pauline	(Hyman) Klein	wife	1854	1936	
Jacob	Klein	son	1873		
Mariam	Klein	daughter	1875		
Julia	Klein	daughter	1877	1943	
Harry	**Kohn**		1877		Brotherhood of Jews in Riverhead 1911
Tilly	Kohn	wife	1883		
Simon	**Leavitt**		1863	1939	Brotherhood of Jews in Riverhead 1911

Table 15.1. Continued.

Rachel	(Truck) Leavitt	wife	1870		
Sarah	Leavitt	daughter	1890		
Harry	Leavitt	son	1892		
Anna	Leavitt	daughter	1894		
Goldie	Leavitt	daughter	1897		
Dewey	Leavitt	son	1899	1980	
Theodore	Leavitt	son	1903	1980	
Max	**Lipetz**		1883	1967	Brother of Morris, Reuben, and Samuel
Fannie	Lipetz	wife	1880	1919	
Lena	Lipetz	daughter	1906		
Morris	Lipetz	son	1908	1994	
Rose	Lipetz	daughter	1910		
Mary	Lipetz	daughter	1911	1930	
Paulina	Lipetz	daughter	1913		
Morris	**Lipetz**		1859	1909	Brother of Max, Reuben, and Samuel
Rebecca	Lipetz	first wife		1903	
Mendel	Lipetz	son	1892		
Goldie	Lipetz	daughter			
Cecelia	Lipetz	second wife			
Reuben	**Lipetz**		1875	1945	Brother of Max, Morris, and Samuel
Rose	(Rubenstein) Lipetz	wife	1879	1939	
Sidney	Lipetz	son	1902	1994	
Eli	Lipetz	son	1907	1997	
Morris	Lipetz	son	1909	1981	
Philip	Lipetz	son	1908	1994	
Miriam	Lipetz	daughter	1912	1996	
Samuel	**Lipetz**		1887		Brother of Max, Morris, and Reuben
Goldie	Lipetz	wife			
Jacob	**Meyer**		1865	1924	Brother of Morris and David from Sag Harbor and Isaac from East Hampton
Anna	(Jacobson) Meyer	wife	1867		Sister of Celia Gutstadt
Miriam	Meyer	daughter	1890		
Fenimore	Meyer	son	1892		
Leah	Meyer	daughter	1896		
Esther	Meyer	daughter	1905		

continued on next page

Table 15.1. Continued.

Israel	**Nelson**		1859		Dry goods peddler
Mary	Nelson	wife	1865		
Anna	Nelson	daughter	1898		
Rosie	Nelson	daughter	1900		
Morris	**Peltz**		1853	1935	Tin Peddler
Annie	(Mindel) Peltz	wife	1850	1943	
Samuel	Peltz	son	1882		m. Annie Brown
Sarah	Peltz	daughter	1883		m. Abraham Ratchick lived in Patchogue
Max	Peltz	son	1885		m. Nellie lived in Patchogue
Jacob	Peltz	son	1888		
Mary	Peltz	daughter	1890		
Harry	Peltz	son	1893	1923	
Samuel	**Peltz**		1882		Son of Morris and Annie
Annie	(Brown) Peltz	wife	1883		
Nathan	**Reitt**		1873		Brotherhood of Jews in Riverhead 1911
Annie	(Levy) Reitt	wife	1874	1934	
Samuel	Reitt	son	1902		
David	**Sandman**		1848		
Hulda	(Lefkowitz) Sandman	wife	1852	1922	
Annie	Sandman	daughter	1875		
Nellie	Sandman	daughter	1876		
Francis	Sandman	daughter	1878		
Louis	Sandman	son	1883		
Edith	Sandman	daughter	1886		
Lena	Sandman	daughter	1887	1918	
Eddie	Sandman	son	1889		
Victor	Sandman	son	1891		Saloon keeper
Samuel	**Saxstein**		1870	1958	President, Brotherhood of Jews in Riverhead 1911
Ida	Saxstein	wife	1878	1946	
Morris	Saxstein	son	1901		
J. Harry	Saxstein	son	1904	1939	
Carl	Saxstein	son	1907	1955	
Julius	Saxstein	son	1909	1980	
Morris	**Segal**		1864		Tailor
Sarah	Segal	wife	1864		
Dora	Segal	daughter	1888		

Table 15.1. Continued.

Alexander	**Weiss**		1878		Brotherhood of Jews in Riverhead 1911
Esther	Weiss	wife			
George	**Wiesen**		1888	1957	Brotherhood of Jews in Riverhead 1911
Emma	Wiesen	wife	1888		
Arnold	Wiesen	son	1912		
Morris	**Wise**		1846	1908	Brother of Mitchell
Emma	Wise	wife	1859	1937	
Mitchell	**Wise**		1841	1905	Brother of Morris
?	Wise	wife			

Table 15.2. Residents of Calverton

Harris	**Karlin**		1864	1942	Farmer
Sarah	(Rodbard) Karlin	wife	1864	1924	
Jacob	Karlin	son	1889	1955	m. Rose Frank
Philip	Karlin	son	1896	1977	
Isaac	Karlin	son	1898	1968	
Charles	Karlin	son	1899	1984	
Sophie	Karlin	daughter	1901	1987	
Hyman	Karlin	son	1903	1974	
Joseph	Karlin	son	1905	1978	
Yetta	Karlin	daughter	1907	1992	
Jacob	**Karlin**		1889	1955	Son of Harris and Sarah
Rose	(Frank) Karlin	wife	1886	1958	Daughter of Charles and Anna from Franklin Square
Charlie	Karlin	son	1915	2003	
Ida	Karlin	son	1917	2019	
Philip	Karlin	son	1918	1997	

Table 15.3. Residents of Center Moriches

Harry	**Bernstein**		1880	1936	Duck farm owner
Annie	(Kurtz) Bernstein	wife	1878	1955	
Mae	Bernstein	daughter	1900		
Richard	Bernstein	son	1902		
Samuel	Bernstein	son	1903		
Abraham	Bernstein	son	1909		

continued on next page

Table 15.3. Continued.

Nathan	**Levi**		1855		Uncle of Harry and Joseph Goldstein from Eastport

Table 15.4. Residents of Eastport

Harry	**Goldstein**		1869	1952	Brother of Joseph
Esther	(Coven) Goldstein	first wife	1874	1915	
Herbert	Goldstein	son	1895		
Lawrence	Goldstein	son	1897	1993	
Jeanette	Goldstein	daughter	1904		
Raymond	Goldstein	son	1905		
Joseph	**Goldstein**		1872		Brother of Harry
Ida	Goldstein	wife	1886		
Geneva	Goldstein	daughter	1899		
Andrew S.	**Levi**		1857	1926	Uncle of Harry and Joseph

Table 15.5. Residents of East Quogue

Max	**Brown**		1868	1952	Farmer
Sarah	(Sacks) Brown	wife	1870	1950	Sister of Harry Sacks
Simon	Brown	son	1896	1942	m. Minnie Kramer
Mary	Brown	daughter	1898	1987	m. Louis Frank, lived in Riverhead
Fannie	Brown	daughter	1900	1991	
Simon	**Brown**		1896		Son of Max and Sarah
Minnie	(Kramer) Brown	wife	1899		Daughter of Samuel from Patchogue
Isaac	**Feinberg**		1862	1946	Fruit peddler
Mary	(Goldberg) Feinberg	wife	1860	1933	
Joseph	Feinberg	son	1878	1916	
Sarah	Feinberg	son	1879		
Israel	Feinberg	son	1884		
Minnie	Feinberg	daughter	1886	1954	
Julius	Feinberg	son	1889		
Samuel	Feinberg	son	1891		m. May Kaplan, lived in Good Ground
Yetta	Feinberg	daughter	1893		
Fannie	Feinberg	daughter	1896	1963	
Simon	Feinberg	son	1897	1984	
David	Feinberg	son	1900		

Table 15.5. Continued.

Rosie	Feinberg	daughter	1905		
Louie	Feinberg	son	1908		
Henry	Feinberg	son	1909		
Harry	**Sacks**		1873	1945	Brother of Sarah Brown
Jennie	(Yoffie) Sacks	wife	1879	1967	
Julius	Sacks	son	1900	1983	
Florence	Sacks	daughter	1903		
Sarah	Sacks	daughter	1905		
Bertha	Sacks	daughter	1908		
Joseph	Sacks	son	1911		
Abraham	Sacks	son	1912		

Table 15.6. Residents of Good Ground (Now Hampton Bays)

Samuel	**Feinberg**		1891	1963	Son of Isaac and Mary from East Quogue
May	(Kaplan) Feinberg	wife	1897	1950	
Sarah	Feinberg	daughter	1917		
Charles	**Frank**		1871	1937	Brother of Israel from Southampton
Yetta	(Horowitz) Frank	wife	1874		
Isaac	Frank	son	1897		
Seymour	Frank	son	1901		

Table 15.7. Resident of Quogue

August	**Mainzer**		1881	1950	Butcher

Table 15.8. Residents of Westhampton Beach

Rose	**Waller**			1967	Sister of Carrie Weixelbaum
Moses	**Weixelbaum**		1875	1956	Butcher
Carrie	(Waller) Weixelbaum	wife	1882	1969	
Milton	Weixelbaum	son	1903		
Jesse	Weixelbaum	son	1904	1979	
Herbert	**Wimpfheimer**		1892	1965	Brother of Irving
Irving	**Wimpfheimer**		1891		Brother of Herbert

Chapter 16

Sag Harbor

*Including Amagansett, East Hampton,
Shelter Island, and Southampton*

The history of the Jewish people is fraught with examples of infighting. On Long Island in the post–World War II era, when synagogues were sprouting up all over Nassau and Suffolk counties, it was not uncommon to find individuals from within organizing under a different agenda who ultimately split off and formed their own congregation. The earliest example of a rivalry between Jewish factions in the same town occurred in Sag Harbor beginning in the latter part of the nineteenth century between immigrants from Russia and those from Hungary.

Adolph Edelstein had a clothing store near the Washington Market by 1872 but was one of only a few Jews living in Sag Harbor in the 1870s. This would change significantly thanks to a French immigrant named Joseph Fahys, who was one of the first manufacturers in the United States to produce watchcases on a large scale. In 1881 Fahys relocated his factory from Carlstadt, New Jersey, to his wife's hometown of Sag Harbor and employed hundreds of workers. The availability of skilled and manual labor positions lured many Jewish immigrants to Sag Harbor, and before long enough had arrived to establish the Jewish Association of United Brethren in 1883. The local group was part of a national Jewish fraternal organization known as Independent Order Ahawas Israel with headquarters in New York City. The Sag Harbor chapter included Sam Freedman, Barney Ginsberg, Samuel Heller, Frank Jaffe, Nathan Mayersohn, Henry Meyer, Max Ollswang, Arnold Spitz, Edel Spodick, and Max Zucker—all of whom were from Russia.

With the Fahys factory bringing new residents to Sag Harbor Jewish merchants such as Morris Meyer recognized an opportunity to start new businesses or grow existing ones. Morris, born in 1860, had established a clothing store in Sag Harbor by 1881 on Washington Street directly across from the watchcase factory. He would eventually bring his younger

Figure 95. Seal of the United Brethren in Sag Harbor. *Source*: American Jewish Historical Society.

brother Jacob into the business known as Meyer Brothers, but that partnership was dissolved in 1888. Jacob retained the store and family name, bringing in another brother, David, while Morris went into business with his brother-in-law, Milton Smith, setting up a competing clothing store at 62 Main Street. The Meyer and Smith enterprise lasted only until 1893, but Meyer continued on his own at the same location. In 1904 he built a new store on the opposite side of Main Street and brought his sons into the business, establishing Morris Meyer & Sons. Beyond being a leading merchant in town, Morris became a land speculator later in life. He made shrewd investments in property in Sag Harbor, Montauk, Amagansett, and

Figure 96. Advertisement for Morris Meyer's clothing store. *Source*: *Sag Harbor Express*, July 23, 1896.

East Hampton, and these increased in value significantly during the Suffolk County land boom of the mid-1920s. Upon his death in 1929 Morris left an estate worth approximately $750,000, an amount equivalent to over $11 million in today's value. Throughout his life Morris was active with civic organizations as a volunteer fireman, a member of the Union Social Club, and a trustee of the village of Sag Harbor for six years. His dedication to the Jewish community rose above all else as a generous financial contributor, and he served three terms as president of the congregation that would become Adas Israel.

The objective of the Jewish Association of United Brethren was to serve the Jewish community by looking out for the welfare of its members and included four key tenets: First, providing a physician for the ill; second, supplying payment of funeral expenses and a location for burial; third, hosting a location for worship; and fourth, promoting proper social and moral standards. In the early years of the United Brethren the second of these tenets meant securing a burial plot in either Brooklyn or Queens. This changed in 1891 when the newly incorporated Jewish Cemetery Association purchased an acre of land from William Osborne on the East Hampton Turnpike for $65. Morris Spodick, a trustee of the Jewish Cemetery Association and son of United Brethren member Edel Spodick, had the unfortunate distinction of first utilizing the burial ground for his eight-day-old child who died on May 24, 1891.

By 1890 the Hungarian Jewish immigrants had followed the lead of their Russian counterparts and formed their own society known as the Independent Jewish Association. Members included Max Grossman, Morris Siegel, H. Trelheift, and men from the Klein and Schwartz families. Adolph, Benjamin, and Herman Schwartz were brothers who were all born in Hungary, all worked in the Fahys watchcase factory, and all had become connected to the Klein family through marriage. Benjamin and Herman married sisters Fanny and Josephine Klein and Adolph Schwartz's daughter Katie married Samuel Klein, Fanny and Josephine's brother. The three couples contributed to the growth of the Hungarians in Sag Harbor by having twelve children. Herman Grossman, unrelated to Max Grossman, was also from Hungary and worked at Fahys as an engraver.

Another Klein named Herman wanted to ensure that members of the Hungarian Jewish community in Sag Harbor had a place to bury their dead. Just as members of the United Brethren had established the Jewish

Figure 97. Herman and Stephanie Grossman in Sag Harbor, c. 1905. *Source*: Courtesy of Karl Grossman.

Cemetery Association, members of the Independent Jewish Association formed the Independent Jewish Cemetery Association. In 1893 Herman Klein purchased a half-acre of land from Sarah Osborne, located on the west side of the East Hampton Turnpike bordered on the north by the Jewish Cemetery Association's property.

Nathan Mayersohn, a devoted Jew his entire life who would become a staunch American, was born in Russia in 1856 and had four sons with his first wife prior to coming to the United States in 1887. Within four years Nathan would marry his second wife, Julia, and together they would have four children, two boys and two girls. Nathan worked at Fahys as a watchcase polisher but also served as secretary of the Jewish Cemetery Association in 1890 and 1893 and as financial secretary of the Jewish Association of United Brethren in 1895 and 1896. His devotion to the United Brethren was recognized at a meeting on December 30, 1895, when Nathan received a gold medal for his commitment to the organization. Mayersohn would continue to rise through the ranks, becoming president in 1897 and again in 1900 when he would oversee the most ambitious project the United Brethren would ever undertake.

Figure 98. Temple Mishcan Israel, the synagogue built by the Jewish Association of United Brethren in Sag Harbor, opened in time for Rosh Hashanah in September 1900. *Source*: Temple Adas Israel, Sag Harbor.

For several years in the 1890s United Brethren would hold services for the High Holidays in town at Crowell's Hall and the Masonic Hall, but Mayersohn and others aspired to have their own permanent synagogue. At the turn of the century there were approximately two hundred Jews living in Sag Harbor with thirty men counted as members of United Brethren. The numbers were sufficient to raise the necessary funds to purchase a plot of land and erect a house of worship. Plans were in place by June 1900 to begin construction at the corner of Elizabeth Street and Atlantic Avenue for the second synagogue to be built on Long Island. It was a two-story building with steps from the street leading up to the sanctuary on the main level. It measured 24' × 30' and included a balcony, adhering to the Orthodox tradition of separate seating for men and women. Another feature of the building was the installation of the latest Weisbach gas system, enabling indoor lighting day or night. Enough of the structure had been completed by the end of September to hold Rosh Hashanah services, with a formal ceremony being held on Sunday, October 28, for the dedication of Temple Mishcan Israel.

Hundreds of residents from Sag Harbor and other towns on the east end turned out for the festivities. Jacob Meyer, former Sag Harbor resident who had moved to Riverhead, opened the synagogue at 2:30 p.m. to allow entrance for select individuals holding a card that gave them admission into the building. The ceremony began with United Brethren president Nathan Mayersohn offering the introductory prayer. David Sandman, another attendee from Riverhead, had the honor of carrying in the Torah and placing it in the ark. Morris Meyer lit the eternal flame, followed by Isaac Bach who took over as master of ceremonies, introducing each of the speakers. They included two rabbis from New York City, a reverend, and George C. Raynor, a lawyer in Sag Harbor who sold his land to United Brethren enabling them to build their synagogue.

Sag Harbor was already a hub for Jewish activity, but a new synagogue gave Jewish residents from East Hampton, Shelter Island, Amagansett, and the bustling village of Southampton another good reason to visit Sag Harbor. Southampton today sees a large spike in visitors during the summer months as a popular resort town, but this has been the case for decades, even as far back as the nineteenth century. Moescha Rosenberg began making annual retreats to Southampton from his residence in New York City beginning in 1896 and even opened a jewelry store in town on Main Street during the summer. Rosenberg also served as secretary of the local chapter of the American Jewish Relief Committee during World War I. In 1905 there were just five year-round Jewish families living in Southampton. Predating them were two men going back to the colonial era: David Elias moved there in 1722, and Joseph Jacobs purchased a house in 1761 with his wife Eleanor and raised five children. The earliest of the nineteenth-century Jewish residents was Max Smith, a peddler who arrived around 1873. Others who settled in Southampton included Henry and Edith Hirschfeld, Benjamin and Dora Rosen, Max and Esther Tisnower, and Israel and Rachel Frank. As a strictly Orthodox Jew, Israel prayed on his own daily and would take his family to Sag Harbor, attending services in the synagogue on the High Holidays. It wasn't until the 1930s that a minyan was held in Southampton, taking place in the living room of the Frank home. Herman and Henrietta Rothenberg were living in Southampton in 1910 with Herman earning a living as a watchcase polisher at Fahys, traveling ten miles each way to and from work. Rothenberg is one of forty-five Jews documented to have worked at the Fahys watchcase factory, but there were likely many more.

Through a series of events born out of financial troubles or mismanagement, United Brethren defaulted on the mortgage of Mishcan Israel synagogue, resulting in foreclosure in 1918. By this time the rift between the Hungarians and Russians had subsided, resulting in the merger of the Jewish Association of United Brethren and the Independent Jewish Association into one synagogue in Sag Harbor. On April 29, 1918, the certificate of incorporation was filed with the Suffolk county clerk that established the new congregation known as Adas Israel. Three of the fifty-two charter members of the congregation, Philip Ballen, Dezso Fischer, and Morris Meyer, came to the rescue and bought back the foreclosed property at public auction and returned the synagogue to the Jewish community.

In 1925 a fire at Fahys destroyed much of the watchcase factory, resulting in decreased production and many workers being laid off. The decline continued through the early years of the depression until the factory closed in 1931. Many of the Jewish merchants remained in Sag Harbor, but the synagogue incurred financial difficulties through the 1940s, causing the building to be open only for Rosh Hashanah and Yom Kippur. In 1948 the decision was made to switch religious affiliation from Orthodox to Conservative and then a few years later to Reform. After years of decline the 1950s brought some optimism from new residents who were moving out east on a seasonal basis as well as some artists and writers who lived in Sag Harbor. In 1956 an empty lot adjacent to the synagogue was purchased allowing for future expansion. Growth continued slowly but surely through the decades and services expanded to being held from Shavuot in May through the end of Sukkot in October. A Hebrew school for the children was established in 2003, and in 2010 Temple Adas Israel became a full-time, year-round congregation.

Table 16.1. Residents of Sag Harbor

Isaac	**Bach**		1860	1926	Dry goods merchant
Regina	(Lowenstein) Bach	wife	1862		
Viola	Bach	daughter	1889		
Philip	**Ballen**		1884	1957	Member Adas Israel 1918
Sophie	(Yerman) Ballen	wife	1888	1948	
Evelyn	Ballen	daughter	1912		
Mildred	Ballen	daughter	1914	1989	
Shirley	Ballen	daughter	1918		
Joseph	**Bergstein**		1870	1946	Member Adas Israel 1918
Sarah	(Tartan) Bergstein	wife	1876		
Aaron	Bergstein	son	1903		
Dora	Bergstein	daughter	1906		
Louis	Bergstein	son	1915		
Harry	Bergstein	son	1917		
Nathan	**Berriman**				Member United Brethren 1900
Max	**Bogner**		1875		Polisher at watchcase factory
Adele	(Seif) Bogner	wife	1877		
William	Bogner	son	1900		
Jacob	Bogner	son	1902		
Madeline	Bogner	daughter	1904		
Julia	Bogner	daughter	1907		
Henry	Bogner	son	1911		
Charles	**Bookstaver**		1875	1957	Member Adas Israel 1918
Annie	(Yarfitz) Bookstaver	wife	1875	1962	
George	Bookstaver	son	1899	1982	
Isidor	Bookstaver	son	1901	1927	
David	Bookstaver	son	1905	2000	
Ethel	Bookstaver	daughter	1909		
Mildred	Bookstaver	daughter	1911	1958	
Samuel	**Bookstaver**		1849	1933	Member Adas Israel 1918
Esther	(Shaver) Bookstaver	wife	1853	1918	
Samuel, Jr.	Bookstaver	son	1879		m. Jennie Ginsburg
George	Bookstaver	son	1892		
Annie	Bookstaver	daughter	1894		
Mollie	Bookstaver	daughter	1896		
Samuel, Jr.	**Bookstaver**		1879		Son of Samuel and Esther
Jennie	(Ginsburg) Bookstaver	wife	1877		Daughter of Morris and Celia

continued on next page

Table 16.1. Continued.

Alexander	Bookstaver	son	1911		
Irving	Bookstaver	son	1913		
Viola	Bookstaver	daughter	1915		
Louise	Bookstaver	daughter	1917	1996	
Jacob	**Cohen**				Member Adas Israel 1918
?	Cohen	wife			
Harry	Cohen	son	1899	1911	
Julius	**Cohen**		1865		Member United Brethren 1906
Sarah	Cohen	wife	1870		
Annie	Cohen	daughter	1895		
Lena	Cohen	daughter	1898		
Harry	Cohen	son	1900		
Hattie	Cohen	daughter	1903		
Samuel	Cohen	son	1905		
Gertrude	Cohen	daughter	1907		
Morris	**Cohen**				Member United Brethren 1900
Udal	**Cohen**				Member United Brethren 1900
Samuel	**Conin**		1863	1916	Watchcase factory laborer
Rosie	Conin	wife	1861		
Annie	Conin	daughter	1883		Watchcase factory polisher
Louis	**Crowitz**		1870	1936	Member Adas Israel 1918
Ida	Crowitz	wife	1869	1937	
David	Crowitz	son	1897	1960	
Gussie	Crowitz	daughter	1901		
Frank	Crowitz	son	1903	1988	
Sophia	Crowitz	daughter	1907		
Samuel	Crowitz	son	1908	1967	
Leonard	Crowitz	son	1913	1932	
Jacob	**Dien**				Member United Brethren 1900
Adolph	**Edelstein**				Clothing store owner
Isidor	**Efron**		1860		Member United Brethren 1906
Lena	Efron	wife	1867	1913	
Rebecca	Efron	daughter	1889		
Cecelia	Efron	daughter	1892		
Jennie	Efron	daughter	1895		

Table 16.1. Continued.

Jacob	**Eisenberg**			1899	Merchant
Rebecca	Eisenberg	wife	1864	1938	
Meyer	Eisenberg	son	1895		
Frank	Eisenberg	son	1898		
Dora	Eisenberg	daughter	1899		
?	Eisenberg	daughter			
?	Eisenberg	daughter			
Nathan	**Eisenberg**		1877		
Sadie	(Schwartz) Eisenberg	wife	1879		
Estelle	Eisenberg	daughter	1901	1994	
Gertrude	Eisenberg	daughter	1907		
Isadore	Eisenberg	son	1910	1983	
Arthur	Eisenberg	son	1911	1990	
Louis	**Epstein**		1879		Bakery owner
Rosa	Epstein	wife	1884		
Gertrude	Epstein	daughter	1907		
Frederick	Epstein	son	1909		
Dezso	**Fischer**		1876	1942	Member Adas Israel 1918
Rachel	(Schwartz) Fischer	wife	1890	1949	Daughter of Adolph and Julia
Mildred	Fischer	daughter	1910		
Sam	**Freedman**				Recording Secy. United Brethren 1895
Dora	(Cotz) Freedman				
Abraham	**Frolich**		1888		Member Adas Israel 1918
Eva	Frolich	wife	1887		
Manuel	Frolich	son	1911		
Annie	Frolich	daughter	1913		
Rose	Frolich	daughter	1915		
Barney	**Ginsberg**				President Jewish Cemetery Assoc. 1893
Morris	**Ginsberg**		1858	1925	Member United Brethren 1906
Celia	Ginsberg	wife	1853	1917	
Jennie	Ginsberg	daughter	1879		m. Samuel Bookstaver
Blanche	Ginsberg	daughter	1880		
Louis	Ginsberg	son	1881		Member United Brethren 1900
Abraham	Ginsberg	son	1888		
Minnie	Ginsberg	daughter	1892		

continued on next page

Table 16.1. Continued.

Harry	**Goldstein**		1864		Member United Brethren 1900
?	Goldstein	wife			
Ida	Goldstein	daughter	1886		
Mary	Goldstein	daughter	1889		
Annie	Goldstein	daughter	1896		
Isaac	**Goldstein**		1870	1910	Worked at watchcase factory
Rose	(Shapiro) Goldstein	wife	1872		Worked at watchcase factory
Jacob	Goldstein	son	1895		Silversmith at watchcase factory
Abraham	Goldstein	son	1898		
Emmanuel	Goldstein	son	1900		
Samuel	**Goldstein**				Member United Brethren 1900
Aaron	**Greenberg**				Member United Brethren 1900
Herman	**Greenberg**		1867	1934	Member Adas Israel 1918
Ellie	Greenberg	wife	1882		
Esther	Greenberg	daughter	1901	1961	
Carrol	Greenberg	son	1904		
Morris	Greenberg	son	1905		
Ervan	Greenberg	son	1908		
Edith	Greenberg	daughter	1912		
Herman	**Greenwald**		1879		Member Adas Israel 1918
Ethel	Greenwald	wife	1884		
Arthur	Greenwald	son	1911		
Herbert	Greenwald	son	1914		
Mourry	Greenwald	son	1918		
Herman	**Grossman**		1885		
Stephanie	(Spiegel) Grossman	wife	1887		Sister of Ernestine Spitz
Max	**Grossman**		1869	1924	VP Independent Jewish Assoc. 1900
Bertha	Grossman	wife	1869		
Harry	Grossman	son	1890		Engraver at watchcase factory
David	Grossman	son	1891		Engine turner at watchcase factory
Jessie	Grossman	son	1894		Engine turner at watchcase factory
Samuel	Grossman	son	1896		Errand boy at watchcase factory

Table 16.1. Continued.

Nellie	Grossman	daughter	1897		
Morris	Grossman	son	1901		
Hannah	Grossman	daughter	1903		
Effie	Grossman	daughter	1905		
Pinkus	**Grossman**		1875	1945	Shoemaker
Anna	(Hacker) Grossman	wife	1875	1919	
Alice	Grossman	daughter	1904	1958	
George	Grossman	son	1907	1972	
Willie	Grossman	son	1915		
David	**Harris**		1857		Member Adas Israel 1918
Annie	Harris	wife	1862		
Henry	Harris	son	1883		
Hilda	Harris	daughter	1887		
Ray	Harris	daughter	1890		
Morris	**Heller**		1873	1951	Member United Brethren 1906
Sprincha	(Rodinsky) Heller	wife		1918	
Ervan	Heller	son	1903		
Edwin	Heller	son	1906		
Samuel	**Heller**		1866	1934	Secretary United Brethren 1900
Ethel	Heller	wife	1869	1955	
Samuel	Heller	son	1890	1973	
Israel	Heller	son	1893	1978	
Esther	Heller	daughter	1896	1989	
Jake	Heller	son	1900		
Jacob	**Hertz**				Member Adas Israel 1918
Joseph	**Hertz**				Member Adas Israel 1918
Philip	**Hertz**		1850		Member Adas Israel 1918
Esther	Hertz	wife	1855		
Jacob	**Hotz**		1881		Member United Brethren 1906
Pauline	Hotz	wife			
Morris	**Hotz**			1908	Member United Brethren 1900
Morris	**Hotz**			1921	Member United Brethren 1900
Annie	(Ollswang) Hotz	wife			Daughter of Max and Rose from Amagansett

continued on next page

Table 16.1. Continued.

?	Hotz	daughter	1902		
?	Hotz	daughter	1903		
?	Hotz	son	1905		
Philip	**Hotz**				Member United Brethren 1900
Esther	(Hirskowitz) Hotz	wife			
Fannie	Hotz	daughter	1883		
Frank	**Jaffe**		1856	1924	President United Brethren 1896
Esther	(Schoolmaster) Jaffe	wife	1859	1946	
Pearl	Jaffe	daughter	1891		Stenographer at watchcase factory
Mortimer	Jaffe	son	1893		
Lionel	Jaffe	son	1896		Apprentice at watchcase factory
Julia	Jaffe	daughter	1898		
Theodore	Jaffe	son	1898	1967	
Samuel	**Jaffe**		1868	1931	Member Jewish Cemetery Assoc. 1893
Bertha	Jaffe	wife	1870	1932	
Lawrence	Jaffe	son	1892	1960	
Morris	Jaffe	son	1894		
Anna	Jaffe	daughter	1898	1948	
Jacob	**Judelowitz**		1865		Shoemaker
Molly	Judelowitz	wife	1868		
Philip	Judelowitz	son	1889		
Joseph	Judelowitz	son	1891		Worked at watchcase factory
Samuel	Judelowitz	son	1893		Worked at watchcase factory
Julius	Judelowitz	son	1895		
Ethel	Judelowitz	daughter	1896		
Annie	Judelowitz	daughter	1898		
Gussie	Judelowitz	daughter	1902		
Nellie	Judelowitz	daughter	1904		
Isaac	**Kirsch**				Member United Brethren 1900
Joseph	**Kirsch**		1861	1912	
?	Kirsch	wife			Member United Brethren 1906
Rebecca	Kirsch	daughter			
Max	**Kirsch**		1884		Member Adas Israel 1918

Table 16.1. Continued.

Lena	Kirsch	wife	1887		
Herman	**Klein**		1875	1942	Son of Samuel and Bertha
Sallie	Klein	wife	1872	1936	
Louis	Klein	son	1901		
May	Klein	daughter	1904		
Pauline	Klein	daughter	1906		
Regina	Klein	daughter	1910		
Morris	**Klein**		1877	1954	Son of Samuel and Bertha
Mary	(Berger) Klein	wife	1881	1967	
Milton	Klein	son	1903	1986	
Regina	Klein	daughter			
Samuel	**Klein**		1853	1928	Chairman Jewish Cemetery Assoc. 1890
Bertha	(Reis) Klein	wife	1856	1931	
Herman	Klein	son	1875	1942	m. Sallie
Julius	Klein	son			
Morris	Klein	son	1877	1954	
Jeanette	Klein	daughter			
Samuel	**Klein**		1870	1921	Brother of Josephine Schwartz and Fannie Schwartz
Katie	(Schwartz) Klein	wife	1875	1963	Daughter of Adolph and Julia
R.	**Levenson**				Member United Brethren 1906
Samuel	**Levin**				Member United Brethren 1900
Belle	**Lowenstein**		1875		Sister of Regina Bach
William	**Marcus**		1887	1956	Member Adas Israel 1918
Edith	Marcus	wife	1886	1947	
Joseph	Marcus	son	1910		
Sarah	Marcus	daughter	1912		
Leanorce	Marcus	son	1913		
Samuel	Marcus	son	1915		
Mildred	Marcus	daughter	1918		
Samuel	**Marer**				Trustee Jewish Cemetery Assoc. 1890
Nathan	**Mayersohn**		1856	1928	President United Brethren 1897 and 1900
?	Mayersohn	first wife			
Louis	Mayersohn	son	1877		Finisher at watchcase factory

continued on next page

Table 16.1. Continued.

William	Mayersohn	son	1879	1906	Member of United Brethren 1900
Meyer	Mayersohn	son	1882		Worked at watchcase factory
Heyman	Mayersohn	son	1884		Worked at watchcase factory
Julia	Mayersohn	second wife	1867	1914	
George	Mayersohn	son	1893	1969	
Oscar	Mayersohn	son	1895	1978	
Esther	Mayersohn	daughter	1897		
Anne	Mayersohn	daughter	1899	1963	
P.	**Mayersohn**				Member United Brethren 1906
David	**Meyer**		1870		Brother of Jacob from Riverhead, Isaac from East Hampton and Morris
Eva	(Ginsburg) Meyer	wife			
Henry	**Meyer**		1841		Cigar manufacturer
Morris	**Meyer**		1860	1929	Brother of Jacob from Riverhead, Isaac from East Hampton and David
Rachel	(Smith) Meyer	wife	1860	1941	
Jacob	Meyer	son	1884	1952	
Harry	Meyer	son	1885	1937	Member Adas Israel 1918
Myron	Meyer	son	1893	1932	Member Adas Israel 1918
Theodore	Meyer	son	1897	1951	
Myron	**Meyerson**		1885	1947	Worked at watchcase factory
Frank	**Miller**				Member Adas Israel 1918
Louis	**Mindel**				Trustee Jewish Cemetery Assoc. 1893
Joshua	**Montefiore**		1762	1843	Lawyer
Isabella	Montefiore	wife			
?	Montefiore	daughter			
?	Montefiore	daughter			
H.	**Nekritz**				Financial Secretary. Jewish Cemetery Assoc. 1893
Jacob	**Peck**				Trustee Jewish Cemetery Assoc. 1893
Charles	**Podowitz**		1884	1961	Member Adas Israel 1918
Anna	Podowitz	wife	1883	1942	
Henry	Podowitz	son	1908		
Abraham	Podowitz	son	1910		
Morris	Podowitz	son	1912	1976	

Table 16.1. Continued.

Jeanette	Podowitz	son	1915		
Samuel	**Posener**				Trustee Jewish Cemetery Assoc. 1890
Aaron	**Press**		1882	1967	Member United Brethren 1906
Katie	Press	wife	1886	1950	
Arthur	Press	son	1904	1993	
Jennie	Press	daughter	1905	1989	
Jacob	Press	son	1907	1974	
Sophia	Press	daughter	1909	1969	
Sadie	Press	daughter	1910		
Mendall	Press	son	1911	1980	
Molly	Press	daughter	1913	1993	
Myer	Press	son	1915	2003	
Benjamin	Press	son	1918		
Solomon	**Raff**		1880	1951	Member Adas Israel 1918
Millee	(Sowetosh) Raff	wife	1887	1971	
Marion	Raff	daughter	1904	1938	
Francis	Raff	daughter	1909	2001	
Ruth	Raff	daughter	1913		
Morris	Raff	son	1914	1994	
Harry	**Reiss**		1872		Member United Brethren 1900
Rosie	Reiss	wife	1876		
Miran	Reiss	son	1898		
Virginia	Reiss	daughter	1900		
Sam	**Rosenberg**				
Samuel	**Rosenthal**		1874		Member Adas Israel 1918
Mary	Rosenthal	wife	1865		
Gertrude	Rosenthal	daughter	1903		
Gilbert	Rosenthal	son	1907		
Bernard	**Schartel**				Member United Brethren 1900
Joseph	**Schockett**		1870	1932	Member United Brethren 1906
Elizabeth	Schockett	wife	1872		
Harry	Schockett	son	1891		
Etta	Schockett	daughter	1894		
Sarah	Schockett	daughter	1898		
Albert	Schockett	son	1900		

continued on next page

Table 16.1. Continued.

Abraham	Schockett	son	1900	1961	
Louis	Schockett	son	1903		
William	Schockett	son	1905		
Gabriel	Schockett	son	1906		
Samuel	Schockett	son	1908	1967	
Adolph	**Schwartz**		1852	1935	Brother of Benjamin and Herman
Julia	Schwartz	wife	1952	1934	
Katie	Schwartz	daughter	1875	1963	m. Samuel Klein
Louis	Schwartz	son	1878	1964	m. Florence lived in Southampton
Morris	Schwartz	son			
Anna	Schwartz	daughter			
Joseph	Schwartz	son	1884	1930	
Rachel	Schwartz	daughter	1890	1949	m. Dezso Fischer
Benjamin	**Schwartz**		1863	1935	Brother of Adolph and Herman
Fannie	(Klein) Schwartz	wife	1865	1940	Sister of Samuel Klein and Josephine Schwartz
Joseph	Schwartz	son	1889		
Irene	Schwartz	daughter	1891	1910	
Rachel	Schwartz	daughter	1893	1971	
Louis	Schwartz	son	1894	1970	
Teresa	Schwartz	daughter	1902		
Estelle	Schwartz	daughter	1904	1956	
Herman	**Schwartz**		1869	1942	Brother of Adolph and Benjamin
Josephine	(Klein) Schwartz	wife	1872	1945	Sister of Samuel Klein and Fannie Schwartz
Teresa	Schwartz	daughter	1897	1956	
Irene	Schwartz	daughter	1899	1985	
Rachel	Schwartz	daughter	1901	1985	
Louis	Schwartz	son	1904	1986	
Garfield	Schwartz	son	1909	1956	
Samuel	**Schwartz**		1838	1908	Brother of Hannah Lenard from Shelter Island
Annie	Schwartz	wife		1920	
Max	Schwartz	son	1881	1962	
Willard	Schwartz	son	1885	1959	
Joseph	**Schapiro**		1875	1959	Worked for Gardiners Bay Oyster Co.

Table 16.1. Continued.

Ida	(Nolan) Schapiro	wife	1883		
Amelia	Schapiro	daughter	1900		
Emmanuel	Schapiro	son	1909		
Morris	**Siegel**			1901	Rabbi, Independent Jewish Assoc. 1900
M.	**Silverstein**				Rabbi, Mishcan Israel 1900
B.	**Silvin**				Shoemaker
?	Silvin	wife			
Sarah	Silvin	daughter	1904	1909	
H.	**Simon**				Member United Brethren 1906
Morris	**Simon**		1874	1945	Brother of Meyer from Patchogue
Clara	(Friedman) Simon	wife	1882	1959	
Dorothy	Simon	daughter	1904	1984	
Freda	**Slutzky**		1840		
Jacob	Slutzky	son	1876		Member United Brethren 1900
Mary	Slutzky	daughter	1879		Finisher at watchcase factory
Morris	**Smith**				Trustee Jewish Cemetery Assoc. 1893
Hanna	Smith	wife			
David	Smith	son	1895	1896	
Samuel	**Speivak**		1885		Member Adas Israel 1918
Bessie	Speivak	wife	1892		
Ethel	Speivak	daughter	1913		
Benjamin	**Spenzer**				Member Adas Israel 1918
Arnold	**Spitz**		1869		Son of Marcus and Lena
Bertha	(Mandel) Spitz	wife	1872		
Annie	Spitz	daughter	1893		
Morris	Spitz	son	1902		
Rose	Spitz	daughter	1903		
Bernhard	**Spitz**		1879	1953	Son of Marcus and Lena
Ernestine	(Spiegel) Spitz	wife	1889	1928	Sister of Stephanie Grossman
Herman	**Spitz**		1881	1947	Son of Marcus and Lena
Katie	(Weiner) Spitz	wife	1884	1966	Daughter of Rebecca
Philip	Spitz	son	1909		
Bertha	Spitz	daughter	1912		
Arthur	Spitz	son	1915	1987	
Jacob	**Spitz**		1875	1950	Son of Marcus and Lena

continued on next page

Table 16.1. Continued.

Malvina	(Wald) Spitz	wife	1886		
Elenor	Spitz	daughter	1909		
Milton	Spitz	son	1911		
Lawrence	Spitz	son	1912		
Marcus	**Spitz**		1848	1919	
Lena	(Weiss) Spitz	wife	1850	1924	
Arnold	Spitz	son	1869		m. Bertha Mandel
Nathan	Spitz	son	1871		
Jacob	Spitz	son	1875	1950	m. Malvina Wald
Bernhard	Spitz	son	1879	1953	m. Ernestine Spiegel
Herman	Spitz	son	1882		m. Katie Weiner
Henrich	Spitz	son	1883	1918	Worked at watchcase factory
Edel	**Spodick**		1859	1928	Trustee Jewish Cemetery Assoc. 1890
Fannie	(Eisenberg) Spodick	wife	1866	1954	
Libby	Spodick	daughter	1885	1919	
Louis	Spodick	son	1888	1856	
Ida	Spodick	daughter	1890	1974	
Harry	Spodick	son	1893	1992	Worked at watchcase factory
Frank	Spodick	son	1894	1961	
Sarah	Spodick	daughter	1896	1990	
Arthur	Spodick	son	1900	1985	
Leroy	Spodick	son	1902	1995	
Goldie	Spodick	daughter	1904	1989	
Morris	**Spodick**				Trustee Jewish Cemetery Assoc. 1890
Sarah	Spodick	wife			
?	Spodick	child	1891	1891	
H.	**Trelheift**				Recording Secretary Independent Jewish Assoc. 1900
Max	**Waldman**		1872	1930	Member United Brethren 1906
Rachael	Waldman	wife	1862	1937	
Nellie	Waldman	daughter	1900		
Rebecca	**Weiner**		1861	1928	
Katie	Weiner	daughter	1884	1966	m. Herman Spitz
Morris	Weiner	son	1892		
Herman	**Weiner**		1883	1929	Member Adas Israel 1918

Table 16.1. Continued.

Hilda	(Eisenberg) Weiner	wife	1891		
Arthur	Weiner	son	1912		
Ethel	Weiner	daughter	1914		
Gustave	**Zaborsky**				Member Adas Israel 1918

Table 16.2. Residents of Amagansett

Max	**Ollswang**		1870	1954	VP United Brethren 1895
Rose	(Hertz) Ollswang	wife	1871	1962	
Annie	Ollswang	daughter	1897		m. Morris Hotz, lived in Sag Harbor
Dorothy	Ollswang	daughter	1894		
Arthur	Ollswang	son	1903		

Table 16.3. Residents of East Hampton

Joseph	**Epstein**		1881		Member Adas Israel 1918
Jacob	**Goldstein**		1866	1934	
Lena	Goldstein	wife	1874	1932	
William	Goldstein	son	1894		
Jeanette	Goldstein	daughter	1894	1979	
Morris	Goldstein	son	1897		
Louis	Goldstein	son	1899		
Rebecca	Goldstein	daughter	1904		
Sam	Goldstein	son	1905		
Myer	Goldstein	son	1907	1919	
Sylvia	Goldstein	daughter	1911		
Aaron	**Isaacs**		1722	1797	Wife and children not Jewish
Aaron	**Jaffee**		1867	1937	Trustee Jewish Cemetery Assoc. 1890
Fanny	Jaffee	second wife	1855		
Ella	Jaffee	daughter	1892		
Isaac	**Meyer**		1870	1932	Brother of David and Morris from Sag Harbor and Jacob from Riverhead
Nellie	Meyer	wife	1880	1948	
Harriet	Meyer	daughter	1903		
Myron	Meyer	son	1905	1917	
Milton	Meyer	son	1915		

continued on next page

Table 16.3. Continued.

Bernhard	**Panzer**		1882	1944	Tailor
Sadie	(Reller) Panzer	wife	1890		
Gertrude	Panzer	daughter	1915		
Irving	Panzer	son	1917		
Samuel	**Spivak**		1884		Jeweler
Bessie	Spivak	wife	1892		
Ethel	Spivak	daughter	1913		

Table 16.4. Residents of Shelter Island

Louis	**Lenard**		1863	1933	Member United Brethren 1900
Hannah	(Schwartz) Lenard	wife	1866	1925	Sister of Samuel Schwartz in Sag Harbor
Minnie	Lenard	daughter	1891		
Rebecca	Lenard	daughter	1893	1959	
Rose	Lenard	daughter	1896		
Janet	Lenard	daughter	1899	1976	

Table 16.5. Residents of Southampton

Morris	**Eisner**		1885	1968	Ladies tailor
Sadie	Eisner	wife	1886	1961	
Isadore	Eisner	son	1909		
Bessie	Eisner	daughter	1913		
David	**Elias**				Moved to Southampton 1722
Israel	**Frank**		1874	1972	Store owner
Rachel	(Warshawsky) Frank	wife	1878	1963	
Bessie	Frank	daughter	1903		
Harry	Frank	son	1905		
Seymour	Frank	son	1909		
Gertrude	Frank	daughter	1912		
Ruth	Frank	daughter	1913		
Abraham	Frank	son	1917		
Abraham	**Goldstein**		1884		Furnishings merchant
Mabel	(Cohn) Goldstein	wife	1884	1953	Daughter of Samuel and Emma from Patchogue
Sylvia	Goldstein	daughter	1913		

Table 16.5. Continued.

Henry	**Hirschfeld**		1851	1916	
Edith	(Greebel) Hirschfeld	wife	1873	1941	Daughter of Sophie from Freeport
Beatrice	Hirschfeld	daughter	1895	1963	
Bernard	Hirschfeld	son	1896	1958	
Milton	Hirschfeld	son	1897		
Joseph	**Jacobs**				Moved to Southampton 1761
Eleanor	Jacobs	wife			
?	Jacobs	child			
?	Jacobs	child			
?	Jacobs	child			
?	Jacobs	child			
?	Jacobs	child			
Benjamin	**Rosen**		1869		Chairman Southampton chapter of the American Jewish Relief Committee
Dora	(Frankel) Rosen	wife	1879		
Harriet	Rosen	daughter	1899		
Annie	Rosen	daughter	1901		
Harry	Rosen	son	1902	1948	
Selma	Rosen	daughter	1911		
Maurice	Rosen	son	1917		
John	**Rosen**		1881		Brother of Benjamin
Ella	Rosen	wife			
Moescha	**Rosenberg**				Secretary Southampton chapter of the American Jewish Relief Committee
Moses	**Roth**		1868		Brother of Goldie Smith
Herman	**Rothenberg**		1861		Member Adas Israel 1918
Henrietta	(Hartstein) Rothenberg	wife	1872		
Samuel	Rothenberg	son	1894		
George	Rothenberg	son	1895	1970	
Sadie	Rothenberg	daughter	1899		
Max	Rothenberg	son	1900		
Louis	**Schwartz**		1878	1964	Son of Adolph and Julia from Sag Harbor
Florence	Schwartz	wife	1882	1961	
Charles	Schwartz	son	1911		
Max	**Smith**		1863	1935	Clothing merchant

continued on next page

Table 16.5. Continued.

Goldie	(Roth) Smith	wife	1868	1945	Secretary Southampton chapter of the American Jewish Relief Committee
Philip	Smith	son	1890		
Ruby	Smith	daughter	1894		
Harold	Smith	son	1897		
Max	**Tisnower**		1865	1937	Member Adas Israel 1918
Esther	Tisnower	wife	1870	1918	
Morris	Tisnower	son	1889		
Isaac	Tisnower	son	1891	1918	Killed in France during WWI
William	Tisnower	son	1892		
Nettie	Tisnower	daughter	1896		
David	Tisnower	son	1901		

Chapter 17

Setauket

Including Port Jefferson and St. James

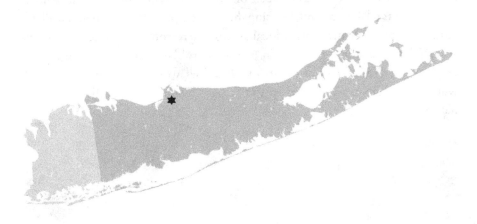

For reasons unknown, young Benjamin Goldberg decided to leave his family and his homeland of Russia in 1882 for the United States. As a seventeen-year-old perhaps he was motivated to pursue the American dream as hundreds of thousands of other eastern European Jews did in the late nineteenth century. Benjamin learned to read and write English and desired to make a living as a merchant. Within a few years he met another immigrant named Rose Moskowitz who arrived in New York from Germany in 1884.

Benjamin's father Abraham was born in Russia in 1830 and married Esther who was fourteen years his junior. One might suspect that by the late 1880s Abraham and Esther were more settled in their ways without a desire to uproot themselves in search of a different way of life. Their daughter Annie, like her older brother, sought a better life; so five years after Benjamin departed for America Annie followed. This left the senior Goldbergs with a decision to make: either stay in Russia to live out their lives or join their children in the United States. They chose the latter and were reunited with Benjamin and Annie on American soil in 1888.

The courtship of Benjamin and Rose progressed to the point where the couple would be married in 1889 and as newlyweds moved to the Long Island community of Setauket. Around the same time Annie met Morris Friedman and married just one year after Benjamin and Rose. They, too, decided to head east and put down roots on the north shore of Suffolk County.

Setauket in the late nineteenth century was a small village on the rise predominantly due to a rubber factory in town owned by Joseph Elberson. His enterprise was the centerpiece of the local economy, providing jobs for immigrant laborers and housing for his employees and their families. Arrangements were made with local stores where company-issued scrip was accepted for purchasing goods. In 1895 the rubber factory was the largest employer in Suffolk County with five hundred workers, a large portion of whom were Jewish, which led to the factory being closed on Rosh Hashanah and Yom Kippur.

Figure 99. Workers inside the rubber factory, c. 1898. *Source*: Three Village Historical Society.

In the early 1890s a small group of men operating under the name Agudas Achim (meaning "association of brothers") would gather regularly for worship and to provide support for the Jewish residents of Setauket. On May 2, 1892, Agudas Achim purchased a lot of five-eighths of an acre from George F. Bayles for $85 and established a cemetery on the land. Less than two years later Louis Rich and Lazarus Seligson met at the home of Aaron Grodenski on November 28, 1893, for the purpose of legally formalizing the establishment of the congregation. Agudas Achim was incorporated with Grodenski, Elias Golden, and Morris Friedman elected as trustees.

The 1890s proved to be prosperous for Benjamin Goldberg and his family. At the dawn of the decade he opened a dry goods store selling his wares to the residents of Setauket as well as those from the nearby community of Port Jefferson. Benjamin's American dream was evolving before his eyes as an immigrant who became a US citizen in 1892. Simultaneously the time

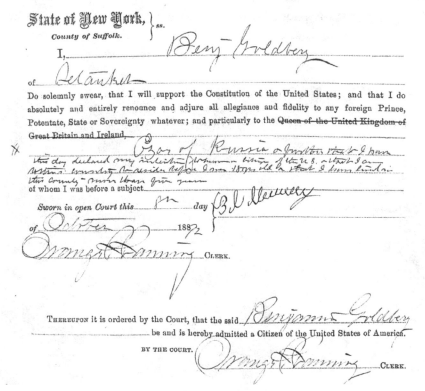

Figure 100. Benjamin Goldberg's record of naturalization that gave him US citizenship on October 8, 1892. *Source*: Suffolk County Clerk's Office.

had come for Benjamin and Rose to start a family. In a span of thirteen years from 1890 to 1902 Rose gave birth to seven children. Benjamin's sister Annie was even more fertile, growing the Friedman family by bearing eight children between 1895 and 1910, giving Abraham and Esther fifteen grandchildren.

The Jewish community of Setauket also enjoyed a period of growth and expansion in the 1890s. Members of Agudas Achim were certainly proud to have dedicated sacred ground to bury their dead; now it was time to set their sights on establishing a permanent location for their members to gather and observe the Orthodox traditions of their Jewish faith. On March 2, 1896, the congregation purchased a plot of land for $200 from Leon Elberson, son of Joseph, the rubber factory owner. The property measured 30' × 150' and was located on Main Street, bordered on the south by the lot and building owned by Benjamin Goldberg. They wasted no time in hiring local carpenter William Deckman to construct an ordinary building measuring 24' × 36' that included a balcony with seating for women. At the time the congregation had fifty-two members, but the synagogue was able to accommodate as many as three hundred worshipers. Construction took six months to complete at a cost of $1,500 and was the first synagogue

Figure 101. The synagogue built for Agudas Achim in 1896 as it appears today. *Source*: Photo by Brad Kolodny.

ever built on Long Island. A dedication took place on September 2 with all the pomp and circumstance appropriate for the occasion. Bunting and colored lanterns adorned the outside of the building with three large arches of green foliage set up near the entrance. Speakers included two rabbis who made the trip out from New York City and a rector from a church in Brooklyn who addressed the large crowd of both Jewish and non-Jewish citizens from Setauket and the surrounding communities.

What should have been a period of optimism and prosperity for the Jewish community of Setauket quickly began to fall apart. Just two years after the synagogue was opened the rubber factory closed, leaving many without a means to support their families. The factory would reopen but with fewer jobs available. Some stayed in Setauket and found new ways to earn a living while others decided to move out of town seeking employment elsewhere, including the rabbi of Agudas Achim who, by September of 1898, had sold his home and land to Morris Friedman. Benjamin's financial situation may have been unstable at the time, as that same year he ran into trouble with the law. Another Setauket resident, Nathan Meyers, asked Goldberg to take some checks to the bank to deposit for him. The two men were certainly more than just acquaintances as they were both Jewish in a small community and also served together as members of the Hebrew Employees Benevolent Association in 1894. Instead of following Nathan's instructions, Benjamin deposited the checks into his own account. Meyers brought charges of theft, and Benjamin was found guilty in court. Goldberg was sentenced to serve four months in the county jail.

The rubber factory continued to fall on hard times. The firm changed names several times and attempts at profitability through management restructuring did not revive the business to its prior glory. In 1904 the factory burned to the ground in a fire that essentially ended the company for good.

The story of the rubber factory runs parallel to the life of the Golden family whose experience was very much intertwined with the rise and fall of this enterprise in Setauket. Elias Golden and his wife Rebecca were married in their native Russia in 1872 and had four boys Isaac, David, Samuel, and Benjamin. The family came to the United States and by 1886 were settled in Setauket, where Elias was employed at the rubber factory and where, from time to time, Rebecca found work as well. Within the next five years the Goldens would have three more children—Lena, Harry,

Figure 102. Elias and Rebecca Golden, c. 1872. *Source*: Courtesy of Nancy Goldstein.

and Mamie. Elias was not only a trustee of Agudas Achim at its inception, but he was also devout in his religious observance and would lead the congregation in prayer on the High Holidays. His booming voice would reach the furthest corner of the balcony in the synagogue, and he dressed the part, wearing a white vest, cutaway coat, and a high silk hat. In 1900 Samuel was employed at the factory as a rubber cutter while Elias had become a clothing peddler and Isaac the proprietor of a saloon. By 1910 Elias and Rebecca left Setauket and moved to the Bronx with Benjamin, Lena, Harry, and Mamie. Samuel and Isaac remained in Setauket as did their brother David who owned a dry goods store on Main Street in 1912.

In 1909 Rose Goldberg developed health problems, including an abscess on her lungs. She suffered in pain for over a year from trouble with her spine and passed away on January 9, 1910, at the age of forty-three. Support for Benjamin and his children was not hard to find from his parents Abraham and Esther and his sister's family the Friedmans, who all lived in close proximity in the area of Setauket known as Chicken Hill.

By 1914 Agudas Achim was no longer in operation. The synagogue lay dormant for thirty-plus years with a few exceptions. During World War I the synagogue was used by the Jewish men who were stationed at nearby Camp Upton. The funeral service for Julius Frank was also held there in 1921.

In 1918 Benjamin sold his dry goods store and residence adjacent to the synagogue to Herman Pinnes, a butcher in Setauket since as early as 1893. Pinnes converted the dry goods store into a new butcher shop, which gave him a more central location than his previous store. By 1930 Benjamin had left Setauket and was living in Patchogue with his daughter Dora, who had married Max Goldin in 1923.

The post–World War II population growth across Long Island gave rise to dozens of new congregations, including one in Setauket that was organized in 1947 called North Shore Jewish Center. Members refurbished the old synagogue on Main Street that was rededicated on July 9, 1950. The first president of the revived congregation was Samuel Golden, son of Isaac and grandson of Elias, who had come to Setauket some seventy years prior. North Shore Jewish Center is an active congregation located in Port Jefferson Station since opening their current synagogue building in 1971.

Figure 103. A panoramic view of Setauket looking west. The dark building on the left side of the road is the rubber factory, and to the right on the other side of the street is the Methodist church. North of the church on Main Street is a double-gable structure that was Benjamin Goldberg's house and store, and the small white building to the right, slightly visible through the trees, is the synagogue. *Source*: Three Village Historical Society.

Table 17.1. Residents of Setauket

Jacob	**Bloch**				Member Hebrew Employees Benevolent Association 1894
Adolph	**Cohn**				Member Hebrew Employees Benevolent Association 1894
Samuel	**Eikov**		1872	1936	Junk peddler
Dora	(Pinnes) Eikov	wife	1873	1911	Sister of Herman Pinnes
Samuel	Eikov	son	1894		
Esther	Eikov	daughter	1898		
Jennie	Eikov	daughter	1901		
Joseph	Eikov	son	1903		
Lester	Eikov	son	1905		
Morris	Eikov	son	1906		
Robert	Eikov	son	1908		
Helen	Eikov	daughter	1909		
Julius	**Frank**		1841	1921	Merchant
Bessie	Frank	wife	1849	1916	
Michael	**Frank**		1860		Clothing store owner
Rebecca	(Silverman) Frank	wife	1872		
Elias	Frank	son	1895		
Annie	Frank	daughter	1897		
Samuel	Frank	son	1899	1941	
Hymen	**Frankel**		1854		Shirt manufacturer
Goldie	(Weindruch) Frankel	wife	1857		
Abraham	Frankel	son	1875		
Jacob	Frankel	son	1877		m. Addie
Rebecca	Frankel	daughter	1878		m. ? Secula
Morris	Frankel	son	1880	1964	
Simon	Frankel	son	1882		
Frank	Frankel	son	1884	1975	
Sarah	Frankel	daughter	1886		
Annie	Frankel	daughter	1891	1942	
George	Frankel	son	1891	1971	
Bernard	Frankel	son	1896		
Jacob	**Frankel**				
Addie	Frankel	wife			
Morris	**Freedman**		1857		Junk dealer
Sarah	(Schlesnick) Freedman	wife	1858		

Table 17.1. Continued.

Rachel	Freedman	daughter	1886		
Dora	Freedman	daughter	1888		m. Leo Rosenberg
Jennie	Freedman	daughter	1890		
Charles	Freedman	son	1893		
Morris	**Friedman**		1865		Trustee Agudas Achim 1893
Annie	(Goldberg) Friedman	wife	1872		Daughter of Abraham and Esther
Julius	Friedman	son	1893	1966	
Rachel	Friedman	daughter	1895		
Lewis	Friedman	son	1897		
Isaac	Friedman	son	1899		
Dora	Friedman	daughter	1901		
Beckie	Friedman	daughter	1906		
Sadie	Friedman	daughter	1908		
Jennie	Friedman	daughter	1910		
Abraham	**Gerstein**		1857	1940	Grocery store owner
Minnie	(Davis) Gerstein	wife	1860		
Edith	Gerstein	daughter	1893		
Dora	Gerstein	daughter	1899		
Nathan	Gerstein	son	1901		
Esther	Gerstein	daughter	1905		
Bernard	Gerstein	son	1908		
Abraham	**Goldberg**		1830		
Esther	Goldberg	wife	1844	1917	
Benjamin	**Goldberg**		1865		Son of Abraham and Esther
Rose	(Moskowitz) Goldberg	wife	1866	1910	
Celia	Goldberg	daughter	1890		
Lena	Goldberg	daughter	1891		
Maxwell	Goldberg	son	1892		
Louis	Goldberg	son	1895		
Dora	Goldberg	daughter	1896		
Solomon	Goldberg	son	1899		
Eva	Goldberg	daughter	1902		
Izik	**Goldberg**		1830		
Yetta	Goldberg	wife	1840		
David	**Golden**		1872		Son of Elias and Rebecca
Elizabeth	(Molasky) Golden	wife	1875		
Lottie	Golden	daughter	1894	1961	

continued on next page

Table 17.1. Continued.

Herman	Golden	son	1896	1952	
Sally	Golden	daughter	1898	1949	
Betty	Golden	daughter	1902		
Elias	**Golden**		1847	1929	Trustee Agudas Achim 1893
Rebecca	(Lavine) Golden	wife	1849	1922	
Isaac	Golden	son	1871	1941	m. Esther Kaschuck
David	Golden	son	1872		m. Elizabeth Molasky
Samuel	Golden	son	1880		Rubber cutter
Benjamin	Golden	son	1884		
Lena	Golden	daughter	1886		
Harry	Golden	son	1888	1918	Killed during WWI in France
Mamie	Golden	daughter	1890		
Isaac	**Golden**		1871	1941	Son of Elias and Rebecca
Esther	(Kaschuck) Golden	wife	1877	1956	
Dora	Golden	daughter	1896		
Sarah	Golden	daughter	1898		
Ida	Golden	daughter	1899	1968	
Samuel	Golden	son	1899		
?	Golden	son	1901		
Charlotte	Golden	daughter	1904		
Maybelle	Golden	daughter	1908	1978	
Louis	**Goldman**				Member Hebrew Employees Benevolent Association 1894
Aaron	**Grodinski**				Trustee Agudas Achim 1893
Klamath	**Helvitch**				Member Hebrew Employees Benevolent Association 1894
Isaac	**Heyman**		1863		Tailor
Frances	Heyman	wife	1860		
Samuel	Heyman	son	1887		
Ida	Heyman	daughter	1895		
Louis	Heyman	son	1897		
Louis	**Hyman**		1858		Member Hebrew Employees Benevolent Association 1894
Eva	Hyman	wife	1862		
Dora	Hyman	daughter	1879		
Minnie	Hyman	daughter	1882		
Harry	Hyman	son	1883		
Robert	Hyman	son	1885		
Annie	Hyman	daughter	1887		
Jennie	Hyman	daughter	1897		

Table 17.1. Continued.

John	**Kashow**		1841		Member Hebrew Employees Benevolent Association 1894
Abby	Kashow	wife	1942		
John	Kashow	son	1859		
Grace	Kashow	daughter	1861		
Florence	Kashow	daughter	1863		
Jacob	**Kramer**				
Jennie	(Pharfar) Kramer	wife			
Nathan	**Meyers**		1861		Member Hebrew Employees Benevolent Association 1894
Jennie	Meyers	wife	1860		
Abram	Meyers	son	1880		
Samuel	Meyers	son	1883		
Annie	Meyers	daughter	1886		
Rebecca	Meyers	daughter	1895		
Edward	Meyers	son	1897		
Eva	Meyers	daughter	1898		
Herman	**Pinnes**		1868		Brother of Dora Eikov
Sara	(Seligson) Pinnes	wife	1875		
Samuel	Pinnes	son	1894		
Evelyn	Pinnes	daughter			
Joseph	Pinnes	son	1900		
Lucy	PInnes	daughter	1905		
Helen	Pinnes	daughter	1908		
Louis	**Rich**				Member Agudas Achim 1893
Leo	**Rosenberg**				
Dora	(Freedman) Rosenberg	wife	1888		Daughter of Morris and Sarah
Max	**Rubenstein**				Member Hebrew Employees Benevolent Association 1894
Samuel	**Russokoff**				Member Hebrew Employees Benevolent Association 1894
Morris	**Sachs**		1850	1900	
?	Sachs	first wife			
Fannie	Sachs	daughter	1875		
Meyer	Sachs	son	1879		
Harry	Sachs	son	1882		
Rebecca	Sachs	second wife	1850	1906	
Joseph	Sachs	son	1887		
Ida	Sachs	daughter	1890		

continued on next page

Table 17.1. Continued.

Nathan	Sachs	son	1895		
?	**Secula**				
Rebecca	(Frankel) Secula	wife	1878		Daughter of Hymen and Goldie
Leah	Secula	daughter	1897		
Lazarus	**Seligson**				Member Agudas Achim 1893
Joel	**Shefkind**		1872		Fruit dealer
Fannie	Shefkind	wife	1878		
Dora	Shefkind	daughter	1897		
Sarah	Shefkind	daughter	1898		
Celia	Shefkind	daughter	1900		
Bessie	Shefkind	daughter	1902		
Minnie	Shefkind	daughter	1903		
Moses	Shefkind	son	1907		
Samuel	**Slessinger**		1864	1944	Tinware peddler
Anna	(Ritch) Slessinger	wife	1867	1934	
Leon	Slessinger	son	1894	1974	
Samuel	Slessinger	son	1895		
Addie	Slessinger	daughter	1897		
Libbie	Slessinger	daughter	1899		
William	Slessinger	son	1902		
Hyman	Slessinger	son	1905		
Edith	Slessinger	daughter	1907		
Morris	**Volk**		1897		

Table 17.2. Residents of Port Jefferson

Benjamin	**Cohn**		1857		Clothing store owner
?	Cohn	first wife			
Leone	Cohn	son	1883		
Donald	Cohn	son	1891		
Barbara	Cohn	second wife	1867		
T. Etta	Cohn	daughter	1896		
Louis	**Davang**		1889		Barber
Ida	Davang	wife	1895		
Ethel	Davang	daughter	1915		
Harry	**Feldman**		1871		Tailor
Ida	Feldman	wife	1873		
Maurice	Feldman	son	1904		

Table 17.2. Continued.

Harris	**Goldberg**		1858		Landlord
Lena	(Rosenberg) Goldberg	wife	1858		
Annie	Goldberg	daughter	1885		
Isaac	Goldberg	son	1886		
Leah	Goldberg	daughter	1887		
Louis	Goldberg	son	1888		
Jacob	Goldberg	son	1891		
Esther	Goldberg	daughter	1893		
Julia	Goldberg	daughter	1898		
Samuel	**Henschel**		1859	1936	Son of Morris and Rachel from Amityville
Martha	(Wolheim) Henschel	wife	1868		
Goldie	Henschel	daughter	1892		
Perry	Henschel	son	1893		
Harry	Henschel	son	1894		
Montifore	Henschel	son	1895	1917	

Table 17.3. Residents of St. James

Julius	**Bernstein**		1881		Machinist
Edith	(Cook) Bernstein	wife		1925	
Bernard	Bernstein	son	1907		
Florence	Bernstein	daughter	1909		
Samuel	**Katz**		1873		
Fanny	(Pyle) Katz	wife	1874	1942	

Appendix

Congregations Established on Long Island before 1919

1. Neta Szarschea, Breslau, January 19, 1875

2. Jewish Association of United Brethren, Sag Harbor, 1883 (became Temple Adas Israel May 2, 1918)

3. Agidath Achim Ansche Bellport, November 29, 1892

4. Agudas Achim, Setauket, December 21, 1893

5. Congregation Tifereth Israel, Glen Cove, November 6, 1899

6. Tifereth Israel, Greenport, November 7, 1902

7. Patchogue Hebrew Congregational Church, February 7, 1904

8. Jewish Brotherhood of Kings Park, July 17, 1906

9. Huntington Hebrew Congregation, March 6, 1907

10. Brotherhood of Jews in Riverhead, 1911

11. Lindenhurst Hebrew Congregation, January 19, 1914

12. B'nai Israel, Freeport, September 12, 1915

13. Hempstead Hebrew Congregation, September 27, 1915

Buildings Constructed for Use as a
Synagogue on Long Island before 1919

1. Agudas Achim*, Setauket, 1896

2. Mishcan Israel^, Sag Harbor, 1900

3. Tifereth Israel^, Greenport, 1904

4. Patchogue Hebrew Congregational Church, 1904

5. Jewish Brotherhood of Kings Park, 1908

6. Huntington Hebrew Congregation*, Huntington Station, 1913

7. B'nai Sholom, Rockville Centre, 1915

8. Lindenhurst Hebrew Congregation, 1915

* building still stands
^ still used as a synagogue today

Acknowledgments

I am grateful for the many people who contributed information, family stories, photographs, and other assistance toward the content included in this book. They include Sam Aronson, Barbara Axmacher, Ellen Bloch, Meghan Bush, Ron Bush, JoMarie Capone, Mary Cascone, Mike Cavanaugh, Marcia Clark, Alexa Cohn, Brad Cohn, Warren Cohn, Lawrence Davidow, Barry Dlouhy, Regina Feeney, Susan Field, Fred Fishel, Leo Fishel, Lloyd Gerard, Joel Glasser, Janet Glassman, Howard Goldberg, Jeri Golden, Nancy Goldstein, Marty Greenberg, Karl Grossman, Lauren Heller, Steven Holbreich, Robert Hughes, Mari Irizarry, Anna Jaeger, Howard Karlin, Marjorie Karlin, Gary Katz, Gertrude Katz, Ron Katz, Warren Katz, Kenneth Kennedy, Natalie Korsavidis, Jennifer Kuttruf, Nancy Leblang, Benjamin Leder, Lloyd Leder, Cindy Leimsider, Judy Leopold, Rabbi Joel Levenson, Steve Lucas, Gary Lutz, Harry Mainzer, Karen Martin, Molly McGirr, Ed Meade, Ralph Meyers, Susan Hirschfeld Mohr, Eileen Moskowitz, Barry Nechis, Jamie Pastor, Noah Pearlstein, Gina Piastuck, Betsy Plevan, Ellen Rodis, Dina Rosenberg, Steve Rung, Cyndy Katz Sigadel, Burt Singer, Phyllis Spector, Aaron Stein, Ben Stein, Gary Stephani, Lois Stern, Dr. Stephen Teich, and Christopher Varmus.

My wife Deborah is not only a computer-savvy designer who helped with the graphics and imagery in the book but has always been incredibly supportive of this work and my other personal endeavors. She has my eternal love and gratitude for all she does for me and our family. Our children Julia and Spencer have also taken time out of their busy lives to assist me. As they get older it is a beautiful thing to see them take an interest and appreciate the importance of our Jewish history.

Bibliography

Barasch, Norman. *The Joy of Laughter: My Life as a Comedy Writer*. Bloomington, IN: iUniverse, 2009.

Clark, Marcia. *The Autobiography of Samuel Clark*. Middletown, DE: Create Space, 2017.

Frank, Abe. *Together but Apart: The Jewish Experience in the Hamptons*. New York: Shengold, 1966.

Jaeger, Anna, and Mary Cascone. *From Breslau to Lindenhurst: 1870 to 1923 / Lindenhurst Historical Society with Anna Jaeger and Mary Cascone*. Charleston, SC: Arcadia, 2018.

Kolodny, Brad. *Seeking Sanctuary: 125 Years of Synagogues on Long Island*. Merrick, NY: Segulah, 2019.

Littleton, Martin W., and Kyle Crichton. *My Partner-in-Law; the Life of George Morton Levy*. New York: Farrar, Straus and Cudahy, 1957.

Marcus, Jacob Rader. *Early American Jewry*. Philadelphia: Jewish Publication Society of America, 1951.

Meyer, Isidore S., and Leo Hershkowitz. *The Lee Max Friedman Collection of American Jewish Colonial Correspondence: Letters of the Franks Family (1733–1748)*. Waltham, MA: American Jewish Historical Society, 1968.

Miller, Rhoda. *Jewish Community of Long Island*. Charleston, SC: Arcadia, 2016.

Portrait and Biographical Record of Suffolk County (Long Island) New York. New York: Chapman, 1896.

Slater, Jeffrey. *A Peddler's Journey*. Bloomington, IN: Xlibris, 2020.

About the Author

Brad Kolodny is the award-winning author of *Seeking Sanctuary: 125 Years of Synagogues on Long Island* and in 2021 established the Jewish Historical Society of Long Island, serving as president. Brad has photographed more than six hundred synagogues in thirteen countries over the last thirty-five years. He has worked for *New York Times* since 1996 and is an active member at Midway Jewish Center in Syosset, New York.

CPSIA information can be obtained
at www.ICGtesting.com
Printed in the USA
BVHW072145080222
628421BV00002B/12